DELIBERATE PRACTICE IN
MULTICULTURAL THERAPY

Essentials of Deliberate Practice Series
Tony Rousmaniere and Alexandre Vaz, Series Editors

ESSENTIALS OF DELIBERATE PRACTICE SERIES

TONY ROUSMANIERE AND ALEXANDRE VAZ, SERIES EDITORS

DELIBERATE PRACTICE IN MULTICULTURAL THERAPY

JORDAN HARRIS

JOEL JIN

SOPHIA HOFFMAN

SELINA PHAN

TRACY A. PROUT

TONY ROUSMANIERE

ALEXANDRE VAZ

AMERICAN PSYCHOLOGICAL ASSOCIATION

Published by
American Psychological Association
750 First Street, NE
Washington, DC 20002
https://www.apa.org

Order Department
https://www.apa.org/pubs/books
order@apa.org

Typeset in Cera Pro by Circle Graphics, Inc., Reisterstown, MD

Printer: Gasch Printing, Odenton, MD
Cover Designer: Mark Karis

Library of Congress Cataloging-in-Publication Data

Names: Harris, Jordan (Psychotherapist), author. | Jin, Joel, author. |
    Hoffman, Sophia, author. | Phan, Selina, author. | Prout, Tracy A.,
    author. | Rousmaniere, Tony, author. | Vaz, Alexandre, author.
Title: Deliberate practice in multicultural therapy / Jordan Harris, Joel
    Jin, Sophia Hoffman, Selina Phan, Tracy A. Prout, Tony Rousmaniere, and
    Alexandre Vaz.
Description: Washington, DC : American Psychological Association, [2024] |
    Series: Essentials of deliberate practice | Includes bibliographical
    references and index.
Identifiers: LCCN 2022061955 (print) | LCCN 2022061956 (ebook) |
    ISBN 9781433836671 (paperback) | ISBN 9781433840883 (ebook)
Subjects: LCSH: Cultural psychiatry. | Psychotherapists--Training of. |
    BISAC: PSYCHOLOGY / Education & Training | EDUCATION / Multicultural
    Education
Classification: LCC RC455.4.E8 H37 2024 (print) | LCC RC455.4.E8 (ebook) |
    DDC 616.89/14--dc23/eng/20230323
LC record available at https://lccn.loc.gov/2022061955
LC ebook record available at https://lccn.loc.gov/2022061956

https://doi.org/10.1037/0000357-000

Printed in the United States of America

10 9 8 7 6 5 4 3 2 1

Contents

Series Preface

Tony Rousmaniere and Alexandre Vaz

We are pleased to introduce the Essentials of Deliberate Practice series of training books. We are developing this book series to address a specific need that we see in many psychology training programs. The issue can be illustrated by the training experiences of Mary, a hypothetical second-year graduate school trainee. Mary has learned a lot about mental health theory, research, and psychotherapy techniques. Mary is a dedicated student; she has read dozens of textbooks, has written excellent papers about multicultural psychotherapy, and receives near-perfect scores on her course exams. However, when Mary sits with her clients at her practicum site, she often has trouble performing the therapy skills that she can write and talk about so clearly. Furthermore, Mary has noticed herself getting anxious when her clients express strong reactions, particularly around issues of identity, culture, and oppression. Sometimes this anxiety is strong enough to make Mary freeze at key moments, limiting her ability to help those clients.

During her weekly individual and group supervision, Mary's supervisor gives her advice informed by best practices in multicultural therapy. The supervisor often supplements that advice by leading Mary through role-plays, recommending additional reading, or providing examples from her own work with clients from a wide range of backgrounds. Mary, a dedicated supervisee who shares tapes of her sessions with her supervisor, is open about her challenges, carefully writes down her supervisor's advice, and reads the suggested readings. However, when Mary sits back down with her clients, she often finds that her new knowledge seems to have flown out of her head, and she is unable to enact her supervisor's advice. Mary finds this problem to be particularly acute with the clients whose cultural backgrounds are different from her own.

Mary's supervisor, who has received formal training in supervision, uses supervisory best practices, including the use of video to review supervisees' work. She would rate Mary's overall competence level as consistent with expectations for a trainee at Mary's developmental level. But even though Mary's overall progress is positive, she experiences some recurring problems in her work. This is true even though the supervisor is confident that she and Mary have identified the changes that Mary should make in her work.

The problem with which Mary and her supervisor are wrestling—the disconnect between her knowledge about psychotherapy and her ability to reliably perform psychotherapy—is the focus of this book series. We started this series because most therapists experience this disconnect, to one degree or another, whether they are beginning trainees or highly experienced clinicians. In truth, we are all Mary.

To address this problem, we are focusing this series on the use of deliberate practice, a method of training specifically designed for improving reliable performance of complex skills in challenging work environments (Rousmaniere, 2016, 2019; Rousmaniere et al., 2017). Deliberate practice entails experiential, repeated training with a particular skill until it becomes automatic. In the context of psychotherapy, this involves two trainees role-playing as a client and a therapist, switching roles every so often, under the guidance of a supervisor. The trainee playing the therapist reacts to client statements, ranging in difficulty from beginner to intermediate to advanced, with improvised responses that reflect fundamental therapeutic skills.

To create these books, we approached leading trainers and researchers of major topics in therapy with these simple instructions: Identify 10 to 12 essential skills for your topic in therapy where trainees often experience a disconnect between cognitive knowledge and performance ability—in other words, skills that trainees could write a good paper about but often have challenges performing, especially with challenging clients. We then collaborated with the authors to create deliberate practice exercises specifically designed to improve reliable performance of these skills and overall responsive treatment (Hatcher, 2015; Stiles et al., 1998; Stiles & Horvath, 2017). Finally, we rigorously tested these exercises with trainees and trainers at multiple sites around the world and refined them based on extensive feedback.

Each book in this series focuses on a specific topic in therapy, but readers will notice that most exercises in these books touch on common factor variables and facilitative interpersonal skills that researchers have identified as having the most impact on client outcome, such as empathy, verbal fluency, emotional expression, persuasiveness, and problem focus (e.g., T. Anderson et al., 2009; Norcross et al., 2019). Thus, the exercises in every book should help with a broad range of clients. Despite the specific theoretical model(s) from which therapists work, most therapists place a strong emphasis on pantheoretical elements of the therapeutic relationship, many of which have robust empirical support as correlates or mechanisms of client improvement (e.g., Norcross et al., 2019). We also recognize that therapy models have already-established training programs with rich histories, so we present deliberate practice not as a replacement but as an adaptable, transtheoretical training method that can be integrated into these existing programs to improve skill retention and help ensure basic competency.

About This Book

This is the 10th book in the Essentials of Deliberate Practice series and is rooted in an anti-racist, multicultural orientation. Multiculturalism has been called the "fourth force" in psychology, a dimension of clinical practice that can strengthen work being done in a cognitive-behavioral, psychodynamic, humanistic, or other type of psychotherapy (Pedersen, 1990). It is often defined as a perspective or way of being that aims to encourage "inclusion and enhances our ability to recognize ourselves in others" (Comas-Díaz, 2011, p. 243). Contemporary multicultural therapy emphasizes the personal development of the therapist, a process that is ongoing and never fully complete. The three pillars of multicultural orientation—cultural humility, cultural opportunities, and cultural comfort (Davis et al., 2018)—inform nearly all the exercises in this book. Multicultural therapy training combines the study of theory, the observation of expert practice, hands-on experiential learning, supervision, and continual self-reflection to develop greater cultural humility (Hook et al., 2017) and cultural comfort (Bartholomew et al., 2021).

Deliberate practice is intended as an additional piece designed to enhance this rich training tradition. Practicing the skills set forth in this book allows trainees to have these skills at their fingertips. Ideally, deliberate practice can help therapists integrate the core skills into their repertoire, allowing them to access needed skills in an automatic fashion in response to the client context. The skills set forth in this book are the basic skills; they are not intended to be holistic nor comprehensive. Deliberate practice is not intended to be the only delivery format through which multicultural therapy skills are acquired. The multicultural therapy skills presented in this book are intended to supplement the development of a multicultural orientation that therapists must also learn to be able to provide culturally responsive care to a range of clients with intersectional identities. Enjoy your learning, enjoy the process!

Thank you for including us in your journey toward psychotherapy expertise. Now let's get to practice!

Acknowledgments

We would like to acknowledge Rodney Goodyear for his significant contribution to starting and organizing this book series. We are grateful to Susan Reynolds, David Becker, Elizabeth Budd, Joe Albrecht, and Emily Ekle at American Psychological Association (APA) Books for providing expert guidance and insightful editing that has significantly improved the quality and accessibility of this book. This book would not have been possible without the contribution of countless students and colleagues who shared their challenging multicultural therapy experiences with us and provided excellent client prompts that form the core of these deliberate practice exercises. We thank Monnica Williams for her valuable feedback on the exercises in this book. We would also like to acknowledge the International Deliberate Practice Society and its members for their many contributions and support for our work. Finally, we are grateful for the invaluable editorial notes and feedback from Inês Amaro, Amy DeSmidt, and Jamie Manser.

The exercises in this book series have undergone extensive testing at training programs around the world. More than 130 testers (trainees, therapists, and supervisors) from 16 countries contributed to testing the exercises. For everyone who volunteered to "test run" this work and provided critically important feedback throughout the method refinement and writing process, we cannot thank you enough.

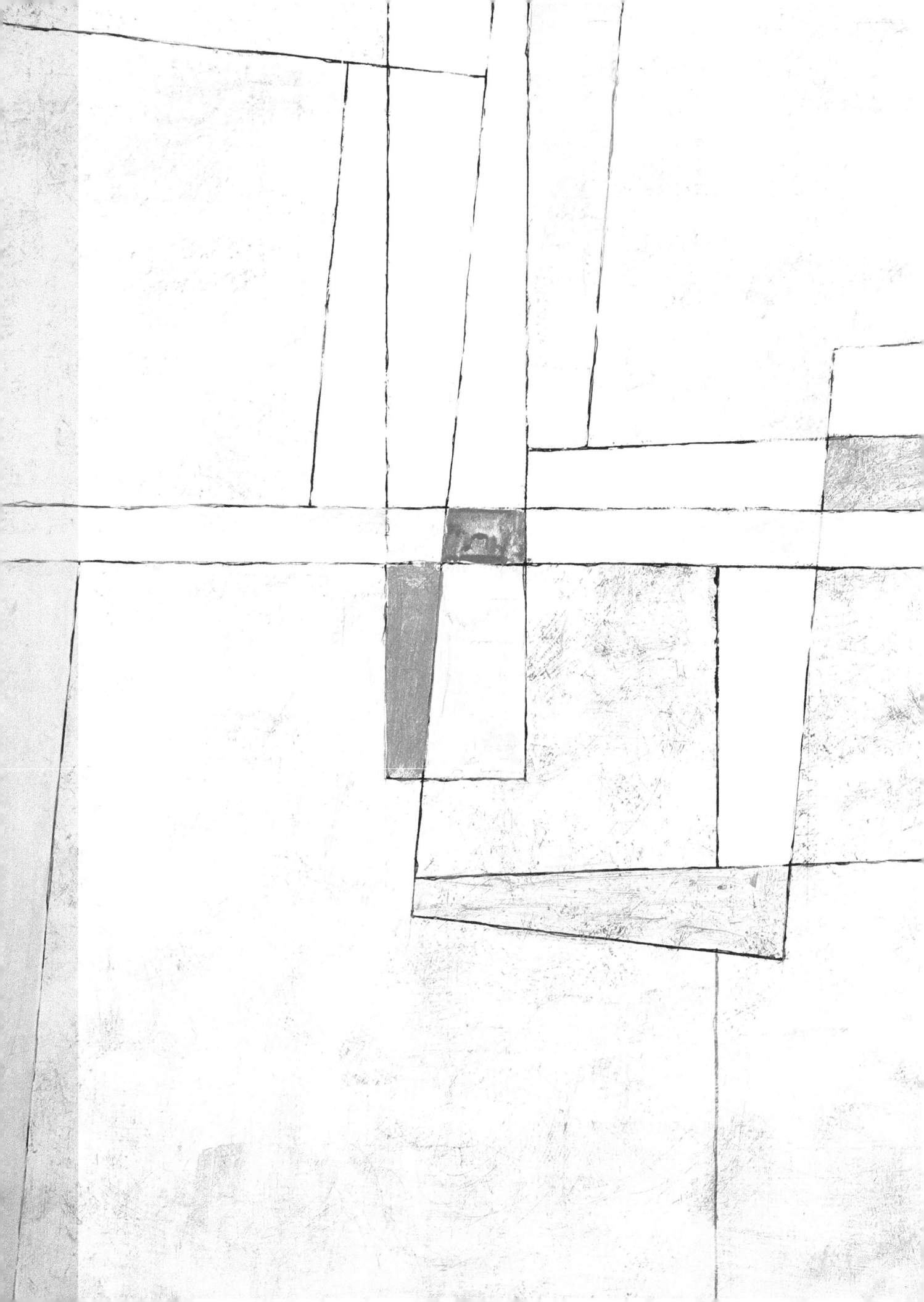

Overview and Instructions

In Part I, we provide an overview of deliberate practice, including how it can be integrated into clinical training programs committed to enhancing multicultural therapy, and instructions for performing the deliberate practice exercises in Part II. **We encourage both trainers and trainees to read both Chapters 1 and 2 before performing the deliberate practice exercises for the first time.**

Chapter 1 provides a foundation for the rest of the book by introducing important concepts related to deliberate practice and its role in psychotherapy training more broadly and multicultural therapy training more specifically. We review multicultural therapy models with an emphasis on the three pillars of a multicultural orientation—cultural humility, cultural opportunities, and cultural comfort—that are emphasized throughout the 12 deliberate practice exercises in Part II. Chapter 2 lays out the basic, most essential instructions for performing the multicultural therapy deliberate practice exercises in Part II. They are designed to be quick and simple and provide you with just enough information to get started without being overwhelmed. Chapter 3 in Part III provides more in-depth guidance, which we encourage you to read once you are comfortable with the basic instructions in Chapter 2.

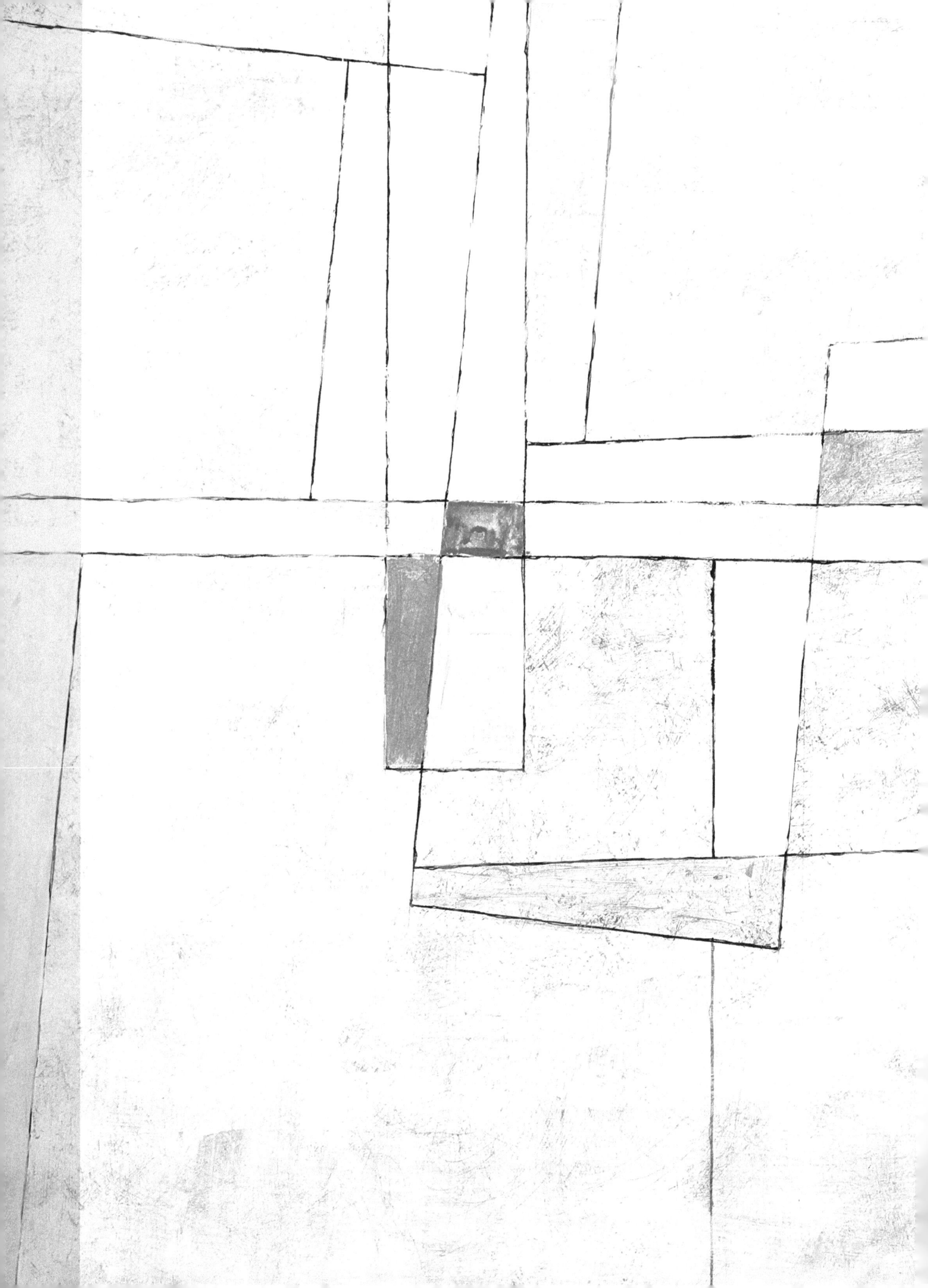

Introduction and Overview of Deliberate Practice and Multicultural Therapy

Multiculturalism has been referred to as the "fourth force" in psychotherapy—a key component of all therapy that supplements and, ideally, enhances whatever therapeutic paradigm the therapist uses—cognitive behavioral, psychodynamic, humanistic, systemic (Pedersen, 1990). All accredited graduate programs require coursework in multiculturalism as part of their psychotherapy training. Countless books and peer-reviewed articles on training in multicultural therapy describe a wide range of best practices for learning how to provide culturally responsive care; these include reading, watching films, completing self-report questionnaires, journaling, examination of implicit bias (e.g., completion of the Implicit Association Test), culturally informed case conceptualizations, and cross-cultural mentorship (Benuto et al., 2018; Jones et al., 2013). Many studies of these methods indicate that students demonstrate increased knowledge as a result of these courses. However, despite our best efforts, there is mixed evidence about the impact of multicultural therapy training on therapist attitudes, awareness, or objective skills (Benuto et al., 2018; Díaz-Lázaro & Cohen, 2001; Lee et al., 2014).

The experience of students in these courses is also mixed, with Black students, bisexual students, and students with disabilities perceiving multicultural therapy training to be of lesser quality than students from other groups (Gregus et al., 2020). Students who self-identify as having intersectional identities from two or more underrepresented groups also report significantly less favorable perceptions of their multicultural training (Gregus et al., 2020). We (the authors) have all taken courses in multicultural therapy, and each of us valued what we learned in each of those courses. But we also longed for more, wishing there was some way to bridge our "book learning" with the deep, repeated, experiential work we knew was necessary for transforming our ability to serve clients from a range of diverse backgrounds. Our collective sense was that the development of a multicultural orientation (before we even knew that term) would require our own personal transformation.

The "therapist as person" has long been understood as a central variable in therapy outcomes. Decades of research on therapeutic alliance, cross-cultural therapy dyads,

https://doi.org/10.1037/0000357-001

Deliberate Practice in Multicultural Therapy, by J. Harris, J. Jin, S. Hoffman, S. Phan, T. A. Prout, T. Rousmaniere, and A. Vaz

and multicultural competencies have attempted to quantify and study empirically the complex variables that influence the therapist's own role in the progress clients make in therapy (see Cabral & Smith, 2011; Flückiger et al., 2018). Each therapist holds their own intersectional identities, and those identities enter the therapy room alongside our clients' own identities. The exercises in this book offer trainees, experienced professionals, and supervisors alike the opportunity to begin the process of self-examination, experiential learning, and the development of procedural knowledge that we know is key to producing lasting change in the therapist's ability to provide multicultural therapy that heals.

Overview of the Deliberate Practice Exercises

The main focus of the book is a series of 13 exercises that have been thoroughly tested and modified based on feedback from a wide range of trainers and trainees. The first 12 exercises each represent a multicultural therapy skill ranging from beginner to advanced. The final exercise is more comprehensive, consisting of improvised mock therapy sessions that teach practitioners how to integrate all these skills into more expansive clinical scenarios. Unlike previous books in the Essentials of Deliberate Practice series, this one does not contain an annotated transcript. We chose not to include one because it would be impossible to capture a wide range of client diversity adequately in a single transcript. Trainers and trainees can instead seek out transcripts from other sources (Cornish et al., 2010; Gundel et al., 2020; Kivlighan & Chapman, 2018; Winkeljohn Black et al., 2021) or video demonstrations of multicultural therapy to supplement the exercises in this book (e.g., Chung, 2021; DeBlaere & Owen, 2020). Table 1.1 presents the 12 skills that are covered in these exercises.

Throughout the exercises, trainees work in pairs under the guidance of a supervisor and role-play as a client and a therapist, switching back and forth between the two roles. Each of the 12 skill-focused exercises consists of multiple client statements grouped by difficulty—beginner, intermediate, and advanced—that calls for a specific skill. For each skill, trainees are asked to read through and absorb the description of the skill, its criteria, and some examples of it. The trainee playing the client then reads the statements, which present possible statements from clients with a wide range of intersectional identities. The trainee playing the therapist then responds in a way that demonstrates the

TABLE 1.1. The 12 Multicultural Therapy Skills Presented in the Deliberate Practice Exercises

Beginner Skills	Intermediate Skills	Advanced Skills
1. Therapist self-awareness: cultural humility I	5. Working with emotions in context	9. Gathering information about safety concerns
2. Assessing client expectations	6. Maintaining a not-knowing stance: cultural humility II	10. Talking about sex and success
3. Reflecting content through a cultural lens	7. Inquiring about cultural implications of the problem: cultural opportunities II	11. Responding to resistance and ambivalence
4. Inquiring about identity: cultural opportunities I	8. Acknowledging therapist limitations	12. Repairing ruptures due to microaggressions

appropriate skill. Trainee therapists will have the option of practicing a response using the one supplied in the exercise or immediately improvising and supplying their own.

After each client statement and therapist response couplet is practiced several times, the trainees will stop to receive feedback from the supervisor. Guided by the supervisor, the trainees will be instructed to try statement–response couplets several times, working their way down the list. In consultation with the supervisor, trainees will go through the exercises, starting with the least challenging and moving through to more advanced levels. The triad (supervisor–client–therapist) will have the opportunity to discuss whether exercises present too much or too little challenge and adjust up or down depending on the assessment.

Trainees, in consultation with supervisors, can decide which skills they wish to work on and for how long. Based on our testing experience, we have found practice sessions last about 1 to 1.25 hours to receive maximum benefit. After this, trainees become saturated and need a break.

Ideally, learners will both gain confidence and achieve competence by practicing these exercises. Competence is defined here as the ability to perform a multicultural therapy skill in a manner that is flexible and responsive to the client. Skills have been chosen that are considered essential to multicultural therapy and that practitioners often find challenging to implement.

The skills identified in this book are not comprehensive in the sense of representing all one needs to learn to become a culturally informed clinician. Some will present particular challenges for trainees. A short history of multicultural therapy models and a brief description of the deliberate practice methodology will be provided in this chapter to explain how we have arrived at the union between them.

The Goals of This Book

The primary goal of this book is to help trainees achieve competence in core multicultural therapy skills. Therefore, the expression of that skill or competency may look somewhat different across clients or even within session with the same client.

The multicultural therapy deliberate practice exercises are designed to achieve the following:

1. Help therapists develop the ability to apply multicultural therapy skills in a range of clinical situations.

2. Move the skills into procedural memory (Squire, 2004) so therapists can access them even when they are tired, stressed, overwhelmed, or discouraged.

3. Provide therapists in training with an opportunity to exercise the particular skill using a style and language that is congruent with who they are.

4. Provide the opportunity to use the multicultural therapy skills in response to varying client statements and affect. This is designed to build confidence to adopt skills in a broad range of circumstances within different client contexts.

5. Provide therapists in training with many opportunities to fail and then correct their failed response based on feedback. This helps build confidence and persistence.

Finally, this book aims to help trainees discover their own personal learning style so that they can continue their professional development long after their formal training is concluded.

Who Can Benefit From This Book?

This book is designed to be used in multiple contexts, including in graduate-level courses, supervision, postgraduate training, and continuing education programs. We assume the following:

1. The trainer is knowledgeable about and competent in multicultural therapy.

2. The trainer is able to provide good demonstrations of how to use multicultural therapy skills across a range of therapeutic situations, via role-play, video, or both, or the trainer has access to examples of multicultural therapy being demonstrated through the many psychotherapy video examples available (see APA PsycTherapy, 2005, 2011; Chung, 2021; Comas-Díaz, 2015; dickey, 2018; Hays, 2016).

3. The trainer is able to provide feedback to students regarding how to craft or improve their application of multicultural therapy skills.

4. Trainees will have accompanying reading, such as books and articles, that explain the theory, research, and rationale of multicultural therapy and each particular skill. Recommended reading for each skill is provided in the sample syllabus (Appendix C).

The exercises covered in this book series were piloted in training sites from 16 countries across four continents (North America, South America, Europe, and Asia). This book is designed for trainers and trainees from different cultural backgrounds. Because culture is inherently embedded in the context and history of a particular place, and the authors of this text are primarily located in the United States, readers may encounter some statements in the book that do not apply to their particular region. Trainees and trainers are encouraged to adapt those statements to be more relevant to their setting.

This book is also designed for those who are training at all career stages, from beginning trainees, including those who have never worked with real clients, to seasoned therapists. All exercises feature guidance for assessing and adjusting the difficulty to precisely target the needs of each individual learner. The term *trainee* in this book is used broadly, referring to anyone in the field of professional mental health who is endeavoring to acquire multicultural psychotherapy skills.

Deliberate Practice in Psychotherapy Training

How does one become an expert in their professional field? What is trainable and what is simply beyond our reach, due to innate or uncontrollable factors? Questions such as these touch on our fascination with expert performers and their development. A mixture of awe, admiration, and even confusion surround people such as Mozart, Leonardo da Vinci, or more contemporary top performers such as basketball legend Michael Jordan and chess virtuoso Garry Kasparov. What accounts for their consistently superior professional results? Evidence suggests that the amount of or time spent on a particular type of training is a key factor in developing expertise in virtually all domains (Ericsson & Pool, 2016). "Deliberate practice" is an evidence-based method that can improve performance in an effective and reliable manner.

The concept of deliberate practice has its origins in a classic study by K. Anders Ericsson and colleagues (1993). They found that the amount of time practicing a skill and the quality of the time spent doing so were key factors predicting mastery and acquisition. They identified five key activities in learning and mastering skills: (a) observing one's own work, (b) getting expert feedback, (c) setting small incremental learning goals just beyond the performer's ability, (d) engaging in repetitive behavioral rehearsal of specific skills, and (e) continuously assessing performance. Ericsson and his colleagues termed this process deliberate practice, a cyclical process that is illustrated in Figure 1.1.

Research has shown that lengthy engagement in deliberate practice is associated with expert performance across a variety of professional fields, such as medicine, sports, music, chess, computer programming, and mathematics (Ericsson et al., 2018). People may associate deliberate practice with the widely known "10,000-hour rule" popularized by Malcolm Gladwell in his 2008 book *Outliers*, although the actual number of hours required for expertise varies by field and by individual (Ericsson & Pool, 2016). This, however, perpetuated two misunderstandings.

The first misunderstanding is that this is the number of deliberate practice hours that everyone needs to attain expertise, no matter the domain. In fact, there can be considerable variability in how many hours are required.

The second misunderstanding is that engagement in 10,000 hours of work performance will lead one to become an expert in that domain. This misunderstanding holds considerable significance for the field of psychotherapy, where hours of work experience with clients has traditionally been used as a measure of proficiency (Rousmaniere, 2016). Research suggests that the amount of experience alone does not predict therapist effectiveness (Goldberg, Babins-Wagner, et al., 2016; Goldberg, Rousmaniere, et al., 2016). It may be that the quality of deliberate practice is a key factor.

Psychotherapy scholars, recognizing the value of deliberate practice in other fields, have recently called for deliberate practice to be incorporated into training for mental health professionals (e.g., Bailey & Ogles, 2019; Hill et al., 2020; Rousmaniere et al., 2017; J. M. Taylor & Neimeyer, 2017; Tracey et al., 2015). There are, however, good reasons to question analogies made between psychotherapy and other professional fields, such as sports or

FIGURE 1.1. Cycle of Deliberate Practice

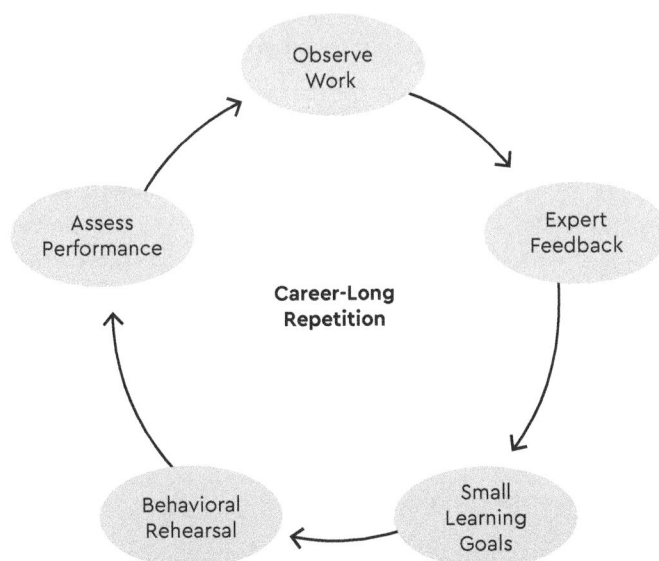

Note. From *Deliberate Practice in Emotion-Focused Therapy* (p. 7), by R. N. Goldman, A. Vaz, and T. Rousmaniere, 2021, American Psychological Association (https://doi.org/10.1037/0000227-000). Copyright 2021 by the American Psychological Association.

music, because by comparison, psychotherapy is so complex and free-form. Sports have clearly defined goals, and classical music follows a written score. In contrast, the goals of psychotherapy shift with the unique presentation of each client at each session. Therapists do not have the luxury of following a score.

Instead, good psychotherapy is more like improvisational jazz (Noa Kageyama, cited in Rousmaniere, 2016). In jazz improvisations, a complex mixture of group collaboration, creativity, and interaction are co-constructed among band members. Like psychotherapy, no two jazz improvisations are identical. However, improvisations are not a random collection of notes. They are grounded in a comprehensive theoretical understanding and technical proficiency that is only developed through continuous deliberate practice. For example, prominent jazz instructor Jerry Coker (1990) listed 18 skill areas that students must master, each of which has multiple discrete skills including tone quality, intervals, chord arpeggios, scales, patterns, and licks. In this sense, more creative and artful improvisations are actually a reflection of a previous commitment to repetitive skill practice and acquisition. As legendary jazz musician Miles Davis put it, "You have to play a long time to be able to play like yourself" (Cook, 2005, p. 34).

The main idea that we would like to stress here is that we want deliberate practice to help therapists become themselves. The idea is to learn the skills so that you have them on hand when you want them. Practice the skills to make them your own. Incorporate those aspects that feel right for you. Ongoing and effortful deliberate practice should not be an impediment to flexibility and creativity. Ideally, it should enhance it. We recognize and celebrate that psychotherapy is an ever-shifting encounter and by no means want it to become or feel formulaic. Strong multicultural therapists eloquently integrate previously acquired skills with properly attuned flexibility. The sample responses provided are meant as templates or possibilities, rather than "answers." Please interpret and apply them as you see fit, in a way that makes sense to you. We encourage flexible and improvisational play!

Simulation-Based Mastery Learning

Deliberate practice uses simulation-based mastery learning (Ericsson, 2004; McGaghie et al., 2014). That is, the stimulus material for training consists of "contrived social situations that mimic problems, events, or conditions that arise in professional encounters" (McGaghie et al., 2014, p. 375). A key component of this approach is that the stimuli being used in training are sufficiently similar to real-world experiences that they provoke similar reactions. This facilitates *state-dependent learning* in which professionals acquire skills in the same psychological environment where they will have to perform them (Fisher & Craik, 1977). For example, pilots train with flight simulators that present mechanical failures and dangerous weather conditions, and surgeons practice with surgical simulators that present medical complications. Training in simulations with challenging stimuli increases professionals' capacity to perform effectively under stress. For the psychotherapy training exercises in this book, the "simulators" are typical client statements that might actually be presented in the course of therapy sessions and call on the use of the particular skill.

Declarative Versus Procedural Knowledge

Declarative knowledge is what a person can understand, write, or speak about. It often refers to factual information that can be consciously recalled through memory and often acquired relatively quickly. In contrast, procedural learning is implicit in memory and "usually requires *repetition of an activity*, and associated learning is demonstrated through *improved task performance*" (Koziol & Budding, 2012, pp. 2694, emphasis added). *Procedural knowledge* is what a person can perform, especially under stress (Squire, 2004). There can be a wide difference between their declarative and procedural knowledge. For example, an "armchair quarterback" is a person who understands and talks about athletics well but would have trouble performing it at a professional ability. Likewise, most dance, music, or theater critics have a very high ability to write about their subjects but would be flummoxed if asked to perform them.

In multicultural therapy training, the gap between declarative and procedural knowledge appears when a trainee or therapist can recognize and perhaps even deeply appreciate, for example, a response that embodies cultural humility while also capitalizing on cultural opportunities, delivered in a way that feels comfortable and solid, but has trouble providing this type of response with real clients even when they want to in a given moment. **The sweet spot for deliberate practice is the gap between declarative and procedural knowledge.** In other words, effortful practice should target those skills that the trainee could write a good paper about but would have trouble actually performing with a real client. We start with declarative knowledge, learning skills theoretically and observing others perform them. Once learned, with the help of deliberate practice, we work toward the development of procedural learning, with the aim of therapists having "automatic" access to each of the skills that they can pull up when necessary.

Let us turn to a little theoretical background on multicultural therapy to help contextualize the skills described in this book and how they fit into the greater training model.

Multicultural Therapy

Multicultural therapy involves the understanding and willingness to learn about the cultural backgrounds of individuals, families, couples, groups, organizations, and communities. Cultural aspects of identity include, but are not limited to, age, disability, race, ethnicity, gender, religion/spirituality, sexual orientation and gender diversity, social class, body size, language, and immigration status. Multicultural therapy is not a specific model of therapy, but rather a perspective that can expand and enhance existing therapy approaches. Psychotherapists' approach to multicultural therapy has evolved significantly over the past 50 years to be more inclusive, complex, and experiential. Early in the 21st century, multicultural therapy training focused on the development of specific multicultural competencies, including recognizing the centrality of culture and their own implicit biases that may impact their interactions with clients (American Psychological Association, 2003). These early models focused primarily on racial and ethnic minorities and soon incorporated broader conceptualizations of *culture*, which is defined as the shared meanings that people interacting within specific contexts or groups have of themselves and their world (La Roche, 2020).

Contemporary models have moved from competency—which suggests a level of success that can be fully achieved, at which point we have successfully met a particular threshold—toward an ongoing process of personal and professional development, referred to as multicultural orientation (MCO; Davis et al., 2018). MCO is a framework organized around three pillars—cultural humility, cultural opportunities, and cultural comfort (Davis et al., 2018). The MCO framework is distinct from multicultural competencies because the language and meaning of *competencies* implies a mastery of awareness, knowledge, and skills, which conflicts with the developmental lifelong process of multicultural learning and cultural humility.

Cultural humility is the foundation—or "organizing virtue" (Davis et al., 2018, p. 91)—of the MCO framework and encourages therapists to remain curious, open, and responsive to clients and aspects of cultural identity that are most important to them (Hook et al., 2013). It describes a "way of being" that includes both intrapersonal (e.g., maintaining an accurate view of yourself, especially your own limitations) and interpersonal (e.g., being other-oriented rather than self-centered) components (Davis et al., 2011). Cultural humility is a lifelong process of self-reflection and self-critique and the development of mutually respectful relationships and partnerships within one's community (Tervalon & Murray-Garcia, 1998). To manage these ideas in relation to providing therapy, one must also be open to self-critique and feedback from supervisors, peers, and clients. Interpersonally, a therapist who consistently pursues cultural humility must also demonstrate an openness and curiosity to others' cultural beliefs and values, especially those that are different from their own (Hook et al., 2017).

Cultural opportunities refer to moments in therapy when the therapist can explore the client's most salient cultural identities, values, and beliefs. Cultural opportunities play an important role in client perception of the therapist and overall therapy outcomes. For example, client ratings of therapist cultural humility are associated with better reported therapy outcomes, whereas clients who perceived that their therapist missed cultural opportunities reported poorer therapy outcomes (Owen et al., 2016).

Cultural comfort is the third pillar of the MCO framework and refers "to the feelings that arise before, during, and after culturally relevant conversations in session between the therapist and client" (Hook et al., 2017, p. 37). A therapist's cultural comfort also lets the client know that the space is safe for discussing culturally relevant issues. Cultural comfort plays a role in demonstrating cultural humility because it is hard to be culturally humble and authentic if a therapist is uncomfortable in being open to and curious about exploring a client's cultural identity. Understanding the comfort or discomfort in response to various topics is important for the therapist to be self-aware and to self-reflect for further exploration and development.

These three pillars of the MCO framework emphasize process-oriented aspects of the therapy relationship, a continual experience of growth and development, and the importance of intersectionality. The emphasis on intersectionality also represents a massive step forward in the development of multicultural therapy and formed the cornerstone of the American Psychological Association's (2017) updated multicultural guidelines (see also Clauss-Ehlers et al., 2019). *Intersectionality*, at its essence, maintains that the various forms of identity (e.g., race, ethnicity, sexual orientation, gender identity, language, country of origin, body size, ability, age, socioeconomic status) do not exist separately from one another but are interwoven. Audre Lorde (1982), a Black, lesbian, American writer, feminist, poet, and civil rights activist, said in a speech at Harvard University, "There is no such thing as a single-issue struggle because we do not live single-issue lives." Intersectionality refers to both the complexities of individual identity and the complex and interlocking systems of oppression that impact individuals who hold membership in multiple socially constructed groups (Crenshaw, 1989). The individual and systemic aspects of intersectionality are dynamic and fluid; in other words, our own identities flexibly shift in reference to time, place, situation, and other contextual factors, and the systems of inequity that marginalize and oppress are also in flux.

As we move through the skills in this book, it is important to remember that traditional "competency" training sometimes leads us to believe that after a clinician becomes "competent" across skills if the client meets us with resistance or ambivalence about treatment or something that occurs in session, that this exists only in the room and within that context. The work of therapy and the interpersonal coconstruction of the therapy room does not exist within a vacuum that is outside of structures of oppression, historic marginalization, purposeful and political pathologizing, and unequal access to services and supports. It is important to acknowledge our own intersectional identities, relationship to marginalization, and proximity or direct access to power and privilege, as well as clients' sometimes necessary, protective, and important resistance and ambivalence to therapy as a process and your interventions.

The MCO framework is based on four basic assumptions: (a) Clients and therapists cocreate dynamic cultural expressions influenced by each other's cultural identities, (b) MCO is a way of being rather than a way of doing, (c) cultural processes such as cultural humility are necessary for connecting with a client's most salient cultural identities, and (d) therapists with a strong multicultural orientation are curious and open to learning more about their own and their client's cultural perspectives (Hook et al., 2013). The multicultural therapy skills in this book can be seen as the basic building blocks to be integrated into the therapist's repertoire and adopted for moment-by-moment use when needed. There are many excellent texts available that can aid in case conceptualization, therapeutic process (Vasquez & Johnson, 2022), and specific therapy skills (Berzoff et al., 2022; Davis et al., 2020; Hays, 2022) with a multicultural therapy framework.

Multicultural Therapy Skills in Deliberate Practice

The Multicultural Therapy Skills Presented in Exercises 1 Through 12

As with all books in the Essentials of Deliberate Practice series, the exercises in this text use a developmentally informed pedagogy in which more advanced skills build on less advanced skills, as indicated in Table 1.1. The beginner-level exercises consist of the most basic skills necessary for multicultural therapy. Therapist self-awareness and cultural humility (Exercise 1) is fundamental when practicing multicultural therapy. It is essential to start any practice centered around multicultural skills development with internal skills. This development of internal awareness as well as awareness of our physical cues is something you can continue to work on throughout your career. Exercise 1 is intended to help you begin the process of developing internal self-awareness and a greater ability to stay present in session, before moving on to the client-facing skills in the later exercises.

Assessing client expectations (Exercise 2), particularly as they relate to the goals and tasks of therapy, is closely related to positive outcomes in therapy (Bordin, 1979). Because the tasks and goals of therapy are so important to client outcomes, it is essential to assess clients' expectations of therapy (Patterson et al., 2008, 2014). Assessing client expectations about the likely outcomes of psychotherapy and the process of the therapeutic endeavor is especially important for clients who have historically had limited access to psychotherapy. Premature termination for racial and ethnic minorities, sexual minorities, and clients who perceive their therapist to have low multicultural competence are high (K. N. Anderson et al., 2019; Owen et al., 2012). Marginalized clients may feel uncertain about how psychotherapy works, what their role in the process entails, and what the boundaries of the relationship and the treatment are. Because of the role of culture and expectations, we recommend therapists clarify with clients how long sessions last, the frequency of sessions, their role as a client, and other aspects of the therapeutic process (Davis et al., 2018).

Reflecting content through a cultural lens (Exercise 3) is an elusively simple skill that must be rooted in cultural humility and also incorporates aspects of cultural opportunities.

This skill requires conveying empathy and understanding of the client's cultural experience without offering any interpretation or concrete guidance. Building on this, inquiring about identity (Exercise 4) offers another opportunity to practice exploring clients' intersectional identities and the ways in which these are fluid and dynamic.

The first of the intermediate exercises is about working with emotions in context (Exercise 5). The experience of emotions is highly contextual and often intersects with various forms of identity, including culture of origin, gender, age, and socioeconomic status (Boiger et al., 2018; Kwon et al., 2013; Mankus et al., 2016). The next intermediate exercise builds on the first cultural humility exercise to help therapists develop and maintain a not-knowing stance (Exercise 6), especially when there has been a moment of misunderstanding, direction confusion, lack of awareness, or active "wrongness" about a facet of a client's identity. Rather than being preoccupied with our own limitations, feelings of guilt, or worries that we might "get something wrong," what if, instead, we say to ourselves, "I am probably going to get something wrong and when I do, how will I remain oriented to the client and their identity and experience?" Moving through the "not knowing" and maintaining a "way of being" infused with cultural humility and nondefensiveness is the focus of this exercise.

Inquiring about cultural implications of the problem (Exercise 7) is one way to convey a multicultural orientation and to demonstrate your comfort with talking about all aspects of identity. Individuals from different cultures may have varying interpretations about the causes of and solutions to psychological distress (Cheng et al., 2013). Feelings of guilt about symptoms and the expression of symptoms also vary across cultural groups (Goodmann et al., 2021). This exercise will give you an opportunity to practice engaging with cultural opportunities and demonstrating cultural comfort with clients.

The final intermediate skill is about acknowledging therapist limitations (Exercise 8). Clients may assume that their therapist completely understands them because of a perceived shared identity. In some therapeutic dyads, clients may also assume that the therapist is so different that the therapist will have difficulty understanding the client's experience and sense of self. These perceived similarities or differences present an opportunity for alliance building and for engaging with important issues of culture and identity. In these moments, therapists can acknowledge their limitations of understanding the client's experiences. This is one of many forms of self-disclosure that are rooted in a position of cultural humility.

The advanced exercises are placed at the end because they require more complex interpersonal and intrapersonal skills. All the skills in the advanced section are dependent on the two earlier cultural humility exercises (Exercises 1 and 6) because they require the therapist to remain other-oriented throughout. Gathering information about safety concerns (Exercise 9) is a first step in addressing suicidal ideation and other risky behaviors, which are often moments when therapists lose contact with the multicultural context in which the client and therapist are rooted. The skill criteria in this exercise are no different from what you might expect in any therapy modality; however, therapists are encouraged to apply them as they think about larger systems of oppression that may be influencing the client's distress and decision making. Talking about sex and success (Exercise 10) is another way to engage with cultural opportunities and the ways in which values and systemic factors shape clients' understanding of themselves in relation to others. Sex and success are important parts of life that hold personalized meanings and may be associated with mixed feelings of enjoyment, pleasure, guilt, shame, or pain. What we do not say to clients—or what we say haltingly or hesitatingly—speaks volumes about what they can and cannot address in therapy. Practicing addressing these topics directly will help you feel more comfortable doing it in sessions with your clients.

The final two discrete skills in this textbook are the two most challenging you will practice. Responding to resistance and ambivalence (Exercise 11) requires the therapist to maintain a warm, nondefensive stance while acknowledging the inherent validity of the client's ambivalence or resistance, given the client's history, identity, and cultural context. Repairing ruptures due to microaggressions (Exercise 12) requires a high degree of cultural humility and also draws on complex interpersonal skills that help facilitate the therapeutic process.

A Note About Cultural Comfort: Vocal Tone, Facial Expression, and Body Posture

In keeping with humanistic approaches to psychotherapy and the literature on facilitative interpersonal skills (T. Anderson & Perlman, 2022) that portend successful therapy, nonverbal and paralinguistic cues expressed by both client and therapist are central components of multicultural therapy. More precisely, these aspects of the therapeutic process can be understood as cultural comfort. When therapists are comfortable integrating cultural language and appear at ease discussing intersectionality, systemic oppression, and working through all of the skills outlined in this book, clients are more likely to perceive their therapist more positively and report meaningful decreases in psychological distress (Bartholomew et al., 2021; Gundel et al., 2020). Deliberate practice exercises provide an opportunity for moment-to-moment feedback from peers and supervisors at the therapist's cultural comfort. You will also find many opportunities for self-reflection as you work through the exercises. Do you feel awkward, genuine, nervous, or relaxed? Ask your partner and supervisor for feedback on these aspects of your responses. This will also provide additional chances to practice receiving feedback nondefensively.

Overview of the Book's Structure

This book is organized into three parts. Part I contains this chapter and Chapter 2, which provides basic instructions on how to perform these exercises. We found through testing that providing too many instructions up front overwhelmed trainers and trainees, and as a result, they skipped past them. Therefore, we kept these instructions as brief and simple as possible to focus on only the most essential information that trainers and trainees will need to get started with the exercises. Further guidelines for getting the most about deliberate practice are provided in Chapter 3, and additional instructions for monitoring and adjusting the difficulty of the exercises are provided in Appendix A. **Do not skip the instructions in Chapter 2, and be sure to read the additional guidelines and instructions in Chapter 3 and Appendix A once you are comfortable with the basic instructions.**

Part II contains the 12 skill-focused exercises, which are ordered based on their difficulty: beginner, intermediate, and advanced (see Table 1.1). They each contain a brief overview of the exercise, example client–therapist interactions to help guide trainees, step-by-step instructions for conducting that exercise, and a list of criteria for mastering the relevant skill. The client statements and sample therapist responses are then presented, also organized by difficulty (beginner, intermediate, and advanced). The statements and responses are presented separately so that the trainee playing the therapist has more freedom to improvise responses without being influenced by the sample responses, which should only be turned to if the trainee has difficulty improvising their own responses. The last exercise in Part II provides opportunities to practice the 12 skills within simulated psychotherapy sessions. Exercise 13 offers suggestions for undertaking mock therapy sessions, as well as client profiles ordered by difficulty (beginner, intermediate, and advanced) that trainees can use for improvised role-plays.

Part III contains Chapter 3, which provides additional guidance for trainers and trainees. While Chapter 2 is more procedural, Chapter 3 covers big-picture issues. It highlights six key points for getting the most out of deliberate practice and describes the importance of appropriate responsiveness, attending to trainee well-being and respecting their privacy, and trainer self-evaluation, among other topics.

Three appendixes conclude this book. Appendix A provides instructions for monitoring and adjusting the difficulty of each exercise as needed. It provides a Deliberate Practice Reaction Form for the trainee playing the therapist to complete to indicate whether the exercise is too easy or too difficult. Appendix B includes a Deliberate Practice Diary Form that can be used to during a training session's final evaluation to process the trainees' experiences. However, its primary purpose is to give trainees a format to explore and record their experiences while engaging in additional, between-session deliberate practice activities without the supervisor. Appendix C presents a sample syllabus demonstrating how the 12 deliberate practice exercises and other support material can be integrated into a wider multicultural therapy course. Instructors may choose to modify the syllabus or pick elements of it to integrate into their own courses.

Downloadable versions of this book's appendixes, including a color version of the Deliberate Practice Reaction Form, can be found in the "Clinician and Practitioner Resources" tab online (https://www.apa.org/pubs/books/deliberate-practice-multicultural-therapy).

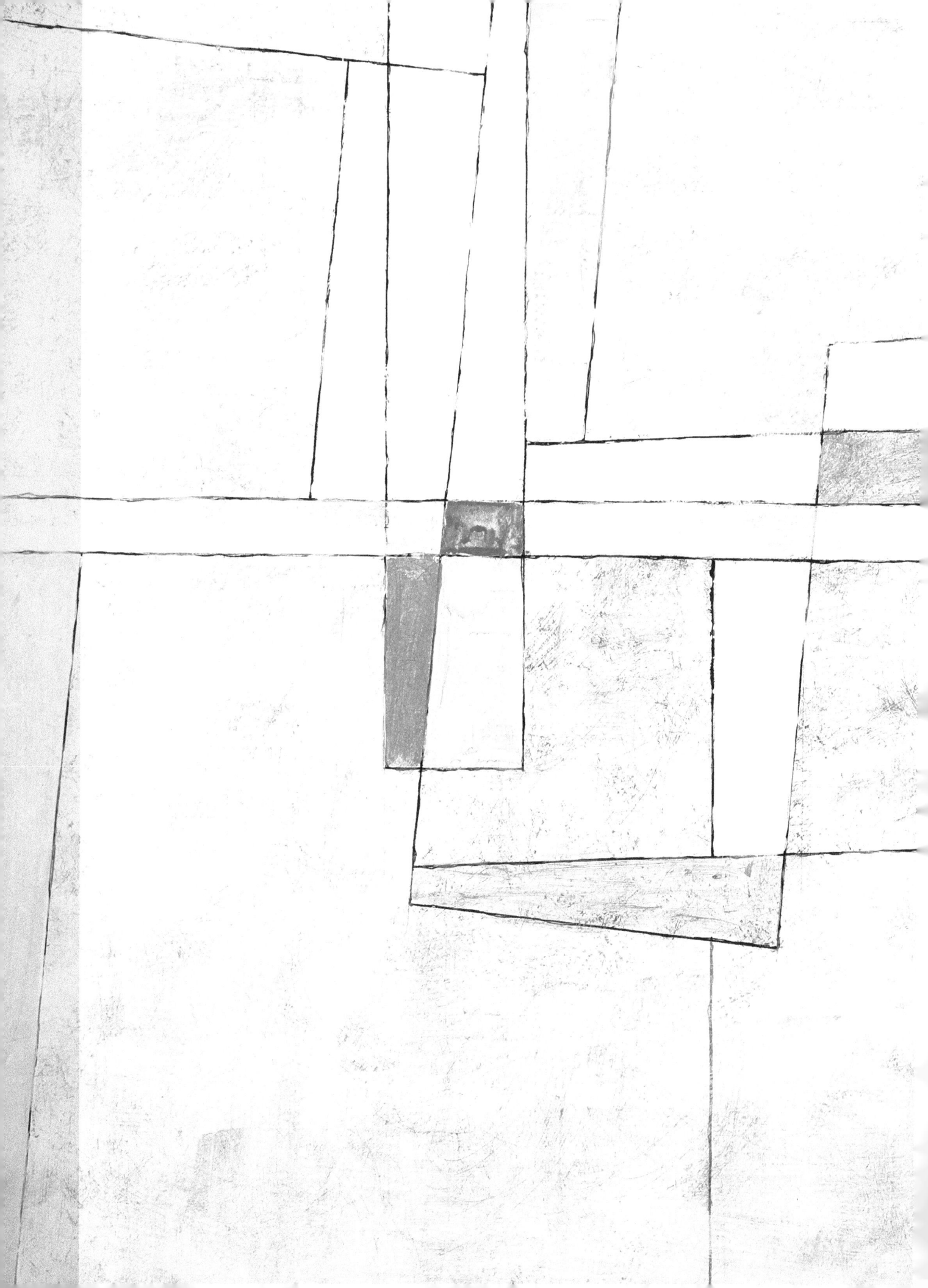

Instructions for the Multicultural Therapy Deliberate Practice Exercises

This chapter provides basic instructions that are common to all the exercises in this book. More specific instructions are provided in each exercise. Chapter 3 also provides important guidance for trainees and trainers that will help them get the most out of deliberate practice. Appendix A offers additional instructions for monitoring and adjusting the difficulty of the exercises as needed after getting through all then client statements in a single difficulty level, including a Deliberate Practice Reaction Form the trainee playing the therapist can complete to indicate whether they found the statements too easy or too difficult. **Difficulty assessment is an important part of the deliberate practice process and should not be skipped.**

Overview

The deliberate practice exercises in this book involve role-plays of hypothetical situations in therapy. The role-play involves three people: One trainee role-plays the therapist, another trainee role-plays the client, and a trainer (professor or supervisor) observes and provides feedback. Alternatively, a peer (e.g., the trainee who role-plays the client) can observe and provide feedback.

This book provides a script for each role-play, each with a client statement and also with an example therapist response. The client statements are graded in difficulty from beginning to advanced, although these difficulty grades are only estimates. The actual perceived difficulty of client statements is very subjective and varies widely by trainee. For example, some trainees may experience a stimulus of a client being angry as be easy to respond to, whereas another trainee may experience it as very difficult. Thus, it is important for trainees to provide difficulty assessments and adjustments to ensure that they are practicing at the right difficulty level: neither too easy nor too hard.

https://doi.org/10.1037/0000357–002

Deliberate Practice in Multicultural Therapy, by J. Harris, J. Jin, S. Hoffman, S. Phan, T. A. Prout, T. Rousmaniere, and A. Vaz

Time Frame

We recommend a 90-minute time block for every exercise, structured roughly as follows:

- First 20 minutes: Orientation. The trainer explains the multicultural therapy skill and demonstrates the exercise procedure with a volunteer trainee.

- Middle 50 minutes: Trainees perform the exercise in pairs. The trainer or a peer provides feedback throughout this process and monitors or adjusts the exercise's difficulty as needed after each set of statements (see Appendix A for more information about difficulty assessment).

- Final 20 minutes: Review, feedback, and discussion.

Preparation

1. Every trainee will need their own copy of this book.

2. Each exercise requires the trainer to fill out a Deliberate Practice Reaction Form after completing all the statements from a single difficulty level. This form is available in the "Clinician and Practitioner Resources" tab online (https://www.apa.org/pubs/books/deliberate-practice-multicultural-therapy) and in Appendix A.

3. Trainees are grouped into pairs. One volunteers to role-play the therapist and one to role-play the client (they will switch roles after 15 minutes of practice). As noted previously, an observer who might be either the trainer or a peer trainee will work with each pair.

The Role of the Trainer

The primary responsibilities of the trainer are to

1. provide corrective feedback, which includes both information about how well the trainees' response met expected criteria and any necessary guidance about how to improve the response, and

2. remind trainees to do difficulty assessments and adjustments after each level of client statements is completed (beginning, intermediate, and advanced).

How to Practice

Each exercise includes its own step-by-step instructions. Trainees should follow these instructions carefully, as every step is important.

Skill Criteria

Each of the first 12 exercises focuses on one essential multicultural therapy skill with two to three skill criteria that describe the important components or principles for that skill.

The goal of the role-play is for trainees to practice improvising responses to the client statement in a manner that (a) is attuned to the client, (b) meets skill criteria as much as possible, and (c) feels authentic for the trainee. Trainees are provided scripts with example therapist responses to give them a sense of how to incorporate the skill criteria into a response. **It is important, however, that trainees do not read the example responses verbatim in the role-plays!** Therapy is highly personal and improvisational; the goal of deliberate practice is to develop trainees' ability to improvise within a consistent framework. Memorizing scripted responses would be counterproductive for helping trainees learn to perform therapy that is responsive, authentic, and attuned to each individual client.

Jordan Harris, Joel Jin, Sophia Hoffman, Selina Phan, and Tracy Prout wrote the scripted example responses. However, trainees' personal style of therapy may differ slightly or greatly from that in the example scripts. It is essential that, over time, trainees develop their own style and voice, while simultaneously being able to intervene according to the model's principles and strategies. To facilitate this, the exercises in this book were designed to maximize opportunities for improvisational responses informed by the skill criteria and ongoing feedback. Trainees will note that some of the scripted responses do not meet all the skill criteria. These responses are provided as examples of flexible application of multicultural therapy skills in a manner that prioritizes attunement with the client.

Review, Feedback, and Discussion

The review and feedback sequence after each role-play has these two elements:

- First, the trainee who played the client **briefly** shares how it felt to be on the receiving end of the therapist response. This can help assess how well trainees are attuning with the client.

- Second, the trainer provides **brief** feedback (less than 1 minute) based on the skill criteria for each exercise. Keep feedback specific, behavioral, and brief to preserve time for skill rehearsal. If one trainer is teaching multiple pairs of trainees, the trainer walks around the room, observing the pairs and offering brief feedback. When the trainer is not available, the trainee playing the client gives peer feedback to the therapist, based on the skill criteria and how it felt to be on the receiving end of the intervention. Alternatively, a third trainee can observe and provide feedback.

Trainers (or peers) should remember to keep all feedback specific and brief and not to veer into discussions of theory. There are many other settings for extended discussion of multicultural therapy theory and research. In deliberate practice, it is of utmost importance to maximize time for continuous behavioral rehearsal via role-plays.

Final Evaluation

After both trainees have role-played the client and the therapist, the trainer provides an evaluation. Participants should engage in a short group discussion based on this evaluation. This discussion can provide ideas for where to focus homework and future deliberate practice sessions. To this end, Appendix B presents a Deliberate Practice Diary Form, which can also be downloaded from the "Clinician and Practitioner Resources" tab online (https://www.apa.org/pubs/books/deliberate-practice-multicultural-therapy).

This form can be used as part of the final evaluation to help trainees process their experiences from that session with the supervisor. However, it is designed primarily to be used by trainees as a template for exploring and recording their thoughts and experiences between sessions, particularly when pursuing additional deliberate practice activities without the supervisor, such as rehearsing responses alone or if two or more trainees want to practice the exercises together—perhaps with another trainee filling the supervisor's role. Then, if they want, the trainees can discuss these experiences with the supervisor at the beginning of the next training session.

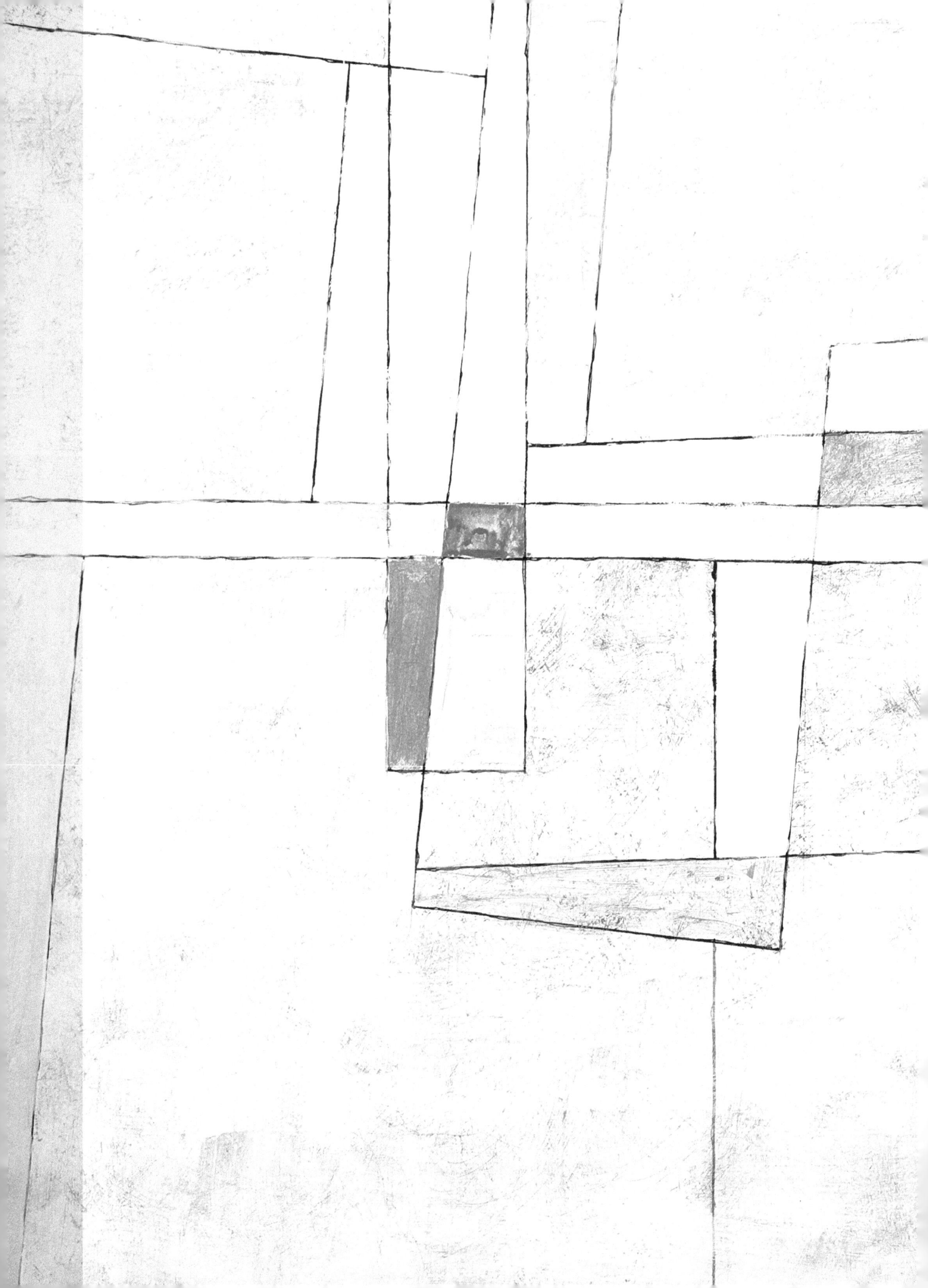

PART

II

Deliberate Practice Exercises for Multicultural Therapy Skills

This section of the book provides 12 deliberate practice exercises for essential multicultural therapy skills. These exercises are organized in a developmental sequence, from those that are more appropriate to someone just beginning multicultural therapy training to those who have progressed to a more advanced level. Although we anticipate that most trainers would use these exercises in the order we have suggested, some trainers may find it more appropriate to their training circumstances to use a different order. We also provide a comprehensive exercise that bring together the multicultural therapy skills using mock multicultural therapy sessions.

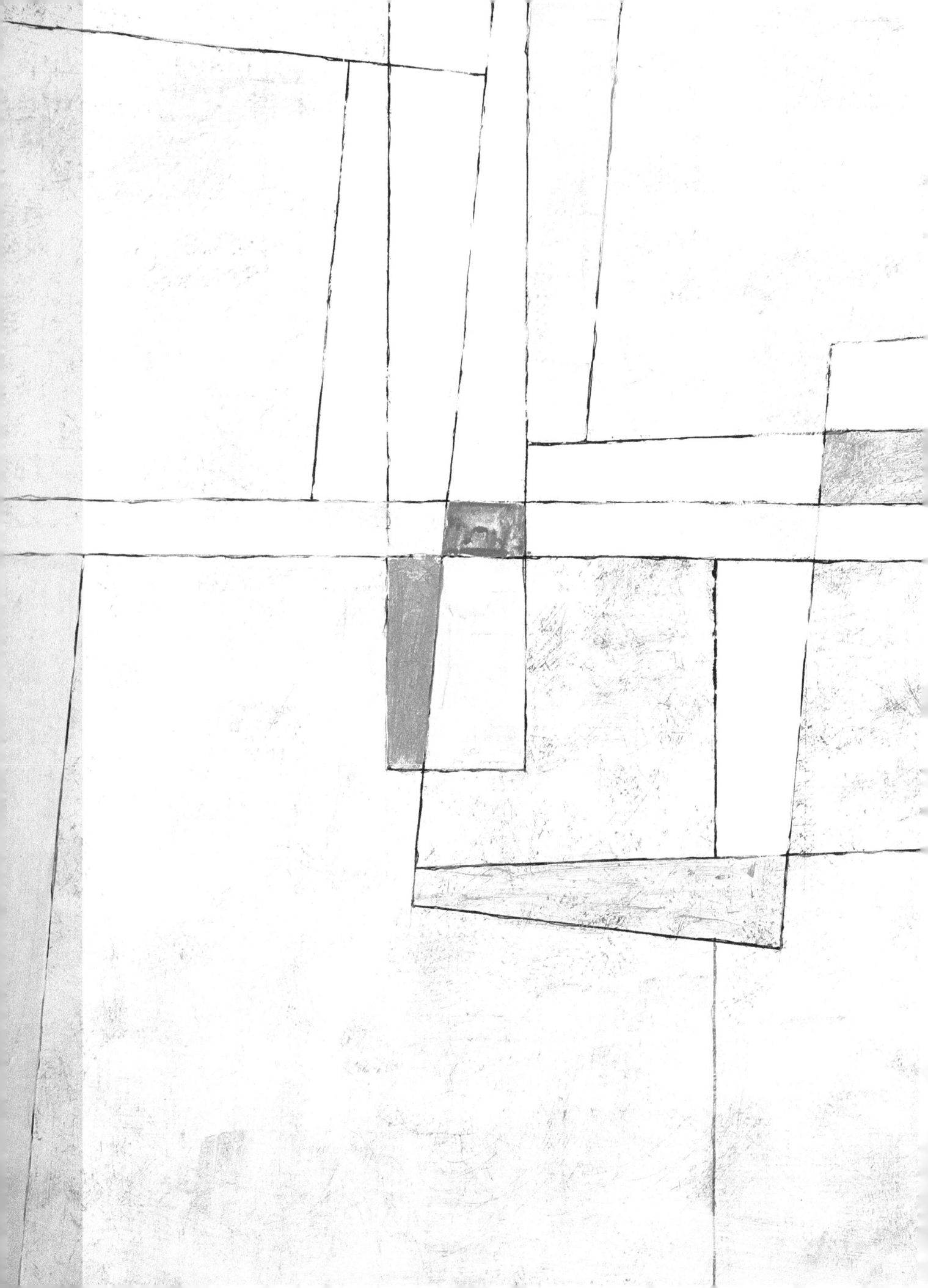

Therapist Self-Awareness: Cultural Humility I

Preparations for Exercise 1

1. Read the instructions in Chapter 2.

2. Download the Deliberate Practice Reaction Form and the Deliberate Practice Diary Form at https://www.apa.org/pubs/books/deliberate-practice-multicultural-therapy (see the "Clinician and Practitioner Resources" tab; also available in Appendixes A and B, respectively).

Skill Description

Skill Difficulty Level: Beginner

This exercise will help you gain greater self-awareness and provide you with opportunities to build your inner skills for developing a stronger multicultural orientation. "Cultural humility" is the practice of meeting clients from different cultural backgrounds with flexibility, understanding of our own biases and privileges, warmth, openness, respect, curiosity, and the acknowledgment that we "don't know what we don't know," but that we strive to understand. In this text, we use the term *culture* to refer to all forms of intersectional identity, including cultural/ethnic background, skin color, language, gender identity, neurodiversity, body size, socioeconomic background, and so on. Cultural humility is developed over time and consists of three pillars: the internal, the interpersonal, and the systemic (Mosher et al., 2017). Cultural humility is an ongoing practice, and central to this practice is being open and oriented to the intersecting, essential, and multifaceted identities of our clients. It is not a competency that is eventually "achieved"; it is an ongoing practice, reiterated and continuously updated through learning, self-reflection, and openness. This exercise is intended to help you begin the process of developing internal self-awareness and cultural humility while also increasing your ability to stay present with a client in session.

https://doi.org/10.1037/0000357-003

Deliberate Practice in Multicultural Therapy, by J. Harris, J. Jin, S. Hoffman, S. Phan, T. A. Prout, T. Rousmaniere, and A. Vaz

Special Instructions for Exercise 1

This exercise follows a different procedure from the other exercises in this book. One trainee will role-play a client who talks about an emotionally arousing topic. The other trainee will not role-play; instead, their task is to monitor their internal thoughts, feelings, and bodily felt responses as they are listening to the client and to disclose only those internal experiences that they feel comfortable sharing. A trainer (professor or supervisor) can observe and provide feedback. The client reads the first statement to the therapist. The therapist monitors their own internal experience and reactions (thoughts, feelings, bodily reactions, and urges) while listening to the client. When the client is finished reading the client statement, the therapist describes aloud any feelings or bodily felt experiences that they feel comfortable disclosing. The therapist should try not to think about the appropriate clinical interventions or responses to the client's words. Instead, the focus is fully on gradually heightening the therapist's awareness of their own internal processes. For example, the therapist could say, "As I hear this, I feel ashamed and I can feel my face flushing or getting hot," "My heart is starting to beat faster," "I feel warmth in my chest," "I feel joy," "I feel very sad, and I get an urge to hug the client," or "I start to feel angry and cross my arms."

Try to notice and describe at least one aspect of your experience. It may be a feeling or sensation you are aware of internally, such as a pit in your stomach or tightening in your throat. It may also involve an externally felt experience, such as flushing of your face or a smile coming across your lips. The goal is to scan continually for inner experiences, although at first many trainees may only notice external responses or have trouble identifying an experience at all. We encourage you to remain as open and curious as possible, being careful not to try and be overly self-effacing or to engage in performative self-reflection. Accordingly, sample responses are not provided for this exercise to encourage therapists to respond in ways that feel true to them. **Only describe out loud experiences that you feel comfortable disclosing and that are true to your experience. Having no response is as valid as having a response. It is very important that trainees have the right not to reveal experiences they wish to keep private.**

SKILL CRITERIA FOR EXERCISE 1
1. Acknowledge your own emotional state—what feelings are coming up?
2. Acknowledge physical reactions that arise—what sensations are coming up in your body?
3. Acknowledge thoughts that arise as you listen openly—what are your thoughts as you absorb what the client has said?

Examples of Therapist Self-Awareness: Cultural Humility I

Note: Underlined text is to be read aloud by the person playing the client to provide context.

Example 1

First session with a 17-year-old client, described as "male" on an intake form.

CLIENT: [*wistful*] Sometimes I wish I was a girl.

THERAPIST: I feel nervous (Criterion 1) when he said this, worried that I may say the wrong thing, (Criterion 2) and my heart started beating faster. (Criterion 3)

Example 2

CLIENT: [*angry*] I don't like cops. Especially White ones.

THERAPIST: I'm White, (Criterion 3) and I start to feel ashamed and anxious; (Criterion 1) I can't make eye contact and feel distracted. (Criterion 2)

or

THERAPIST: I also feel distrustful of police, (Criterion 3) so I could feel myself getting agitated (Criterion 2) and excited (Criterion 1) as he spoke.

Example 3

CLIENT: [*frustrated*] Yeah, well, where I'm from, stuff like this happens. You probably wouldn't understand.

THERAPIST: I feel nervous (Criterion 1) and become flushed and hot in my face, (Criterion 2) wondering if she is right, that I won't be able to understand. (Criterion 3)

INSTRUCTIONS FOR EXERCISE 1

Step 1: Role-Play and Feedback

- The client either says the first beginner patient statement or uses it as an improvisation prompt (i.e., there is no need to repeat every word, but the client needs to convey the general content and tone of the statement).
- The therapist does not respond to the client but instead describes their experience out loud, sharing whatever thoughts, feelings, or bodily experiences they feel comfortable sharing.
- The trainer (or, if not available, the client) provides **brief** feedback.

Step 2: Repeat

- Repeat Step 1 for all the statements **in the current difficulty level** (beginner, intermediate, or advanced).

Step 3: Assess and Adjust Difficulty

- The therapist completes the Deliberate Practice Reaction Form (see Appendix A) and decides whether to make the exercise easier or harder or to repeat the same difficulty level.

Step 4: Repeat for Approximately 15 Minutes

- Repeat Steps 1 to 3 for at least 15 minutes.
- The trainees then switch therapist and client roles and start over.

Now it's your turn! Follow Steps 1 and 2 from the exercise instructions.

Remember: The goal of the role-play is for trainees to practice improvising responses to the client statements in a manner that (a) uses the skill criteria and (b) feels authentic for the trainee. **Example therapist responses for each client statement are provided at the end of this exercise. Trainees should attempt to improvise their own responses before reading the example responses.**

    Note: Underlined text is to be read aloud by the person playing the client to provide context.

BEGINNER-LEVEL CLIENT STATEMENTS FOR EXERCISE 1
Beginner Client Statement 1
Seventeen-year-old, described as "male" on an intake form, in your first session.
[**Wistful**] Sometimes I wish I was a girl.
Beginner Client Statement 2
[**Angry**] I don't like cops. Especially White ones.
Beginner Client Statement 3
[**Dismissive**] Look, I'm a cis, straight, White dude. I've got no right to complain about my issues.
Beginner Client Statement 4
[**Angry**] There was yet another microaggression in my college Zoom class today from my professor. I'm so sick of this.
Beginner Client Statement 5
[**Frustrated**] I really don't want to come here. There's no way you can understand what it's like to be me.
Beginner Client Statement 6
[**Anxious**] There are things I can't talk about with you because of my parents' status in this country.

Assess and adjust the difficulty before moving to the next difficulty level (see Step 3 in the exercise instructions).

INTERMEDIATE-LEVEL CLIENT STATEMENTS FOR EXERCISE 1
Intermediate Client Statement 1
[Frustrated] Yeah, well, where I'm from, stuff like this happens. You probably wouldn't understand.
Intermediate Client Statement 2
The client is a 15-year-old nonbinary person.   **[Dismissive]** Someone like you can't help me.
Intermediate Client Statement 3
[Curious] I saw you have that gay pride flag sticker on your door. Are you gay?
Intermediate Client Statement 4
[Anxious, almost whispering] Part of the reason I feel so anxious in class is because I'm worried I'll say something that will offend the students of color in my class.
Intermediate Client Statement 5
[Matter-of-fact] When I feel anxious, I just realize I don't have to worry because the world is nothingness. I'm an atheist. You're not religious, are you?
Intermediate Client Statement 6
[Casual] You're nice and all, but I'm guessing you've never been followed around a convenience store because of the way you look, right?

Assess and adjust the difficulty before moving to the next difficulty level (see Step 3 in the exercise instructions).

ADVANCED-LEVEL CLIENT STATEMENTS FOR EXERCISE 1
Advanced Client Statement 1
The client corrects you after you used the word *gay.* **[Annoyed]** I'm actually pansexual. Do you even know what that means?
Advanced Client Statement 2
[Frustrated] I'm just sick of all the Black Lives Matter signs and protests. I get it, OK. Enough.
Advanced Client Statement 3
[Frightened] I've been having nightmares lately where I'm being attacked by other [insert one aspect of your own identity, e.g., "gay people," "Asian American people"].
Advanced Client Statement 4
[Angry] I bet I can guess how you voted in the last election.
Advanced Client Statement 5
[Exasperated] Honestly, we've been working together for a few months, and I wanted to give therapy a chance, but I can't let another microaggression from you go by without saying something.
Advanced Client Statement 6
[Demoralized] Have you ever even treated a fat person before? I bet you're going to suggest diet and exercise like everyone else. That's not even what I'm here for.

🛑 **Assess and adjust the difficulty here (see Step 3 in the exercise instructions). If appropriate, follow the instructions to make the exercise even more challenging (see Appendix A).**

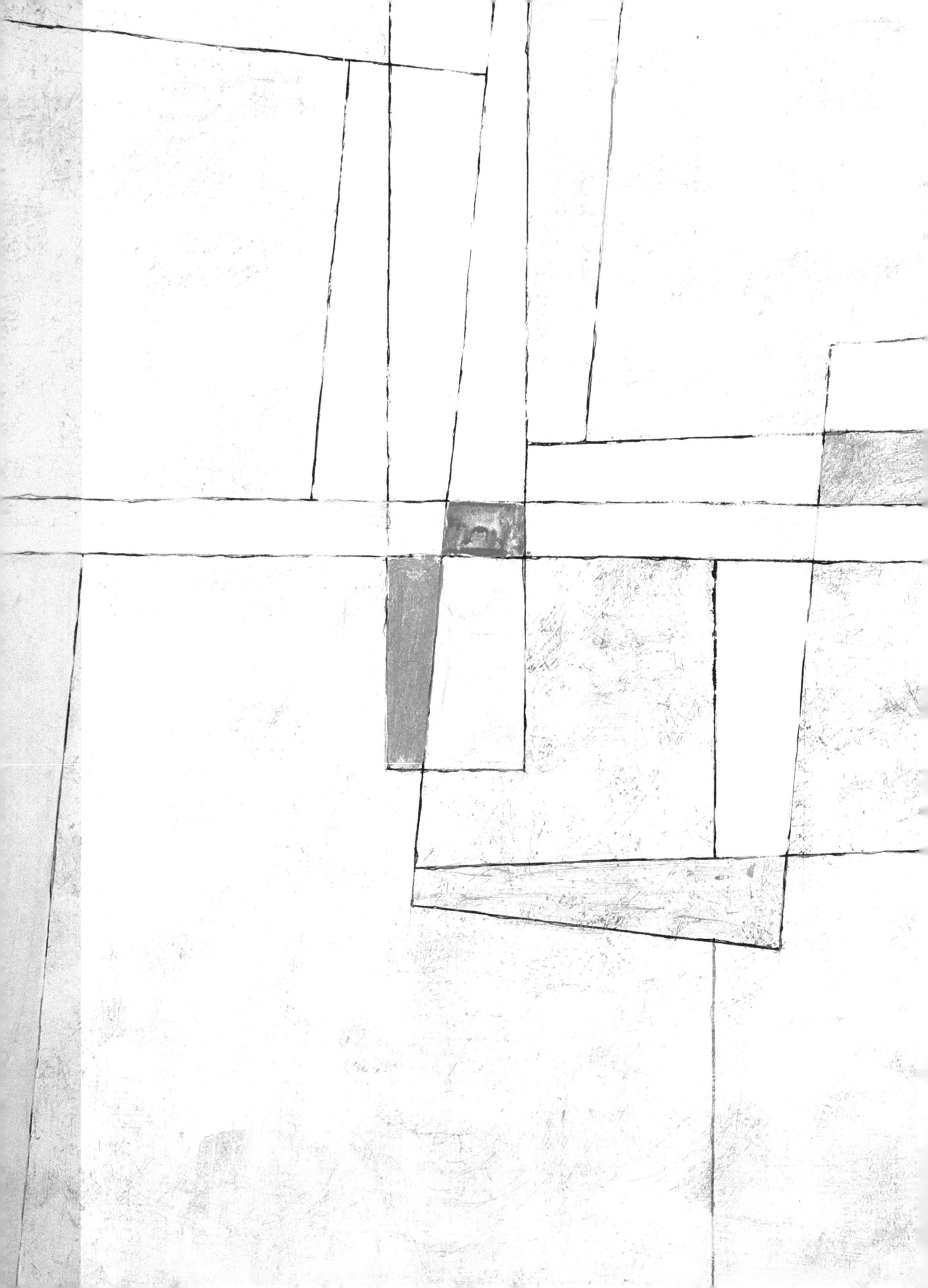

Assessing Client Expectations

Preparations for Exercise 2

1. Read the instructions in Chapter 2.

2. Download the Deliberate Practice Reaction Form and the Deliberate Practice Diary Form at https://www.apa.org/pubs/books/deliberate-practice-multicultural-therapy (see the "Clinician and Practitioner Resources" tab; also available in Appendixes A and B, respectively).

Skill Description

Skill Difficulty Level: Beginner

The aim of this exercise is to help you develop skills to assess clients' expectations of therapy. Client–therapist agreement on the tasks and goals of therapy is critical to building a strong therapeutic alliance and is one of the most consistent predictors of positive outcomes in psychotherapy (Bordin, 1979; Flückiger et al., 2018; Horvath et al., 2011). Clients—especially those who have historically had limited access to psychotherapy— may feel uncertain about how psychotherapy works, what their role in the process entails, and what the boundaries of the relationship and the treatment are. This becomes even more important when working with marginalized people, as some research suggests that dropout rates for racial and ethnic minorities are high (Owen et al., 2012). This is important even when cultural and marginalized identities are not immediately evident. For example, one's sexual orientation is not necessarily immediately apparent; however, premature termination appears to be higher among sexual minorities and clients who perceive their therapist to have low multicultural competence (K. N. Anderson et al., 2019). Because of the role of culture and expectations, we recommend therapists clarify with clients how long sessions last, the frequency of sessions, their role as a client, and other aspects of the therapeutic process.

https://doi.org/10.1037/0000357-004

Deliberate Practice in Multicultural Therapy, by J. Harris, J. Jin, S. Hoffman, S. Phan, T. A. Prout, T. Rousmaniere, and A. Vaz

SKILL CRITERIA FOR EXERCISE 2

1. Validate the client's statement.
2. Using a tentative and open tone, ask a question about the client's expectations of the therapy process.
3. If relevant, ask the client about or comment on the potential role of identity in shaping expectations for therapy.

Examples of Therapists Assessing Client Expectations

Note: Underlined text is to be read aloud by the person playing the client to provide context.

Example 1

The client is using a wheelchair.

CLIENT: [*tentative*] So, I've never done therapy before. I'm not totally sure how this works. It's been hard to find a therapist whose office was accessible for me.

THERAPIST: That makes sense, thanks for bringing it up. (Criterion 1) I'm glad you were able to find me. I can imagine that challenges in finding an accessible office shape how you might think or feel about therapy. (Criterion 3) Coming in today, did you have any expectations for what therapy would look like? (Criterion 2)

Example 2

CLIENT: [*assertive*] I don't believe in depression. It's not a thing in my culture. I just feel a little low. I build myself up with positive thoughts. I just need you to build me up with more positive thoughts because I can't do that anymore.

THERAPIST: You're really good at building yourself up. That's a great skill to have! (Criterion 1) Can you give me an example of what you expect this process to be like? (Criterion 2) I'm also curious about your culture and how that plays a role in your beliefs about depression. (Criterion 3)

Example 3

CLIENT: [*uncertain*] I'm here because my pastor told me to come see someone. Is this religious counseling? I don't want anything that's going to go against my religion.

THERAPIST: I'm glad you took your pastor's advice. (Criterion 1) I'd really like to hear more about your faith in our sessions. (Criterion 3) When you came in today, what did you expect? What was the picture you had in mind about what would happen? (Criterion 2)

INSTRUCTIONS FOR EXERCISE 2
Step 1: Role-Play and Feedback
• The client says the first beginner client statement. The therapist **improvises** a response based on the skill criteria.
• The trainer (or, if not available, the client) provides **brief** feedback based on the skill criteria.
• The client then repeats the same statement, and the therapist again improvises a response. The trainer (or client) again provides brief feedback.
Step 2: Repeat
• Repeat Step 1 for all the statements **in the current difficulty level** (beginner, intermediate, or advanced).
Step 3: Assess and Adjust Difficulty
• The therapist completes the Deliberate Practice Reaction Form (see Appendix A) and decides whether to make the exercise easier or harder or to repeat the same difficulty level.
Step 4: Repeat for Approximately 15 Minutes
• Repeat Steps 1 to 3 for at least 15 minutes.
• The trainees then switch therapist and client roles and start over.

Now it's your turn! Follow Steps 1 and 2 from the exercise instructions.

Remember: The goal of the role-play is for trainees to practice improvising responses to the client statements in a manner that (a) uses the skill criteria and (b) feels authentic for the trainee. **Example therapist responses for each client statement are provided at the end of this exercise. Trainees should attempt to improvise their own responses before reading the example responses.**

    Note: Underlined text is to be read aloud by the person playing the client to provide context.

BEGINNER-LEVEL CLIENT STATEMENTS FOR EXERCISE 2
Beginner Client Statement 1
The client is using a wheelchair. **[Tentative]** So, I've never done therapy before. I'm not totally sure how this works. It's been hard to find a therapist whose office was accessible.
Beginner Client Statement 2
[Eager] I don't know anyone who goes to therapy, but on my favorite online show, they talk about therapy on there. So, I thought I'd give it a try.
Beginner Client Statement 3
[Sad] I never thought I would be here. My family believes that people who need therapy are weak.
Beginner Client Statement 4
[Self-deprecating] Everyone thinks we're so strong. I mean I need help too. I need to work through a few issues.
Beginner Client Statement 5
[Assertive] I don't believe in depression. It's not a thing in my culture. I just feel a little low. I build myself up with positive thoughts. I just need you to build me up with more positive thoughts because I can't do that anymore.

🛑 **Assess and adjust the difficulty before moving to the next difficulty level (see Step 3 in the exercise instructions).**

INTERMEDIATE-LEVEL CLIENT STATEMENTS FOR EXERCISE 2
Intermediate Client Statement 1
[Forceful] The lawyer said it would look good in court if I came here without anyone asking. She said it would show I was already working on my issues.
Intermediate Client Statement 2
[Uncertain] I chose you because we have the same background. I'm guessing I just start talking and you'll give me some advice?
Intermediate Client Statement 3
[Angry] My wife said I needed to come. I don't really talk about feelings. It's not really something men do. At least not where I'm from.
Intermediate Client Statement 4
[Hopeful] Do you do tarot cards? I heard about tarot cards on a therapy podcast, and I think that would help me.
Intermediate Client Statement 5
The client is a cisgender man. **[Hostile]** I'm just saying I've never done this before. I'm here because my boyfriend said he'd dump me if I didn't get a handle on things.

🛑 **Assess and adjust the difficulty before moving to the next difficulty level (see Step 3 in the exercise instructions).**

ADVANCED-LEVEL CLIENT STATEMENTS FOR EXERCISE 2
Advanced Client Statement 1
The client is a cisgender woman in an army uniform and has a prosthetic limb.
[Confident] Yeah, I'm here for the anger management class. This is a class, right?
Advanced Client Statement 2
[Matter-of-fact] I had a spiritual mentor before. That was great. She really understood body positivity and supported my identity as a fat person. I'm worried that someone in a body like yours won't get it.
Advanced Client Statement 3
[Uncertain] I'm here because my pastor told me to come see someone. Is this religious counseling? I don't want anything that's going to go against my religion.
Advanced Client Statement 4
[Matter-of-fact] Can we pray together? That's really what I need.
Advanced Client Statement 5
[Anxious] Therapy isn't something Black people do. But my doctor recommended it along with the medication she's prescribing me. Have you worked with someone like me before?

> **Assess and adjust the difficulty here (see Step 3 in the exercise instructions). If appropriate, follow the instructions to make the exercise even more challenging (see Appendix A).**

Example Therapist Responses: Assessing Client Expectations

Remember: Trainees should attempt to improvise their own responses before reading the example responses. **Do not read the following responses verbatim unless you are having trouble coming up with your own responses!**

EXAMPLE RESPONSES TO BEGINNER-LEVEL CLIENT STATEMENTS FOR EXERCISE 2
Example Response to Beginner Client Statement 1
That makes sense, thanks for bringing it up. (Criterion 1) I'm glad you were able to find me. I can imagine that challenges in finding an accessible office shape how you might think or feel about therapy. (Criterion 3) Coming in today, did you have any expectations for what therapy would look like? (Criterion 2)
Example Response to Beginner Client Statement 2
That's great. You're trying something new. (Criterion 1) From watching the show, what did you expect therapy to be like? (Criterion 2) I'd also love to know more about the show you watch and why it's important to you. (Criterion 3)
Example Response to Beginner Client Statement 3
So, it probably took a lot for you to come here today. That's a perspective I've heard from a lot of folks. (Criterion 1) As we talk, I'd really like to hear more about your family, their beliefs, and the ways in which you might think differently. (Criterion 3) What did you imagine would happen in therapy, and do you think that means you're weak? (Criterion 2)
Example Response to Beginner Client Statement 4
You've already taken that first step of acknowledging you need some help. (Criterion 1) Maybe you can tell me more about what your expectations are for therapy. (Criterion 2) I'd also like to know more about what you mean when you say, "Everyone thinks we're so strong." (Criterion 3)
Example Response to Beginner Client Statement 5
You're really good at building yourself up. That's a great skill to have! (Criterion 1) Can you give me an example of what you expect this process to be like? (Criterion 2) I'm also curious about your culture and how that plays a role in your beliefs about depression. (Criterion 3)

EXAMPLE RESPONSES TO INTERMEDIATE-LEVEL CLIENT STATEMENTS FOR EXERCISE 2
Example Response to Intermediate Client Statement 1
Yeah, it's great that you're already taking steps to address your issues. (Criterion 1) What do you know about therapy and how this process works? (Criterion 2) I can also imagine that being involved with the justice system informs how you're thinking about our work together. (Criterion 3)
Example Response to Intermediate Client Statement 2
Great question. (Criterion 1) Sometimes therapy involves advice, or action steps, or helping you get to know and understand yourself more deeply. I'd really like to learn what feels most important to you in therapy. (Criterion 2) And you mentioned that our shared background is important—what about my background seems similar to yours? (Criterion 3)
Example Response to Intermediate Client Statement 3
I appreciate you taking a chance in coming in and for letting me know how countercultural this is for you. (Criterion 1) Is your expectation that therapy is mainly talking about feelings? (Criterion 2) I'd also like to know more about where you're from and what it means to be a man in your culture. (Criterion 3)
Example Response to Intermediate Client Statement 4
You've already taken steps like listening to podcast to help yourself. That's a great first step. (Criterion 1) I don't do tarot cards, but I'd like to understand more about your spiritual beliefs and the kinds of things you're looking for help with. (Criterion 3) When you set the appointment, what were you hoping we'd work on in therapy? (Criterion 2)
Example Response to Intermediate Client Statement 5
This is the first time you're trying this, and it sounds like the stakes are high. (Criterion 1) Your relationship with your boyfriend must be important to you, and I'd like to know more about it. (Criterion 3) First, can we talk about what you expected therapy to be like? (Criterion 2)

EXAMPLE RESPONSES TO ADVANCED-LEVEL CLIENT STATEMENTS FOR EXERCISE 2
Example Response to Advanced Client Statement 1
I'm glad you're here. This is a little different than a class because it's one-on-one and I'll have the opportunity to get to know you better than in a group format. (Criterion 1) I notice you're in uniform, and I'm curious about how being a female veteran relates to your experience with angry feelings. What kind of things were you expecting we'd do in a first session? (Criterion 3)
Example Response to Advanced Client Statement 2
That's a big deal. Sounds like she was a force for good in your life and that she really understood your identity as a fat person. (Criterion 1) You're right that our bodies are different sizes. Can you tell me more about what you're expecting therapy to be like and the things you're worried I might not understand because of my body size? (Criterion 3)
Example Response to Advanced Client Statement 3
I'm glad you took your pastor's advice. (Criterion 1) When you came in today, what did you expect? I want us to collaborate in a way that supports your religious faith. (Criteria 2 and 3)
Example Response to Advanced Client Statement 4
Sounds like your spirituality is really important to you. That's great that you have that as a resource. (Criteria 1 and 3) Have you had spiritual counseling before? Maybe you thought this would be like that?
Example Response to Advanced Client Statement 5
Thanks for letting me know how countercultural this is for you. (Criterion 1) I have worked with many Black clients, but that doesn't mean I know anything about your individual experience. (Criterion 3) What are you thinking might happen in therapy that goes against your culture?

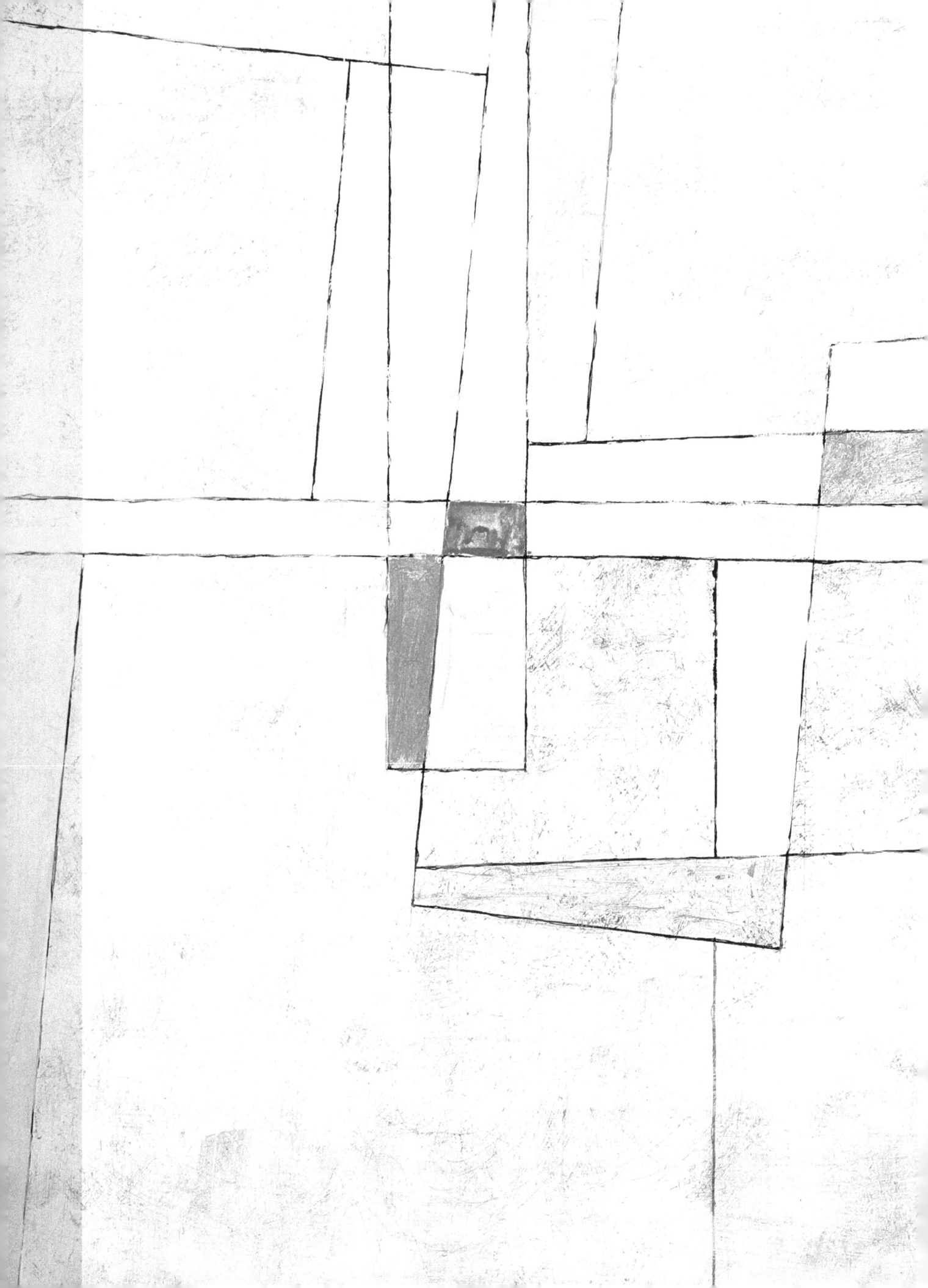

Reflecting Content Through a Cultural Lens

Preparations for Exercise 3

1. Read the instructions in Chapter 2.

2. Download the Deliberate Practice Reaction Form and the Deliberate Practice Diary Form at https://www.apa.org/pubs/books/deliberate-practice-multicultural-therapy (see the "Clinician and Practitioner Resources" tab; also available in Appendixes A and B, respectively).

Skill Description

Skill Difficulty Level: Beginner

Maintaining a culturally informed framework, even when reflecting clients' statements, is a skill that helps build a strong therapeutic relationship. A therapist conveys their empathy and understanding of the client's cultural experience by making a statement (not asking a question) that reflects back the client's experience using different words. This technique is not done by simply repeating the client's statement verbatim. The therapist does not offer their opinion or any advice. The goal of reflecting content through a cultural lens is to demonstrate to the client that their experience is clearly understood by the therapist. Clients who perceive their therapists as comfortable, genuine, and relaxed—demonstrating cultural comfort—when exploring culture and intersectionality also experience greater reductions in distress (Bartholomew et al., 2021). Additionally, when therapists seize cultural opportunities early on in treatment, this sets the tone for the entirety of therapy, helping clients be more open to discuss the ways in which their distress intersects with identity and past experiences of marginalization (Owen et al., 2016). This helps the client to process their experience and continue moving toward self-acceptance and growth. It also helps lay the foundation for cultural opportunities, cultural humility, and cultural comfort.

https://doi.org/10.1037/0000357–005

Deliberate Practice in Multicultural Therapy, by J. Harris, J. Jin, S. Hoffman, S. Phan, T. A. Prout, T. Rousmaniere, and A. Vaz

SKILL CRITERIA FOR EXERCISE 3

1. Make a statement that reflects back the client's experience, in the context of cultural and identity factors, using your own words.
2. Use a tone that is supportive and exploratory.

Examples of Therapists Reflecting Content Through a Cultural Lens

Example 1

CLIENT: [*worried*] I don't want my parents to drop me off at school this year. People have a hard time understanding them. I just don't want anyone to think I'm different because of them.

THERAPIST: You're worried about what people will think of you because your parents are different from theirs. (Criteria 1 and 2)

Example 2

CLIENT: [*sad*] I'm going to miss my best friend when she leaves for college. She's the only other person who knew what it was like to have separated parents like me.

THERAPIST: You've felt really close with this friend, so this must be a big loss. It sounds like she was a rare person in your life who truly understood what it's been like to have your parents separate. (Criteria 1 and 2)

Example 3

CLIENT: [*happy*] I finally found others from my home country who had to seek asylum.

THERAPIST: You've been patient. You're excited to find others who share a similar journey here. (Criteria 1 and 2)

INSTRUCTIONS FOR EXERCISE 3

Step 1: Role-Play and Feedback

- The client says the first beginner client statement. The therapist **improvises** a response based on the skill criteria.
- The trainer (or, if not available, the client) provides **brief** feedback based on the skill criteria.
- The client then repeats the same statement, and the therapist again improvises a response. The trainer (or client) again provides brief feedback.

Step 2: Repeat

- Repeat Step 1 for all the statements **in the current difficulty level** (beginner, intermediate, or advanced).

Step 3: Assess and Adjust Difficulty

- The therapist completes the Deliberate Practice Reaction Form (see Appendix A) and decides whether to make the exercise easier or harder or to repeat the same difficulty level.

Step 4: Repeat for Approximately 15 Minutes

- Repeat Steps 1 to 3 for at least 15 minutes.
- The trainees then switch therapist and client roles and start over.

Now it's your turn! Follow Steps 1 and 2 from the exercise instructions.

Remember: The goal of the role-play is for trainees to practice improvising responses to the client statements in a manner that (a) uses the skill criteria and (b) feels authentic for the trainee. **Example therapist responses for each client statement are provided at the end of this exercise. Trainees should attempt to improvise their own responses before reading the example responses.**

BEGINNER-LEVEL CLIENT STATEMENTS FOR EXERCISE 3
Beginner Client Statement 1
[Worried] I don't want my parents to drop me off at school this year. People have a hard time understanding them. I just don't want anyone to think I'm different because of them.
Beginner Client Statement 2
[Motivated] I haven't gone to church in a long time, but I want to try it out again.
Beginner Client Statement 3
[Sad] I don't want to go to high school next year. I can't play in the band, and that's why school is fun. I heard you get made fun of for being in a school band.
Beginner Client Statement 4
[Grateful] I think I finally found some friends! There's a student group at my college that's only for queer students, and the faculty advisor is out too.
Beginner Client Statement 5
[Sad] I'm going to miss my best friend when she leaves for college. She's the only other person who knew what it was like to have separated parents like me.

🛑 **Assess and adjust the difficulty before moving to the next difficulty level (see Step 3 in the exercise instructions).**

INTERMEDIATE-LEVEL CLIENT STATEMENTS FOR EXERCISE 3
Intermediate Client Statement 1
[Frustrated] I feel anxious every time I'm in this one mall. I can tell that the security guards are tailing me around the stores. They never follow my friends though.
Intermediate Client Statement 2
[Happy] I finally found others from my home country who had to seek asylum.
Intermediate Client Statement 3
[Worried] It's so easy for my other friends because they don't have to work part time or babysit their siblings. I have to help out my family. But after my job and chores, I can't focus on my homework. I hope my grades will be alright.
Intermediate Client Statement 4
[Sad] It's the little things on campus though. I'm having a hard time getting into buildings and using the restrooms.
Intermediate Client Statement 5
[Confused] So we've been talking about how my parents might play a role in my current romantic relationships. Well, my dad's always told me to "push through." I guess he was extra tough on me to be a man, you know, as his son. I'm not sure what that would have to do with my breakup right now though.

🛑 **Assess and adjust the difficulty before moving to the next difficulty level (see Step 3 in the exercise instructions).**

ADVANCED-LEVEL CLIENT STATEMENTS FOR EXERCISE 3
Advanced Client Statement 1
[Angry] They hired me to do an impossible job. I was bound to fail. Did they hire me just to make the team diverse?
Advanced Client Statement 2
[Depressed] Another professor kept going on about how this university is Catholic and shouldn't be for gay people. I've heard it all since being here, but it felt like the professor was aiming at me.
Advanced Client Statement 3
[Guilty] I'm thinking of going back to the reservation. My grandma says she misses me a lot, and it's been hard getting to know others at the university.
Advanced Client Statement 4
[Depressed] Sometimes I wish I didn't look so dark. I think I'm the only Latina in this prep school and I stand out so much.
Advanced Client Statement 5
[Angry] It's as if they've never seen a coder who's a woman and Black. I've had to work twice as hard as everyone else to get recognized.

> **Assess and adjust the difficulty here (see Step 3 in the exercise instructions). If appropriate, follow the instructions to make the exercise even more challenging (see Appendix A).**

Example Therapist Responses: Reflecting Content Through a Cultural Lens

Remember: Trainees should attempt to improvise their own responses before reading the example responses. **Do not read the following responses verbatim unless you are having trouble coming up with your own responses!**

EXAMPLE RESPONSES TO BEGINNER-LEVEL CLIENT STATEMENTS FOR EXERCISE 3
Example Response to Beginner Client Statement 1
You're worried about what people will think of you because your parents are different from theirs. (Criteria 1 and 2)
Example Response to Beginner Client Statement 2
It's been a while. And it sounds like something is shifting inside of you, pulling you back to a community of faith that might feel like a home. (Criteria 1 and 2)
Example Response to Beginner Client Statement 3
High school can feel so daunting! Band is important to you, and maybe you're worried others will make fun of you. (Criteria 1 and 2)
Example Response to Beginner Client Statement 4
I can see how happy you feel. You're finally finding friends who might really be able to understand your experience. (Criteria 1 and 2)
Example Response to Beginner Client Statement 5
You've felt really close with this friend, so this must be a big loss. It sounds like she was a rare person in your life who truly understood what it's been like to have your parents separate. (Criteria 1 and 2)

EXAMPLE RESPONSES TO INTERMEDIATE-LEVEL CLIENT STATEMENTS FOR EXERCISE 3
Example Response to Intermediate Client Statement 1
I can really understand how anxiety-provoking and frustrating that must be. Security guards are treating you differently compared to others. (Criteria 1 and 2)
Example Response to Intermediate Client Statement 2
You've been patient. You're excited to find others who share a similar journey here. (Criteria 1 and 2)
Example Response to Intermediate Client Statement 3
Wow, you're juggling so much while being a student. You're feeling anxious trying to keep up with helping your family and your studies. (Criteria 1 and 2)
Example Response to Intermediate Client Statement 4
These are basic issues of access that haven't been addressed on your campus. Having all these challenges at school must make it hard to be there and to feel like you belong. (Criteria 1 and 2)
Example Response to Intermediate Client Statement 5
That's an important reflection, this memory of how your dad taught you that a man ought to "push through." But maybe it's a little confusing that I'm asking about how this might be related to your recent breakup. (Criteria 1 and 2)

EXAMPLE RESPONSES TO ADVANCED-LEVEL CLIENT STATEMENTS FOR EXERCISE 3
Example Response to Advanced Client Statement 1
You're finding something at work is unfair. You're questioning why you've been hired in the first place. (Criteria 1 and 2)
Example Response to Advanced Client Statement 2
Tolerating these professors as a gay student has left you feeling exhausted and targeted. (Criteria 1 and 2)
Example Response to Advanced Client Statement 3
It sounds like you're feeling conflicted being away from the reservation, especially your grandma who means so much to you. (Criteria 1 and 2)
Example Response to Advanced Client Statement 4
Noticing that you stand out at this school, you feel really down. It can be hard to feel like you are different from everyone around you. (Criteria 1 and 2)
Example Response to Advanced Client Statement 5
You've worked harder than all your colleagues to get where you are. And yet, it's like they can't accept your expertise and recognize your value. (Criteria 1 and 2)

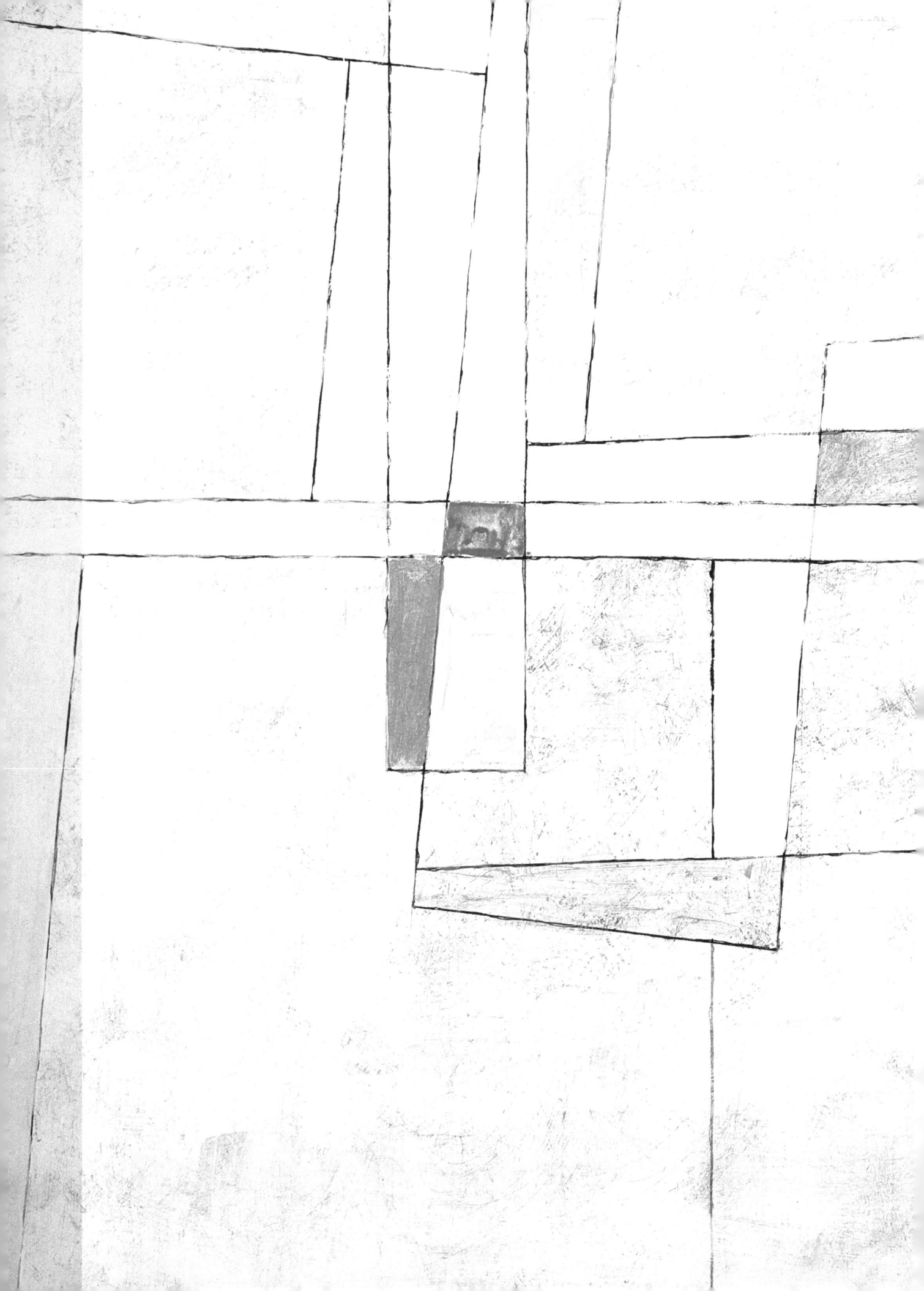

Inquiring About Identity: Cultural Opportunities I

Preparations for Exercise 4

1. Read the instructions in Chapter 2.

2. Download the Deliberate Practice Reaction Form and the Deliberate Practice Diary Form at https://www.apa.org/pubs/books/deliberate-practice-multicultural-therapy (see the "Clinician and Practitioner Resources" tab; also available in Appendixes A and B, respectively).

Skill Description

Skill Difficulty Level: Beginner

The goal of this exercise is to begin building your skills in exploring clients' cultural and intersectional identities. Cultural opportunities are the moments in psychotherapy when there is an opening to attend directly to aspects of clients' cultural identity, including aspects of race/ethnicity, gender, sexual orientation, religion, socioeconomic status, ability, and body size. One of the challenges of seizing upon cultural opportunities is developing the ability to respond in an attuned, contextual way. When doing this exercise, we recommend trying out different responses until you find you are able to stay connected to the client's concern and address issues of culture and identity without getting side-tracked. Addressing culture and identity in psychotherapy is a complex task, requiring the therapist to follow the natural unfolding of the therapeutic process (Owen et al., 2016). Although it is not necessary to engage every single cultural opportunity in an actual therapy session, it is important to encourage clients to explore and integrate their cultural identity whenever possible. There is some evidence that seeking cultural opportunities is especially important with clients who have multiple aspects of identity that are salient for them (e.g., intersectionality; Anders et al., 2021).

https://doi.org/10.1037/0000357-006

Deliberate Practice in Multicultural Therapy, by J. Harris, J. Jin, S. Hoffman, S. Phan, T. A. Prout, T. Rousmaniere, and A. Vaz

SKILL CRITERIA FOR EXERCISE 4

1. Empathically affirm the client's concern or statement.
2. Explore the client's cultural or intersectional identity as it relates to the client's concern or statement.

Examples of Therapists Inquiring About Identity

Example 1

CLIENT: [*worried*] I don't really want to transfer to this rich, private high school. I won't know anybody there, and all the kids drive nice cars. What if there's nobody like me?

THERAPIST: Going to a new school, especially one that is known for being "rich," can be really tough! (Criterion 1) It sounds like issues of wealth and status play a role in how you see yourself compared with others. Can you tell me more about that? (Criterion 2)

Example 2

CLIENT: [*embarrassed*] I almost didn't come to this session. I bet you rarely work with men.

THERAPIST: So, coming here today was really hard . . . and yet you made it. I'm glad you're telling me about your reluctance. (Criterion 1) It sounds like being a man is pretty central to your identity. I'd be glad to tell you more about my experience working with other male clients. But I'm also really curious about this part of you. What feels important about knowing your therapist has worked with other men? (Criterion 2)

Example 3

CLIENT: [*exhausted*] I had to figure out how to submit my college applications alone. My mom couldn't help because she's never been to college—no one in my family has ever been.

THERAPIST: You're right, there's something about being the first person in your family to go to college that's really important—and sometimes hard because you feel like you have to go it alone. (Criterion 1) Can you share more about that part of your background? (Criterion 2)

INSTRUCTIONS FOR EXERCISE 4

Step 1: Role-Play and Feedback

- The client says the first beginner client statement. The therapist **improvises** a response based on the skill criteria.
- The trainer (or, if not available, the client) provides **brief** feedback based on the skill criteria.
- The client then repeats the same statement, and the therapist again improvises a response. The trainer (or client) again provides brief feedback.

Step 2: Repeat

- Repeat Step 1 for all the statements **in the current difficulty level** (beginner, intermediate, or advanced).

Step 3: Assess and Adjust Difficulty

- The therapist completes the Deliberate Practice Reaction Form (see Appendix A) and decides whether to make the exercise easier or harder or to repeat the same difficulty level.

Step 4: Repeat for Approximately 15 Minutes

- Repeat Steps 1 to 3 for at least 15 minutes.
- The trainees then switch therapist and client roles and start over.

Now it's your turn! Follow Steps 1 and 2 from the exercise instructions.

Remember: The goal of the role-play is for trainees to practice improvising responses to the client statements in a manner that (a) uses the skill criteria and (b) feels authentic for the trainee. **Example therapist responses for each client statement are provided at the end of this exercise. Trainees should attempt to improvise their own responses before reading the examples.**

BEGINNER-LEVEL CLIENT STATEMENTS FOR EXERCISE 4
Beginner Client Statement 1
[Worried] I don't really want to transfer to this rich, private high school. I won't know anybody there, and all the kids drive nice cars. What if there's nobody like me?
Beginner Client Statement 2
[Embarrassed] I almost didn't come to this session. I bet you rarely work with men.
Beginner Client Statement 3
[Exhausted] I had to figure out how to submit my college applications alone. My mom couldn't help because she's never been to college—no one in my family has ever been.
Beginner Client Statement 4
[Frustrated] It's always the men controlling the lives of women. This is my life, isn't it?
Beginner Client Statement 5
[Grateful] You're the first therapist who's mentioned my wheelchair. I've been wanting to talk about this part of me.

Assess and adjust the difficulty before moving to the next difficulty level (see Step 3 in the exercise instructions).

INTERMEDIATE-LEVEL CLIENT STATEMENTS FOR EXERCISE 4
Intermediate Client Statement 1
[Irritated] Being a bisexual woman dating a man is complicated. People make a lot of assumptions.
Intermediate Client Statement 2
[Sad] People at work still misgender me. I'm starting to wonder if it's even worth it to correct people.
Intermediate Client Statement 3
[Frustrated] I want to be able to stand up to my parents more, but it would come across as disrespectful.
Intermediate Client Statement 4
[Sad] I always dreamed of becoming an engineer, but it's expected that I do something more "feminine."
Intermediate Client Statement 5
[Concerned] I'm afraid to start my new job. Bosses in the past haven't understood the way my brain functions.

🛑 **Assess and adjust the difficulty before moving to the next difficulty level (see Step 3 in the exercise instructions).**

ADVANCED-LEVEL CLIENT STATEMENTS FOR EXERCISE 4
Advanced Client Statement 1
[Euthymic] I feel really safe to be myself with you. I normally have to fit myself into a box to make others comfortable.
Advanced Client Statement 2
[Annoyed] I have a coworker who always makes a face and wrinkles her nose when I heat up my lunch. It happens at least three times a week. She doesn't do that to anyone else.
Advanced Client Statement 3
[Hurt] I can tell that you're younger than me and that you really are trying to understand. But I don't think therapy will work because of our age difference. My kids, who are probably around your age, never want to listen to me.
Advanced Client Statement 4
[Upset] I hate going to family gatherings because everyone speaks the same language, which I don't understand. My parents made me speak only English to fit in, but now I don't fit in with my family.
Advanced Client Statement 5
[Determined] I think I need to change my hair to be taken seriously at work.

Assess and adjust the difficulty here (see Step 3 in the exercise instructions). If appropriate, follow the instructions to make the exercise even more challenging (see Appendix A).

Example Therapist Responses: Inquiring About Identity

Remember: Trainees should attempt to improvise their own responses before reading the example responses. **Do not read the following responses verbatim unless you are having trouble coming up with your own responses!**

EXAMPLE RESPONSES TO BEGINNER-LEVEL CLIENT STATEMENTS FOR EXERCISE 4
Example Response to Beginner Client Statement 1
Going to a new school, especially one that is known for being "rich," can be really tough! I'm glad you mentioned that part about having nice cars. (Criterion 1) It sounds like issues of wealth and status play a role in how you see yourself compared to others. Can you tell me more about that? If there are kids who drive nice cars and not, then how do you describe yourself? (Criterion 2)
Example Response to Beginner Client Statement 2
So, coming here today was really hard . . . and yet you made it. I'm glad you're telling me about your reluctance. I appreciate you bringing up what it's like for men to seek therapy. (Criterion 1) It sounds like being a man is pretty central to your identity. I'd be glad to tell you more about my experience working with other male clients. But I'm also really curious about this part of you. What feels important about knowing your therapist has worked with other men? Could you tell me more about what it means to be a man? (Criterion 2)
Example Response to Beginner Client Statement 3
You're right, there's something about being the first person in your family to go to college that's really important—and sometimes hard because you feel like you have to go it alone here. (Criterion 1) Can you share more about that part of your identity? (Criterion 2)
Example Response to Beginner Client Statement 4
I can hear you wanting more control of your life, as opposed to men dictating your life. (Criterion 1) Can you tell me more about what that means for you as a woman? (Criterion 2)
Example Response to Beginner Client Statement 5
It must be frustrating to feel like this part of you has been overlooked. (Criterion 1) I wonder how this has affected your past experiences in therapy as therapists didn't attend to your use of a wheelchair. (Criterion 2)

EXAMPLE RESPONSES TO INTERMEDIATE-LEVEL CLIENT STATEMENTS FOR EXERCISE 4
Example Response to Intermediate Client Statement 1
People are misunderstanding who you are, who you're attracted to, and that you're not simple in identities. (Criterion 1) If we pay attention to you as a whole, as a bisexual woman, how would you define yourself? What are those assumptions you want to question? (Criterion 2)
Example Response to Intermediate Client Statement 2
It sounds exhausting to have to constantly fight this battle. It's another stressor at work, trying to be known for who you are. (Criterion 1) Can you tell me more about your gender identity and how it has developed over the years? (Criterion 2)
Example Response to Intermediate Client Statement 3
You're wanting to share with your parents what you think and want, yet you're afraid something about that could be seen as disrespectful by your parents, perhaps related to your family or cultural values. That's really tricky. (Criterion 1) Can you share more about these parts of your identity? (Criterion 2)
Example Response to Intermediate Client Statement 4
You have these dreams for yourself that are opposed by the expectations that others are placing on you. According to them, there isn't a fit. (Criterion 1) What are your expectations of who you are and what you can do? (Criterion 2)
Example Response to Intermediate Client Statement 5
You have these past experiences with bosses that are reminding you of how stressful work can be as you start this new job, specifically related to how you process and make sense of work. (Criterion 1) Can you tell me more about that, of how your brain functions and what that means about how you operate in the world? (Criterion 2)

EXAMPLE RESPONSES TO ADVANCED-LEVEL CLIENT STATEMENTS FOR EXERCISE 4

Example Response to Advanced Client Statement 1

I'm glad you're feeling safer here. That's important as we work together. At the same time, you may feel some anxiety or fear because of what we're working on. Perhaps similar to how you feel with others in that box. I hope you can let me know when that happens too. (Criterion 1) Can you tell me how you're feeling safer here with me and not in this box, compared to when you're with others? (Criterion 2)

Example Response to Advanced Client Statement 2

You're treated differently by this coworker as you eat the food you like. I imagine this takes a toll on you as you notice this frequently over time. (Criterion 1) Can you tell me what food you enjoy and what food means in the context of your culture and identity? (Criterion 2)

Example Response to Advanced Client Statement 3

I appreciate you sharing this with me. You're concerned if I'll listen intently to what you have to say, especially because your kids, who like me are younger than you are, don't listen. (Criterion 1) Certainly I can help you find a better fit. But if you're willing, can you tell me more about being older and not having a listening ear from those who are younger, particularly from your kids? (Criterion 2)

Example Response to Advanced Client Statement 4

If you're unable to speak the language your family does, and they don't use much English, I can see how you feel isolated. You want to connect, and it's hard to. (Criterion 1) Can you tell me more about being an English speaker within your family? (Criterion 2)

Example Response to Advanced Client Statement 5

I can tell you want to fit in and do well at work. Yet there's something challenging at work, perhaps related to how you're treated because of how you look. (Criterion 1) Can you share more about the significance of your hair, both to you personally and how it relates to your role at work? (Criterion 2)

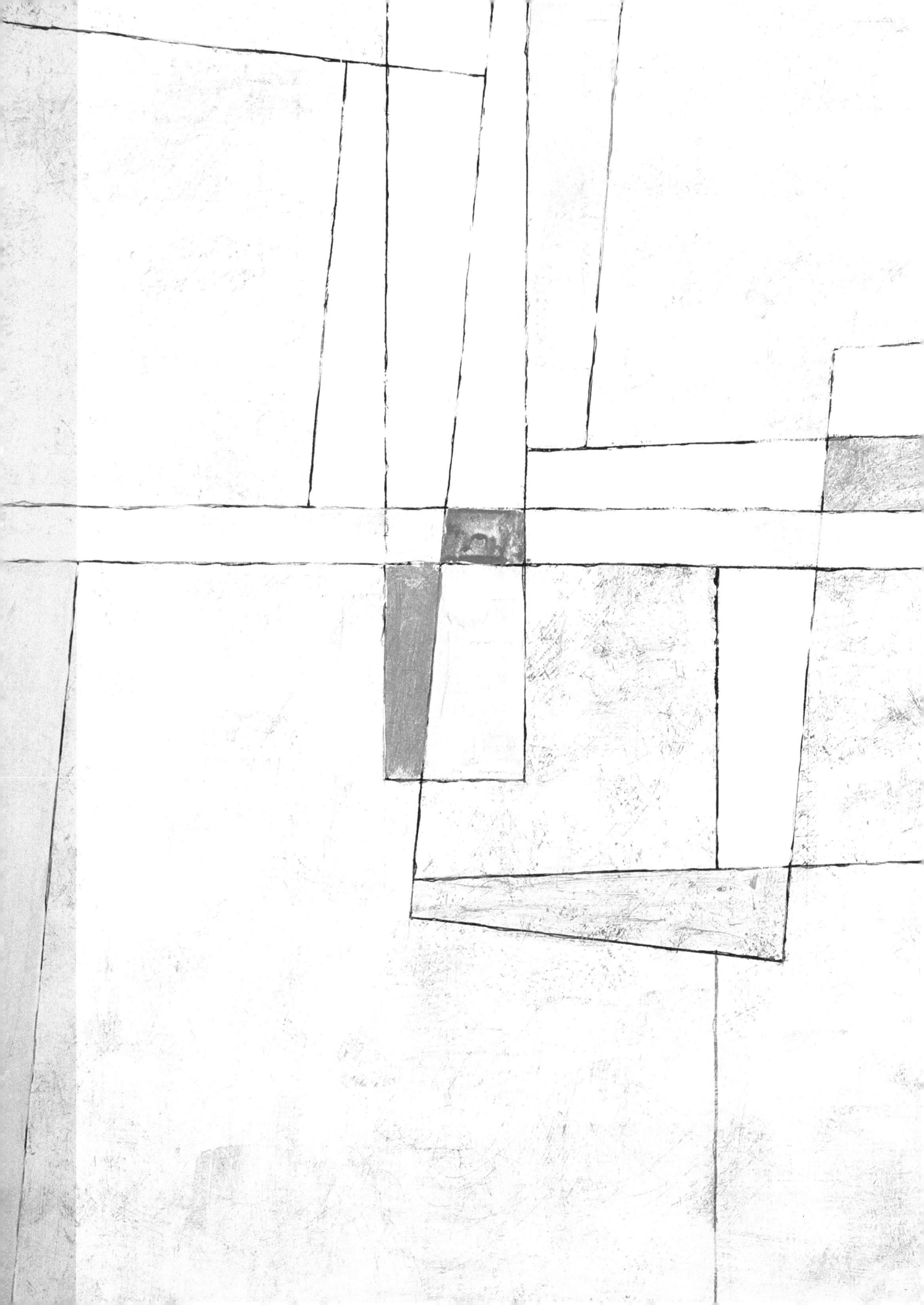

Working With Emotions in Context

Preparations for Exercise 5

1. Read the instructions in Chapter 2.

2. Download the Deliberate Practice Reaction Form and the Deliberate Practice Diary Form at https://www.apa.org/pubs/books/deliberate-practice-multicultural-therapy (see the "Clinician and Practitioner Resources" tab; also available in Appendixes A and B, respectively).

Skill Description

Skill Difficulty Level: Intermediate

The goal of working with emotions in context is to understand the client's experience of emotions as it relates to their culture and identities. Depending on one's cultural identities, emotions are experienced, expressed, perceived, and regulated differently (Mesquita et al., 2017). Sociocultural values influence emotional functioning and must be considered when working with clients. For example, the emotional experience of anger and shame is largely predicted by an individual's culture of origin (Boiger et al., 2018). Similarly, factors such as gender (Kwon et al., 2013), age, socioeconomic status (Mankus et al., 2016), and many other aspects of identity impact emotional expression and awareness.

Many clients have experienced *emotional acculturation*, which describes the ways in which emotional expression and experience change as a result of sustained contact with another cultural environment (De Leersnyder, 2017; De Leersnyder et al., 2020). As people move between different cultural frames of reference, the ways in which they experience and express emotions can change significantly. Interestingly, there is some evidence that acculturating to the dominant culture, whereby there is greater similarity between the individual's and the mainstream culture's patterns of emotion and emotion regulation, is associated with fewer somatic symptoms (Consedine et al., 2014).

https://doi.org/10.1037/0000357-007

Deliberate Practice in Multicultural Therapy, by J. Harris, J. Jin, S. Hoffman, S. Phan, T. A. Prout, T. Rousmaniere, and A. Vaz

This exercise provides the opportunity to practice exploring emotions in the context of personal identity. By encouraging clients to reconnect to emotional experience in the context of intersectional identity and cultural background, clinicians can remain flexibly attuned to the needs of their clients.

SKILL CRITERIA FOR EXERCISE 5
1. Reflect a core meaning from the client's statement.
2. Curiously explore if culture and/or identity influence the client's emotional experience.

Examples of Therapists Working With Emotions in Context

Example 1

CLIENT: [*anxious*] I'm not really sure how I'm feeling. We didn't talk about feelings growing up.

THERAPIST: Sometimes it's really hard to understand what's going on inside emotionally, especially if you didn't have the opportunity or language to explore these things when you were young. (Criterion 1) Can you tell me more about your family's background and how that relates to your uncertainty around feelings? (Criterion 2)

Example 2

CLIENT: [*sad*] Honestly, sometimes I wonder if I'm cut out to be a parent. All the teachers at my son's school just see a poor, Black, single mom. They have no idea how much I'm juggling.

THERAPIST: You really are working overtime to keep everything in your family moving smoothly and also trying to take care of yourself through therapy and the other supports you have. I see this so clearly. (Criterion 1) Your mention of being poor, single, Black, and a mother made me really curious. It sounds like the teachers are missing something important. Can you tell me more about how it feels to feel like others aren't truly seeing you? (Criterion 2)

Example 3

CLIENT: [*crying*] I can't believe I'll never see my husband again. I can't believe God would take him away from me so soon.

THERAPIST: This has been such a tragic and painful loss. (Criterion 1) I hear you wondering about God's role in all of this, and it makes me curious about how you feel inside when you can't make sense of things in the context of your relationship with God. (Criterion 2)

INSTRUCTIONS FOR EXERCISE 5
Step 1: Role-Play and Feedback
• The client says the first beginner client statement. The therapist **improvises** a response based on the skill criteria. • The trainer (or, if not available, the client) provides **brief** feedback based on the skill criteria. • The client then repeats the same statement, and the therapist again improvises a response. The trainer (or client) again provides brief feedback.
Step 2: Repeat
• Repeat Step 1 for all the statements **in the current difficulty level** (beginner, intermediate, or advanced).
Step 3: Assess and Adjust Difficulty
• The therapist completes the Deliberate Practice Reaction Form (see Appendix A) and decides whether to make the exercise easier or harder or to repeat the same difficulty level.
Step 4: Repeat for Approximately 15 Minutes
• Repeat Steps 1 to 3 for at least 15 minutes. • The trainees then switch therapist and client roles and start over.

Now it's your turn! Follow Steps 1 and 2 from the exercise instructions.

Remember: The goal of the role-play is for trainees to practice improvising responses to the client statements in a manner that (a) uses the skill criteria and (b) feels authentic for the trainee. **Example therapist responses for each client statement are provided at the end of this exercise. Trainees should attempt to improvise their own responses before reading the examples.**

BEGINNER-LEVEL CLIENT STATEMENTS FOR EXERCISE 5
Beginner Client Statement 1
[Anxious] I'm not really sure how I'm feeling. We didn't talk about feelings growing up.
Beginner Client Statement 2
[Sad] Honestly, sometimes I wonder if I'm cut out to be a parent. All the teachers at my son's school just see a poor, Black, single mom. They have no idea how much I'm juggling.
Beginner Client Statement 3
[Crying] I can't believe I'll never see my husband again. I can't believe God would take him away from me so soon.
Beginner Client Statement 4
[Angry, distant] I don't want to talk about it. Transphobia is just part of my everyday existence.
Beginner Client Statement 5
[Proud] I'm grateful that my parents are living with us. It's my chance to give back to them and take care of them as they took care of me.

🛑 **Assess and adjust the difficulty before moving to the next difficulty level (see Step 3 in the exercise instructions).**

INTERMEDIATE-LEVEL CLIENT STATEMENTS FOR EXERCISE 5
Intermediate Client Statement 1
[**Worried**] I don't want people to see me or treat me differently just because of my facial paralysis. It's not my fault I got this after my stroke. I just want to be normal.
Intermediate Client Statement 2
[**Ashamed, embarrassed**] Nobody can know that I'm in therapy. It's looked down upon in my community. I tell my family and friends that I have this weekly class for professional development.
Intermediate Client Statement 3
[**Angry**] I got so mad at my friend the other day. I tried to open up to him about my sexuality, and he asked me all these judgmental, offensive questions. I thought I could trust him, but I was wrong.
Intermediate Client Statement 4
[**Hopeless**] The news has really been affecting me. I feel so hopeless about the future. Like half the world doesn't even want me to exist.
Intermediate Client Statement 5
[**Looking downward, sad**] I guess we weren't chosen by God to have children. This is the sixth pregnancy I've lost and I feel nothing.

🛑 **Assess and adjust the difficulty before moving to the next difficulty level (see Step 3 in the exercise instructions).**

ADVANCED-LEVEL CLIENT STATEMENTS FOR EXERCISE 5
Advanced Client Statement 1
[Resentful, fists clenched] It's fine. It's totally fine. People like me can't show our anger . . . unless we wanna get shot.
Advanced Client Statement 2
[Hopeless] My partner is going to leave me if I don't tell my parents about our relationship.
Advanced Client Statement 3
[Flat affect] I got passed over for promotion. I'm pretty sure it was simply because I'm a woman. If you were my boss, you probably would have passed me over too, huh?
Advanced Client Statement 4
[Annoyed] How does that make me feel? I don't know. You tell me. You're the one with the big fancy degree. How do you think it makes me feel?
Advanced Client Statement 5
[Conflicted, ambivalent] Part of me wants to get better and stay sober, but there's the other part of me that doesn't want to feel the pain and hurt from all the things I missed out on in my childhood. I wish I could let go of my story and just move on.

Assess and adjust the difficulty here (see Step 3 in the exercise instructions). If appropriate, follow the instructions to make the exercise even more challenging (see Appendix A).

Example Therapist Responses: Working With Emotions in Context

Remember: Trainees should attempt to improvise their own responses before reading the example responses. **Do not read the following responses verbatim unless you are having trouble coming up with your own responses!**

EXAMPLE RESPONSES TO BEGINNER-LEVEL CLIENT STATEMENTS FOR EXERCISE 5
Example Response to Beginner Client Statement 1
Sometimes it's really hard to understand what's going on inside emotionally, especially if you didn't have the opportunity or language to explore these things when you were young. (Criterion 1) Can you tell me more about your family's background and how that relates to your uncertainty around feelings? (Criterion 2)
Example Response to Beginner Client Statement 2
You really are working overtime to keep everything in your family moving smoothly and also trying to take care of yourself through therapy and the other supports you have. I see this so clearly. (Criterion 1) Your mention of being poor, single, Black, and a mother made me really curious. It sounds like the teachers are missing something really important. Can you tell me more about how it feels when others aren't truly seeing you? (Criterion 2)
Example Response to Beginner Client Statement 3
This has been such a tragic and painful loss. (Criterion 1) I hear you wondering about God's role in all of this, and it makes me curious about how you feel inside when you can't make sense of things in the context of your relationship with God. (Criterion 2)
Example Response to Beginner Client Statement 4
That is a lot to carry and withstand day in and day out. So much so that you don't want to talk about it. (Criterion 1) I hear a sense of hopelessness in your voice. Would it be possible for you to share with me what makes it hard to even talk about being trans? Especially in a world that is hostile to your identity. (Criterion 2)
Example Response to Beginner Client Statement 5
Wow. You're doing something really important. A way to give back to the people who raised you. (Criterion 1) Can you tell me more about how your cultural values inform your experience of having your parents live with you? (Criterion 2)

EXAMPLE RESPONSES TO INTERMEDIATE-LEVEL CLIENT STATEMENTS FOR EXERCISE 5

Example Response to Intermediate Client Statement 1

This is such a huge and difficult change in your life. There is a real longing in what you said—a wish to undo what has happened. (Criterion 1) Can you tell me more about this idea of "being normal" and how it feels to think you aren't "normal"? (Criterion 2)

Example Response to Intermediate Client Statement 2

Therapy feels like something that needs to be hidden, like maybe you're a little embarrassed. (Criterion 1) You mentioned how therapy is viewed in your community. How does coming to therapy feel to you? (Criterion 2)

Example Response to Intermediate Client Statement 3

Wow. It sounds like he really let you down and hurt your feelings. I can imagine that it's hard to know who to trust with this part of your identity. (Criterion 1) Maybe you're also wondering if you can trust me. How does it feel to share about your sexuality with me? (Criterion 2)

Example Response to Intermediate Client Statement 4

There is so much in the news that is hard to tolerate and digest. (Criterion 1) I'd like to understand what specifically is feeling like an attack on you and parts of your identity. Can you tell me more? (Criterion 2)

Example Response to Intermediate Client Statement 5

I'm so sorry you are going through this loss yet again. (Criterion 1) Can you tell me more about how your relationship with God and your faith affect your emotional experience around these losses? (Criterion 2)

EXAMPLE RESPONSES TO ADVANCED-LEVEL CLIENT STATEMENTS FOR EXERCISE 5

Example Response to Advanced Client Statement 1

You have to be so careful, and it feels unsafe to show what you really feel. (Criterion 1) I have some idea, but I'd like to understand specifically what you mean when you say "people like me." What part of your identity leads you to feel so silenced? (Criterion 2)

Example Response to Advanced Client Statement 2

You're really stuck between your partner's needs and your parents' judgment. (Criterion 1) I'd like to understand more about what you're feeling. What is the emotional experience for you when you're caught between this pressure to disclose and the felt need for secrecy? (Criterion 2)

Example Response to Advanced Client Statement 3

I'm so sorry you got passed over for promotion. That must feel so deflating. (Criterion 1) I'm curious about your sense that I would pass you over too. Is there something that has happened in our relationship, maybe a sense that I view you as "less than" because you are a woman? Can we talk about your feelings around this? (Criterion 2)

Example Response to Advanced Client Statement 4

I have been asking you a lot of probing questions about your emotional experience. And maybe you feel that we are operating on two different levels—your real-world experience and me, with my fancy degree in this fancy office. (Criterion 1) Does this difference in our perceived socioeconomic status make it hard to open up in this room? (Criterion 2)

Example Response to Advanced Client Statement 5

You are really torn. It sounds like you've been able to see how using substances protected you in some ways from having to contend with the past. (Criterion 1) I'd like to understand your story more, to stand alongside you so you don't have to do it alone and you don't have to escape into substances. Without having to go into too much painful detail, what parts of your history are the ones you'd most like to let go of? (Criterion 2)

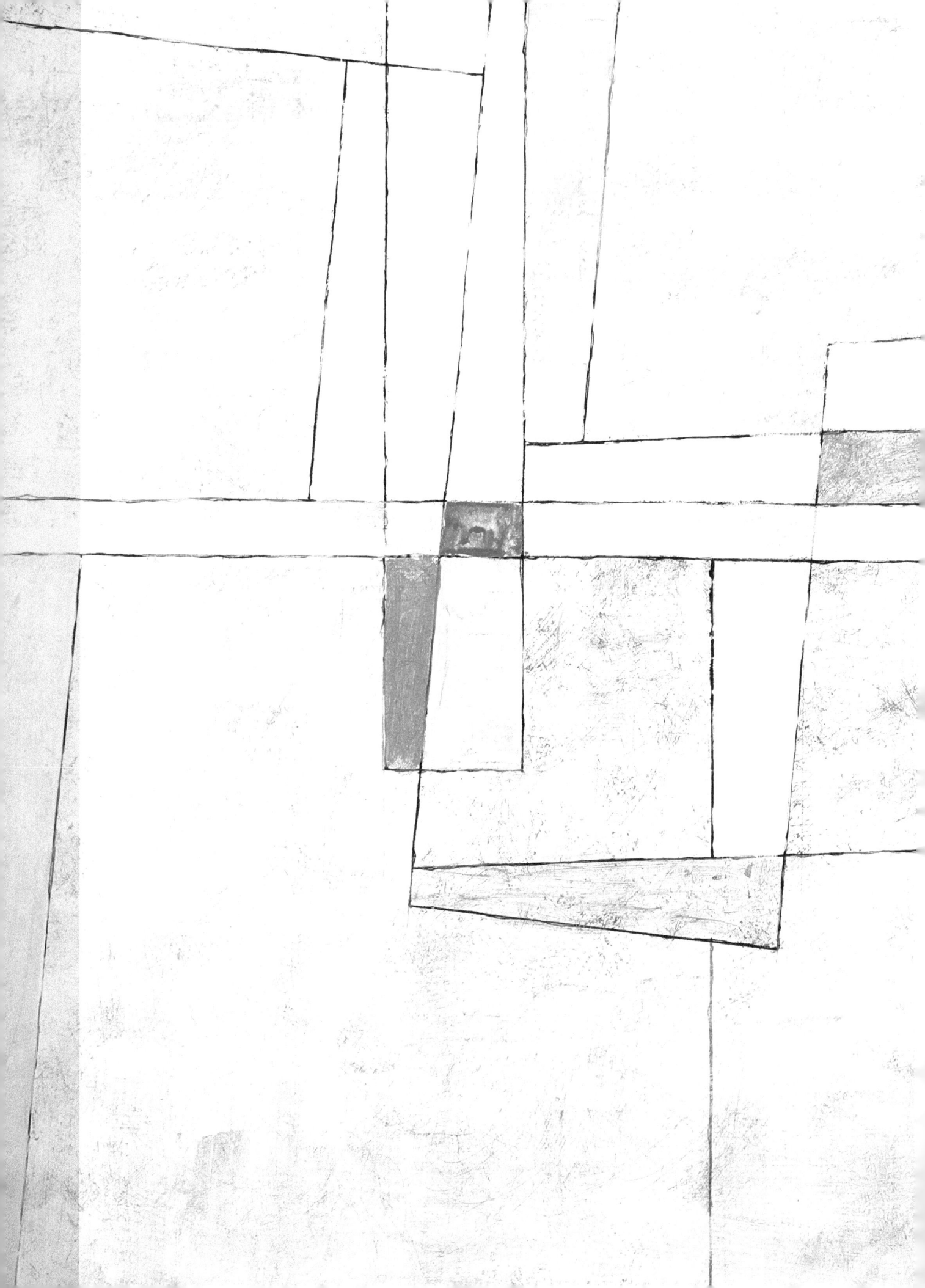

Maintaining a Not-Knowing Stance: Cultural Humility II

Preparations for Exercise 6

1. Read the instructions in Chapter 2.

2. Download the Deliberate Practice Reaction Form and the Deliberate Practice Diary Form at https://www.apa.org/pubs/books/deliberate-practice-multicultural-therapy (see the "Clinician and Practitioner Resources" tab; also available in Appendixes A and B, respectively).

Skill Description

Skill Difficulty Level: Intermediate

The shift from "competency" to "humility" is a shift from a "way of doing" to a "way of being" (Hook et al., 2017). In this exercise, we explore one facet of this "way of being": maintaining the "not knowing" stance. A "way of being" requires us to be (a) curious without being anthropological, (b) humble about the limits of our knowledge without being overly self-effacing or self-flagellating, and (c) respectful and open in the face of our own mistakes without being excessively anxious about the inevitability of missteps or misunderstandings.

In this exercise, you will be asked to respond to client scenarios in which there has been a moment of misunderstanding, direction confusion, lack of awareness, or active "wrongness" about a facet of a client's identity. The moving through the "not knowing" and maintaining a "way of being" characterized by cultural humility throughout the potential rupture is the focus of this exercise.

https://doi.org/10.1037/0000357–008

Deliberate Practice in Multicultural Therapy, by J. Harris, J. Jin, S. Hoffman, S. Phan, T. A. Prout, T. Rousmaniere, and A. Vaz

SKILL CRITERIA FOR EXERCISE 6
1. Calmly and succinctly acknowledge something you do not understand or know.
2. Gently ask for clarification.

Examples of Therapists Maintaining a Not-Knowing Stance

Note: Underlined text is to be read aloud by the person playing the client to provide context.

Example 1

The client is a transgender woman.

CLIENT: [*sad*] I just feel so different when I visit my family since starting HRT.[1]

THERAPIST: I'm not sure what HRT is. (Criterion 1) Would you feel comfortable explaining that to me? (Criterion 2)

or

THERAPIST: I'm interested to hear more about your family, but first, you used an abbreviation just then: HRT. I want to make sure I know what that means before we keep going. (Criterion 1) It feels important to me understanding your experience well. (Criterion 2)

Example 2

CLIENT: [*frustrated*] I know you don't speak Spanish, but it would be a lot easier if I could speak Spanish here sometimes.

THERAPIST: That makes sense to me! But since I don't speak Spanish, (Criterion 1) maybe we can decide together how to approach those times? (Criterion 2)

or

THERAPIST: Even though I don't speak Spanish it sounds like that would be valuable. (Criterion 1) Should we try anyway and see how it feels even if I don't fully understand it? (Criterion 2)

Example 3

The client corrects you after you used the word "gay."

CLIENT: [*annoyed*] I'm pansexual—not gay. Do you even know what that means?

THERAPIST: I'm actually not quite sure what that means, (Criterion 1) would you mind helping me understand the difference? (Criterion 2)

or

THERAPIST: I think we bumped up against the limits of my vocabulary just then—I made the wrong assumption about using the word "gay" to describe you. (Criterion 1) Maybe you can explain more about how you view your identity so I can get to know you a bit more, so I don't make that mistake again. (Criterion 2)

1. The client is using an abbreviated term for *hormone replacement therapy* that some transgender people undergo.

INSTRUCTIONS FOR EXERCISE 6
Step 1: Role-Play and Feedback
<ul><li>The client says the first beginner client statement. The therapist **improvises** a response based on the skill criteria.</li><li>The trainer (or, if not available, the client) provides **brief** feedback based on the skill criteria.</li><li>The client then repeats the same statement, and the therapist again improvises a response. The trainer (or client) again provides brief feedback.</li></ul>
Step 2: Repeat
<ul><li>Repeat Step 1 for all the statements **in the current difficulty level** (beginner, intermediate, or advanced).</li></ul>
Step 3: Assess and Adjust Difficulty
<ul><li>The therapist completes the Deliberate Practice Reaction Form (see Appendix A) and decides whether to make the exercise easier or harder or to repeat the same difficulty level.</li></ul>
Step 4: Repeat for Approximately 15 Minutes
<ul><li>Repeat Steps 1 to 3 for at least 15 minutes.</li><li>The trainees then switch therapist and client roles and start over.</li></ul>

Now it's your turn! Follow Steps 1 and 2 from the exercise instructions.

Remember: The goal of the role-play is for trainees to practice improvising responses to the client statements in a manner that (a) uses the skill criteria and (b) feels authentic for the trainee. **Example therapist responses for each client statement are provided at the end of this exercise. Trainees should attempt to improvise their own responses before reading the example responses.**

Note: Underlined text is to be read aloud by the person playing the client to provide context.

BEGINNER-LEVEL CLIENT STATEMENTS FOR EXERCISE 6
Beginner Client Statement 1
The client is a transgender woman.   [Sad] I just feel so different when I visit my family since starting HRT.
Beginner Client Statement 2
The client describes in detail a memory of a dish that her grandmother makes around the holidays that you have never eaten.   [Hopeful] You've tried it, right?
Beginner Client Statement 3
[Thoughtful] I don't think there is a word in English for the emotion I am trying to describe.
Beginner Client Statement 4
[Forcefully] I was raised to believe in God and pray, not to go to therapy to whine about my problems.
Beginner Client Statement 5
[Tentative] I think I might be poly. My partner and I are thinking about exploring that together.
Beginner Client Statement 6
[Happy] The client says something in a language you do not speak.

🛑 **Assess and adjust the difficulty before moving to the next difficulty level (see Step 3 in the exercise instructions).**

INTERMEDIATE-LEVEL CLIENT STATEMENTS FOR EXERCISE 6
Intermediate Client Statement 1
[Sad] I doubt you know how it feels to be followed around a store the way that I have been.
Intermediate Client Statement 2
[Hopeless] Can you imagine how it feels to be rejected by your family for who you are? I bet you can't.
Intermediate Client Statement 3
[Matter-of-fact] Families from my country don't work like the families I see here. It's different.
Intermediate Client Statement 4
[Amused] You know how immigrant parents are, right?
Intermediate Client Statement 5
[Curious] I was reading an article about racial trauma online and how therapists who treat folks of color are supposed to know about it. Do you?
Intermediate Client Statement 6
[Bitter] Going to the grocery store as a poor kid, counting quarters with my mom, it has an effect. You know what I mean?

🤚 **Assess and adjust the difficulty before moving to the next difficulty level (see Step 3 in the exercise instructions).**

ADVANCED-LEVEL CLIENT STATEMENTS FOR EXERCISE 6
Advanced Client Statement 1
The client corrects you when you use the word "gay."
[Annoyed] I'm pansexual—not gay. Do you even know what that means?
Advanced Client Statement 2
[Listless] You and I aren't the same. I wish I had a therapist who looked like me.
Advanced Client Statement 3
You struggle with pronouncing a client's name during an intake session.
[Accommodating] You pronounced my name wrong, but you can just use the Americanized name I use at school.
Advanced Client Statement 4
[Frustrated] I live my life based on certain spiritual beliefs. I feel like I've tried to explain before what God means to me, and you just don't get it.
Advanced Client Statement 5
[Angry] I hate when you ask me how something "feels" for me. You don't have to move through the world in a wheelchair. I'm tired of explaining how it feels. I wish you just knew.
Advanced Client Statement 6
[Frightened] Everywhere I go I feel unsafe because of the color of my skin. I worry about my kid every day at school. Do you know what that feels like?

Assess and adjust the difficulty here (see Step 3 in the exercise instructions). If appropriate, follow the instructions to make the exercise even more challenging (see Appendix A).

Example Therapist Responses: Maintaining a Not-Knowing Stance

Remember: Trainees should attempt to improvise their own responses before reading the example responses. **Do not read the following responses verbatim unless you are having trouble coming up with your own responses!**

EXAMPLE RESPONSES TO BEGINNER-LEVEL CLIENT STATEMENTS FOR EXERCISE 6
Example Response to Beginner Client Statement 1
I'm not sure what HRT is. (Criterion 1) Would you feel comfortable explaining that to me? (Criterion 2) or I'm interested to hear more about your family, but first, you used an abbreviation just then: HRT. I want to make sure I know what that means before we keep going. (Criterion 1) It feels important to me understanding your experience well. (Criterion 2)
Example Response to Beginner Client Statement 2
I haven't! (Criterion 1) I want to make sure I understand what is special about your grandma's dish. Will you tell me more? (Criterion 2)
Example Response to Beginner Client Statement 3
Should we try to work together and find something close? (Criterion 2) Or maybe I can listen and afterward we can see if I get my understanding of it correct? (Criterion 1)
Example Response to Beginner Client Statement 4
I'd like to understand more about the faith you were raised with. I'm not sure I know 100% what you mean. (Criterion 1) Would you mind telling me more? (Criterion 2)
Example Response to Beginner Client Statement 5
I'm not sure I know what "poly" means. (Criterion 1) Do you mind if we take a second to explore it before we talk about you and your partner? I want to make sure I'm hearing you well when you talk about it. (Criterion 2)
Example Response to Beginner Client Statement 6
That felt like you said something important just then. (Criterion 1) Would you mind translating it for me? (Criterion 2) or A little while ago you used a word that I'm not quite sure I know the meaning of. (Criterion 1) When that happens, should I stop you and ask for translation, or do you think it would be better if I just listened and tried to understand it in context? (Criterion 2)

EXAMPLE RESPONSES TO INTERMEDIATE-LEVEL CLIENT STATEMENTS FOR EXERCISE 6

Example Response to Intermediate Client Statement 1

You're right, I haven't had that experience. (Criterion 1) But I do want to hear more about how it feels for you, if you want to tell me. (Criterion 2)

Example Response to Intermediate Client Statement 2

I'm wondering if you can tell me more about it so that I can imagine it better? (Criterion 2) It sounds like you're worried I can't understand this experience if I've never had it. (Criterion 1)

Example Response to Intermediate Client Statement 3

Will you help me get a better sense of what you mean by "different"? (Criterion 2) I want to make sure we are on the same page. This feels important to your story. (Criterion 1)

Example Response to Intermediate Client Statement 4

I think I have a sense of what you mean, but I definitely haven't had your specific experience. (Criterion 1) Would you mind telling me a little more? (Criterion 2)

Example Response to Intermediate Client Statement 5

I do—would you like to hear my sense of what it means? (Criterion 1) I'd be curious to hear yours—this feels important. (Criterion 2)

or

I don't. (Criterion 1) But this feels important. Can we take a second to make sure I understand what you took away from the article? (Criterion 2)

Example Response to Intermediate Client Statement 6

I think I do, but I'm guessing your experience was very specific to you. (Criterion 1) Do you mind expanding a little on that? (Criterion 2)

EXAMPLE RESPONSES TO ADVANCED-LEVEL CLIENT STATEMENTS FOR EXERCISE 6

Example Response to Advanced Client Statement 1

I'm actually not quite sure what that means. (Criterion 1) Would you mind helping me understand the difference? (Criterion 2)

or

I think we bumped up against the limits of my vocabulary just then—I made the wrong assumption about using the word "gay" to describe you. (Criterion 1) Maybe you can explain more about how you view your identity so I can get to know you a bit more, so I don't make that mistake again. (Criterion 2)

Example Response to Advanced Client Statement 2

No, we don't look the same, and it's totally valid that it feels easier to work with someone who looks like you. (Criterion 1) I'm wondering if there is anything I can do to help you feel more seen here? (Criterion 2)

Example Response to Advanced Client Statement 3

I'm sorry about that! (Criterion 1) I'm wondering if we can talk for a second about which name you'd like me to use in therapy so you can feel most yourself here. (Criterion 2)

Example Response to Advanced Client Statement 4

I'd really like to "get it." It sounds like I haven't up until this point. (Criterion 1) Let's see if we can work out a way so that I do get it. (Criterion 2) It sounds like it's been frustrating to have me continue to not quite get it.

Example Response to Advanced Client Statement 5

Yeah, I use the word "feels" a lot and it sounds like it would be better if I just knew. (Criterion 1) I wonder if we can figure out a way to work through that. I can only imagine how frustrating that must be. What else do I need to know to do a better job understanding your experience? (Criterion 2)

Example Response to Advanced Client Statement 6

You're pointing out a really important difference between the two of us. I don't know what it's like to have that pervasive sense of being unsafe. (Criterion 1) Part of our work together will be my working to enter into your experience. Can you tell me more about what it has been like for you and your child? (Criterion 2)

or

You know, we both have dark skin. But your experience and mine may differ. (Criterion 1) I think I have a decent sense of that unsafe feeling, but I'd really like to understand your personal experience, your history, and the specific fears you have for your child. (Criterion 2)

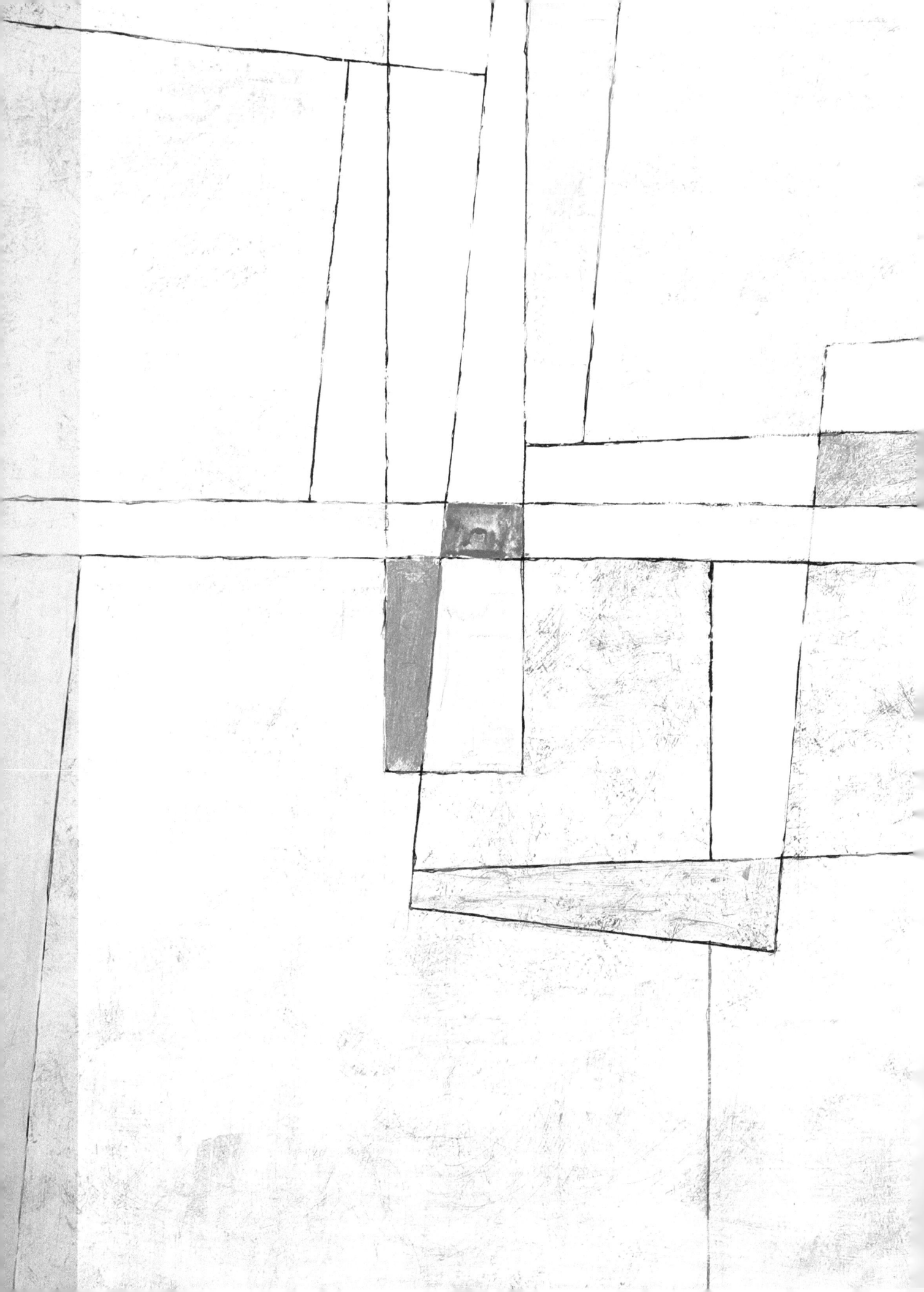

Inquiring About Cultural Implications of the Problem: Cultural Opportunities II

Preparations for Exercise 7

1. Read the instructions in Chapter 2.

2. Download the Deliberate Practice Reaction Form and the Deliberate Practice Diary Form at https://www.apa.org/pubs/books/deliberate-practice-multicultural-therapy (see the "Clinician and Practitioner Resources" tab; also available in Appendixes A and B, respectively).

Skill Description

Skill Difficulty Level: Intermediate

The goal of learning more about the cultural implications of clients' presenting problems is to build a stronger therapeutic alliance and demonstrate attentiveness to the client's intersectional identity. A key component of the therapist's multicultural orientation is being open to "cultural opportunities"—the moments within a session when there is an opening to attend directly to clients' cultural identity (Davis et al., 2018; Owen et al., 2016). An important opportunity to address cultural identity and its salience in the client's life is to inquire about the cultural implications of the client's presenting problem. Sometimes clients will readily engage in talking about the cultural implications of their distress. For example, individuals from individualistic or collectivist cultures may experience different levels of perceived control (Cheng et al., 2013). Feelings of guilt about symptoms and the expression of symptoms also vary across cultural groups (Goodmann et al., 2021). At times clients may be unaware of or uncomfortable talking about cultural implications of their presenting problems. Therapists have an ethical responsibility to inquire about the cultural implications of the client's symptoms

https://doi.org/10.1037/0000357-009

Deliberate Practice in Multicultural Therapy, by J. Harris, J. Jin, S. Hoffman, S. Phan, T. A. Prout, T. Rousmaniere, and A. Vaz

and presenting problems because this conveys to the client that the therapist is comfortable discussing culture. Making space for all aspects of the client's identity is a central component of the psychotherapy process. To that end, in this exercise, you will practice inquiring about cultural implications of the problem.

SKILL CRITERIA FOR EXERCISE 7

1. Using the client's words, acknowledge the client's main concern.
2. Using the context provided, tentatively ask an open-ended question about possible intersectionality issues in the client's presenting problem.

Examples of Therapists Inquiring About Cultural Implications

Note: Underlined text is to be read aloud by the person playing the client to provide context.

Example 1

The client is a cisgender woman.

CLIENT: [*matter-of-fact*] I have a panic attack when my husband and I fight.

THERAPIST: Yeah, whenever you guys fight you have a panic attack. (Criterion 1) Is there any part of these arguments that affects you differently because you're a woman? (Criterion 2)

Example 2

The client comes from a conservative religious background.

CLIENT: [*anxious*] I'm not attracted to my partner. I mean I am and I'm not. I feel so much pressure to get married.

THERAPIST: You feel a lot of pressure to be married. (Criterion 1) Is there a part here that's anchored to your religious background? (Criterion 2)

Example 3

The client comes from a cultural background that values the group over the individual.

CLIENT: [*annoyed*] My wife is suicidal, and her sister keeps coming over and "helping" us. It's really frustrating, but we need the support right now.

THERAPIST: You really need the help. (Criterion 1) Is this more weighty because of your cultural heritage? (Criterion 2)

INSTRUCTIONS FOR EXERCISE 7
Step 1: Role-Play and Feedback
• The client says the first beginner client statement. The therapist **improvises** a response based on the skill criteria.   • The trainer (or, if not available, the client) provides **brief** feedback based on the skill criteria.   • The client then repeats the same statement, and the therapist again improvises a response. The trainer (or client) again provides brief feedback.
Step 2: Repeat
• Repeat Step 1 for all the statements **in the current difficulty level** (beginner, intermediate, or advanced).
Step 3: Assess and Adjust Difficulty
• The therapist completes the Deliberate Practice Reaction Form (see Appendix A) and decides whether to make the exercise easier or harder or to repeat the same difficulty level.
Step 4: Repeat for Approximately 15 Minutes
• Repeat Steps 1 to 3 for at least 15 minutes.   • The trainees then switch therapist and client roles and start over.

Now it's your turn! Follow Steps 1 and 2 from the exercise instructions.

Remember: The goal of the role-play is for trainees to practice improvising responses to the client statements in a manner that (a) uses the skill criteria and (b) feels authentic for the trainee. **Example therapist responses for each client statement are provided at the end of this exercise. Trainees should attempt to improvise their own responses before reading the examples.**

Note: Underlined text is to be read aloud by the person playing the client to provide context.

BEGINNER-LEVEL CLIENT STATEMENTS FOR EXERCISE 7
Beginner Client Statement 1
The client comes from a conservative religious background.
[Sad] He cheated and lied and cheated. So I got a divorce. It's been harder than I thought it would be.
Beginner Client Statement 2
The client comes from a cultural background that values togetherness.
[Sad] Since moving here, I've felt so lonely. No one's invited me over.
Beginner Client Statement 3
The client is Asian American.
[Frustrated] I was in the cafeteria and a group of them walked by and one of them said, "God, that stinks." She was talking about my food!
Beginner Client Statement 4
The client is a cisgender man.
[Frustrated] I always got told I was dramatic.
Beginner Client Statement 5
The client is a cisgender woman.
[Angry] I'm not respected at work. No one's listening to me.

🛑 **Assess and adjust the difficulty before moving to the next difficulty level (see Step 3 in the exercise instructions).**

INTERMEDIATE-LEVEL CLIENT STATEMENTS FOR EXERCISE 7
Intermediate Client Statement 1
The client is a transgender woman.
[Hopeless] They say I've got a conversion disorder. I've been to so many doctors.
Intermediate Client Statement 2
The client is a nonbinary person.
[Angry] The secretary wouldn't let me in the school. My partner called and told them I was coming, but they pretended not to know who I am.
Intermediate Client Statement 3
The client is in a wheelchair.
[Sad] My partner was in the hospital and I couldn't visit them.
Intermediate Client Statement 4
The client comes from a religious background that values marriage.
[Insistent] My partner has completely changed since we got married. This is not the person I married.
Intermediate Client Statement 5
The client is a parent of a neurodivergent child.
[Hopeless] The teacher keeps giving my kid demerits. I've had so many meetings with those people.

🛑 **Assess and adjust the difficulty before moving to the next difficulty level (see Step 3 in the exercise instructions).**

ADVANCED-LEVEL CLIENT STATEMENTS FOR EXERCISE 7
Advanced Client Statement 1
The client is a bisexual cisgender woman.
[Defeated] My partner doesn't trust me. He keeps thinking I will cheat on him with my female friends.
Advanced Client Statement 2
The client is a cultural minority.
[Dejected] Let's just say her parents didn't like me. I never had a chance.
Advanced Client Statement 3
The client is a gay cisgender man.
[Frustrated] I keep having panic attacks. There was so much wrong with where I grew up. I guess you'd call it trauma.
Advanced Client Statement 4
The client identifies as Black and was adopted by White parents.
[Disappointed] I always felt like an outsider with my mom. And Grandma would make comments.
Advanced Client Statement 5
The client is a Black cisgender woman.
[Dismissive] I'm pretty used to it. People always ask about my hair.

> Assess and adjust the difficulty here (see Step 3 in the exercise instructions). If appropriate, follow the instructions to make the exercise even more challenging (see Appendix A).

Example Therapist Responses: Inquiring About Cultural Implications

Remember: Trainees should attempt to improvise their own responses before reading the example responses. **Do not read the following responses verbatim unless you are having trouble coming up with your own responses!**

EXAMPLE RESPONSES TO BEGINNER-LEVEL CLIENT STATEMENTS FOR EXERCISE 7
Example Response to Beginner Client Statement 1
Divorcing can be hard, even when you know it's the right move for you. (Criterion 1) Is there a part of this that's weightier because of your religious background? (Criterion 2)
Example Response to Beginner Client Statement 2
It's been a lonely move. (Criterion 1) How does your cultural background influence this? (Criterion 2)
Example Response to Beginner Client Statement 3
What a rude thing to say. (Criterion 1) Is this more than rude? Do you think your coworkers' attitudes about Asian Americans play into this? (Criterion 2)
Example Response to Beginner Client Statement 4
People told you all the time that you were dramatic. (Criterion 1) Does this also go against what it means to be a man? (Criterion 2)
Example Response to Beginner Client Statement 5
People aren't listening and they should be. (Criterion 1) Just wondering, is there any part of this that's because you're a woman? (Criterion 2)

EXAMPLE RESPONSES TO INTERMEDIATE-LEVEL CLIENT STATEMENTS FOR EXERCISE 7
Example Response to Intermediate Client Statement 1
The doctors seem out of their depth. (Criterion 1) Do you think maybe they are treating you like this because you're trans? (Criterion 2)
Example Response to Intermediate Client Statement 2
That's so frustrating! They wouldn't let you in the school. (Criterion 1) How much of this, do you think, is because you're nonbinary? (Criterion 2)
Example Response to Intermediate Client Statement 3
Oh no. When they needed you, you couldn't be with them. (Criterion 1) Was there also an element of ableism? Had that crossed your mind? (Criterion 2)
Example Response to Intermediate Client Statement 4
Wow, so it's like being married to a stranger. (Criterion 1) How much of this change is religious? Is there a religious part? (Criterion 2)
Example Response to Intermediate Client Statement 5
Yes, that sounds exhausting to continually be meeting with the school. (Criterion 1) I'm guessing at least some of this is because your child is neurodivergent. (Criterion 2)

EXAMPLE RESPONSES TO ADVANCED-LEVEL CLIENT STATEMENTS FOR EXERCISE 7
Example Response to Advanced Client Statement 1
That sounds hard, not having your partner's trust. (Criterion 1) Does some of this have to do with you being bi? (Criterion 2)
Example Response to Advanced Client Statement 2
You already started out behind. (Criterion 1) Did it cross your mind that maybe this was due to being a minority? (Criterion 2)
Example Response to Advanced Client Statement 3
Yeah, growing up for you was so traumatic. (Criterion 1) How much of that was because you're gay, do you think? (Criterion 2)
Example Response to Advanced Client Statement 4
You felt like an outsider in your own family. (Criterion 1) At what level was this because you're a minority? (Criterion 2)
Example Response to Advanced Client Statement 5
This is pretty normal for you. (Criterion 1) How does this hit you as a minority? (Criterion 2)

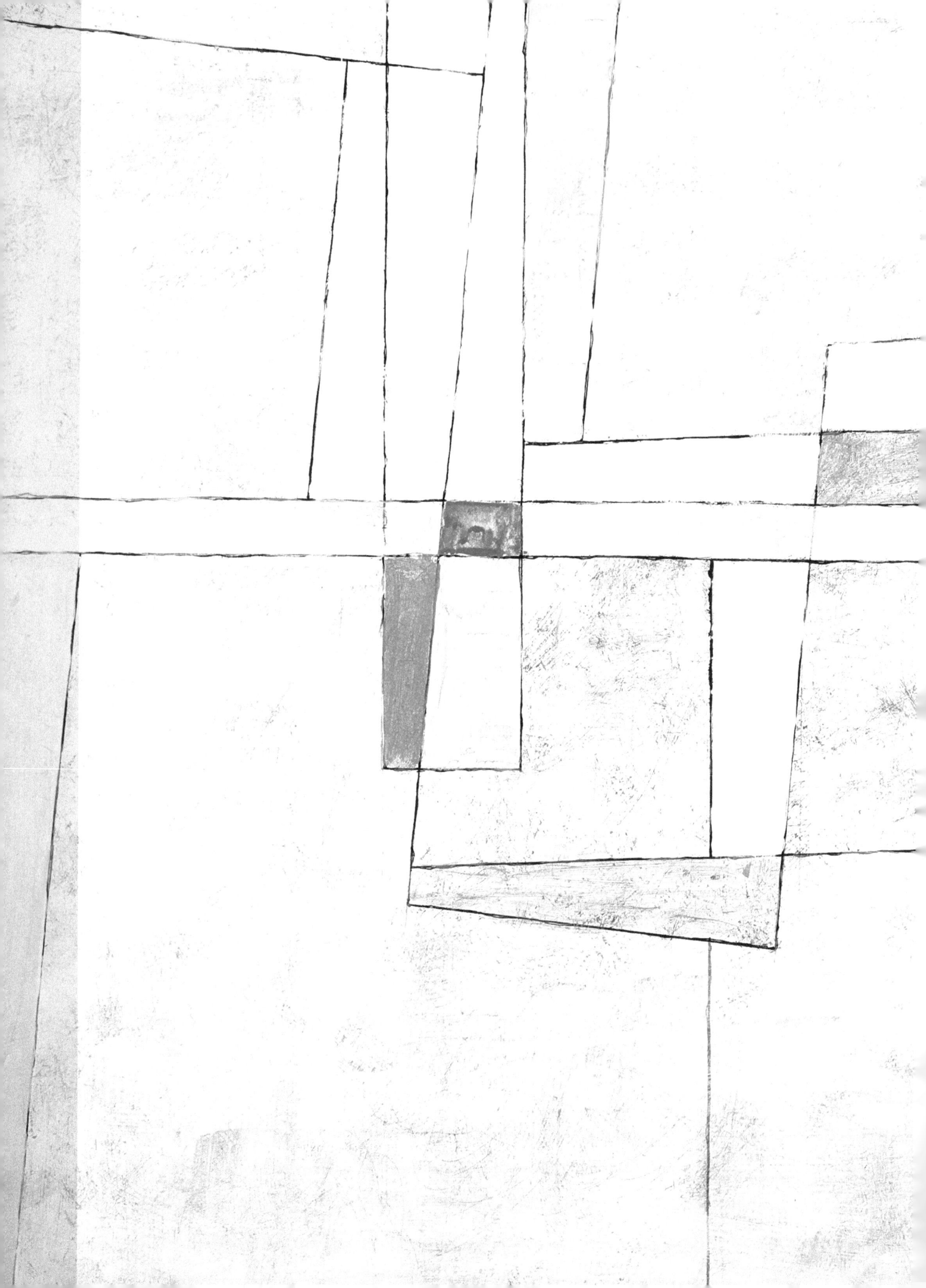

Acknowledging Therapist Limitations

Preparations for Exercise 8

1. Read the instructions in Chapter 2.

2. Download the Deliberate Practice Reaction Form and the Deliberate Practice Diary Form at https://www.apa.org/pubs/books/deliberate-practice-multicultural-therapy (see the "Clinician and Practitioner Resources" tab; also available in Appendixes A and B, respectively).

Skill Description

Skill Difficulty Level: Intermediate

The goal of this exercise is to help you practice acknowledging therapist limitations that can help strengthen the therapeutic alliance between you and your clients. Acknowledging limitations as a therapist is a clear way to practice cultural humility because the therapist seeks further understanding of the client while acknowledging their own position of privilege or "not knowing" (Owen et al., 2016). Therapists can use this skill to approach cultural opportunities that the client initiates, especially when a client is curious about whether the therapist will understand them (Owen et al., 2016).

Acknowledging therapist limitations is highly individualistic, tailored to the needs of the client and rooted in the intersectional identities of the client and therapist. Often, these opportunities overlap with self-disclosure because they involve the therapist revealing information about their knowledge or experience. Whether you disclose and what you choose to share will be unique to you. This practice of vulnerability will also be based on the particular therapeutic situation, treatment modality, clinical characteristics of the client, and your own background. The therapist may choose to disclose, verbally or implicitly, personal information (Hill et al., 2018). Self-disclosure can be beneficial;

https://doi.org/10.1037/0000357-010

Deliberate Practice in Multicultural Therapy, by J. Harris, J. Jin, S. Hoffman, S. Phan, T. A. Prout, T. Rousmaniere, and A. Vaz

for example, there are benefits associated with LGBTQ+ therapists disclosing their sexual orientation or gender identity to queer clients (Guthrie, 2006; Kronner & Northcut, 2015). Intentional and brief self-disclosure can allow the therapist to respond genuinely to the client's curiosity, limit the client's isolation, or strengthen the relationship through cultural similarities (Sunderani & Moodley, 2020). This exercise does not include self-disclosures in the skill criteria or in the sample therapist responses given that deciding whether and what to disclose is highly personal. Trainees can consult with their supervisors on appropriate self-disclosures and integrate them into clinical training as needed.

Following an acknowledgment of therapist limitations, the therapist can return the focus to the client by opening an opportunity to explore the client's own cultural background and experiences further. In this way, the therapist remains culturally humble to the client and open to engaging in cultural opportunities that are salient for them (Owen et al., 2016).

SKILL CRITERIA FOR EXERCISE 8

1. Acknowledge your limitations in terms of your ability to understand the client's experiences.
2. Ask a question to further explore the client's cultural background.

Examples of Therapists Acknowledging Limitations

Example 1

CLIENT: [*relieved*] Finally I can work with a therapist who'll know what it's like. I want to work with someone who understands being raised by parents like mine.

THERAPIST: I may not understand exactly what your parents were like even though we might share similarities. (Criterion 1) What was it like growing up with your parents? (Criterion 2)

Example 2

CLIENT: [*curious*] Well, high school is awful, everyone's so mean. Will you know what it's like? You're way older than me.

THERAPIST: You're right, we're not the same age, so I may not know what you're going through exactly. (Criterion 1) But I'd like to know. What makes high school awful for you right now? (Criterion 2)

Example 3

CLIENT: [*curious*] My parents have been divorced my whole life. I don't expect you to know what I'm going through.

THERAPIST: I don't know exactly what it's like to go through a divorce. (Criterion 1) But I'd like to know what it's like for you. Could you share more what's most challenging about this divorce? (Criterion 2)

INSTRUCTIONS FOR EXERCISE 8

Step 1: Role-Play and Feedback

- The client says the first beginner client statement. The therapist **improvises** a response based on the skill criteria.
- The trainer (or, if not available, the client) provides **brief** feedback based on the skill criteria.
- The client then repeats the same statement, and the therapist again improvises a response. The trainer (or client) again provides brief feedback.

Step 2: Repeat

- Repeat Step 1 for all the statements **in the current difficulty level** (beginner, intermediate, or advanced).

Step 3: Assess and Adjust Difficulty

- The therapist completes the Deliberate Practice Reaction Form (see Appendix A) and decides whether to make the exercise easier or harder or to repeat the same difficulty level.

Step 4: Repeat for Approximately 15 Minutes

- Repeat Steps 1 to 3 for at least 15 minutes.
- The trainees then switch therapist and client roles and start over.

Now it's your turn! Follow Steps 1 and 2 from the exercise instructions.

Remember: The goal of the role-play is for trainees to practice improvising responses to the client statements in a manner that (a) uses the skill criteria and (b) feels authentic for the trainee. **Example therapist responses for each client statement are provided at the end of this exercise. Trainees should attempt to improvise their own responses before reading the examples.**

BEGINNER-LEVEL CLIENT STATEMENTS FOR EXERCISE 8
Beginner Client Statement 1
[Relieved] Finally I can work with a therapist who'll know what it's like. I want to work with someone who understands being raised by parents like mine.
Beginner Client Statement 2
[Curious] Well, high school is awful, everyone's so mean. Will you know what it's like? You're way older than me.
Beginner Client Statement 3
[Curious] My parents have been divorced my whole life. I don't expect you to know what I'm going through.
Beginner Client Statement 4
[Shy] I'm fluent in English, but I'll need to translate some Spanish in my head. Is that OK?
Beginner Client Statement 5
[Frustrated] Everyone in this small town is so rude, you know? I'm surprised there are any nice people like me and you here.

Assess and adjust the difficulty before moving to the next difficulty level (see Step 3 in the exercise instructions).

INTERMEDIATE-LEVEL CLIENT STATEMENTS FOR EXERCISE 8
Intermediate Client Statement 1
[Excited] I'm so excited to work with some who specializes in LGBTQ+ issues! You've probably heard it all at this point.
Intermediate Client Statement 2
[Confused] I read something about you on a blog. I've wondered if you have a disability as well because you'd probably understand my disability better.
Intermediate Client Statement 3
[Relieved] I really wanted to work with someone who understands my religious faith. I'm glad you were able to take me on as a client with your specialty in religion and spirituality.
Intermediate Client Statement 4
[Curious] It's hard to share when no one ever understands what it's really like to be raised religiously orthodox in a small community. Will you get me?
Intermediate Client Statement 5
[Frustrated] You sit in this nice office while people like me have to work multiple shifts to get by.
Intermediate Client Statement 6
[Skeptical] I know you've worked with others who've transitioned, but I might need a therapist who has had personal experience with gender transitions.

Assess and adjust the difficulty before moving to the next difficulty level (see Step 3 in the exercise instructions).

ADVANCED-LEVEL CLIENT STATEMENTS FOR EXERCISE 8
Advanced Client Statement 1
[Confrontational] You have to know what it's like to raise kids. Otherwise, you won't be able to get me.
Advanced Client Statement 2
[Depressed] I'm not sure if it's worth mentioning to you. I had to find any means to immigrate and live in this country. I don't know if it was worth it. But staying back home would have meant death. You wouldn't understand.
Advanced Client Statement 3
[Angry] I thought you were biracial and would understand my history. I expected you to be a different therapist because of your identity.
Advanced Client Statement 4
[Disgusted] You look very young. I don't expect you to know my loneliness. Have you watched all your friends die?
Advanced Client Statement 5
[Angry] How can you help me quit drinking if you're not in recovery yourself?

> **Assess and adjust the difficulty here (see Step 3 in the exercise instructions). If appropriate, follow the instructions to make the exercise even more challenging (see Appendix A).**

Example Therapist Responses: Acknowledging Therapist Limitations

Remember: Trainees should attempt to improvise their own responses before reading the example responses. **Do not read the following responses verbatim unless you are having trouble coming up with your own responses!**

EXAMPLE RESPONSES TO BEGINNER-LEVEL CLIENT STATEMENTS FOR EXERCISE 8
Example Response to Beginner Client Statement 1
I may not understand exactly what your parents were like even though we might share similarities. (Criterion 1) What was it like growing up with your parents? (Criterion 2)
Example Response to Beginner Client Statement 2
You're right, we're not the same age so I may not know what you're going through exactly. (Criterion 1) But I'd like to know. What makes high school awful for you right now? (Criterion 2)
Example Response to Beginner Client Statement 3
I don't know exactly what it's like to go through a divorce. (Criterion 1) But I'd like to know what it's like for you. Could you share more what's most challenging about this divorce? (Criterion 2)
Example Response to Beginner Client Statement 4
Of course. Even though I may not fully understand, I'd like you to hear more of the language you're comfortable with. (Criterion 1) What are some emotionally important Spanish words? (Criterion 2)
Example Response to Beginner Client Statement 5
I can see what you mean, but being a "nice person" could mean a lot of things. (Criterion 1) What do you think makes someone nice? (Criterion 2)

EXAMPLE RESPONSES TO INTERMEDIATE-LEVEL CLIENT STATEMENTS FOR EXERCISE 8
Example Response to Intermediate Client Statement 1
I'm glad you're looking forward to our sessions together. I don't want to assume that I can fully understand your experiences though. (Criterion 1) What about your gender and sexual orientation is important to discuss today? (Criterion 2)
Example Response to Intermediate Client Statement 2
I don't have a disability, which gives me a different perspective to listen to you. (Criterion 1) I want to understand your story, though. Where can you start so I can hear how your disability has impacted you? (Criterion 2)
Example Response to Intermediate Client Statement 3
I'm glad we are able to work together too. But I might not know everything about what makes your faith important to you. (Criterion 1) What's an important part of your faith for me to keep in mind? (Criterion 2)
Example Response to Intermediate Client Statement 4
I may not get every piece of how you were raised. (Criterion 1) Still, I don't want to miss what's important to you. How have you been misunderstood in the past having been raised orthodox and in a small community? (Criterion 2)
Example Response to Intermediate Client Statement 5
You're right, we have different work situations. (Criterion 1) How might this difference impact our work together? (Criterion 2)
Example Response to Intermediate Client Statement 6
That sounds important to you. We can look for a therapist with a better fit if you'd like, since I don't have personal experience. (Criterion 1) And I'm open to see if we could still work together as well. What about your transition is important for you to be able to connect with a therapist? (Criterion 2)

EXAMPLE RESPONSES TO ADVANCED-LEVEL CLIENT STATEMENTS FOR EXERCISE 8
Example Response to Advanced Client Statement 1
Right, I may not get you because I haven't raised kids. (Criterion 1) Could I hear more about how being a parent is important to you? (Criterion 2)
Example Response to Advanced Client Statement 2
You've had to do everything you can to survive experiences I can't even imagine, so I may not understand now. (Criterion 1) Would it be worth it if I knew a bit more of your story so that we can work together even better? (Criterion 2)
Example Response to Advanced Client Statement 3
You're angry that I'm not biracial like you. (Criterion 1) I hear that your biracial identity is important to you. Can you tell me more about the significance of being biracial? (Criterion 2)
Example Response to Advanced Client Statement 4
I don't know that particular kind of loneliness—of seeing friends die. (Criterion 1) Given this difference, would you still like to see if we can work together on grieving for your friends? (Criterion 2)
Example Response to Advanced Client Statement 5
I'm not in recovery, but there are many things that have led me to work with people like you. (Criterion 1) What part of your recovery is important for me to understand? (Criterion 2)

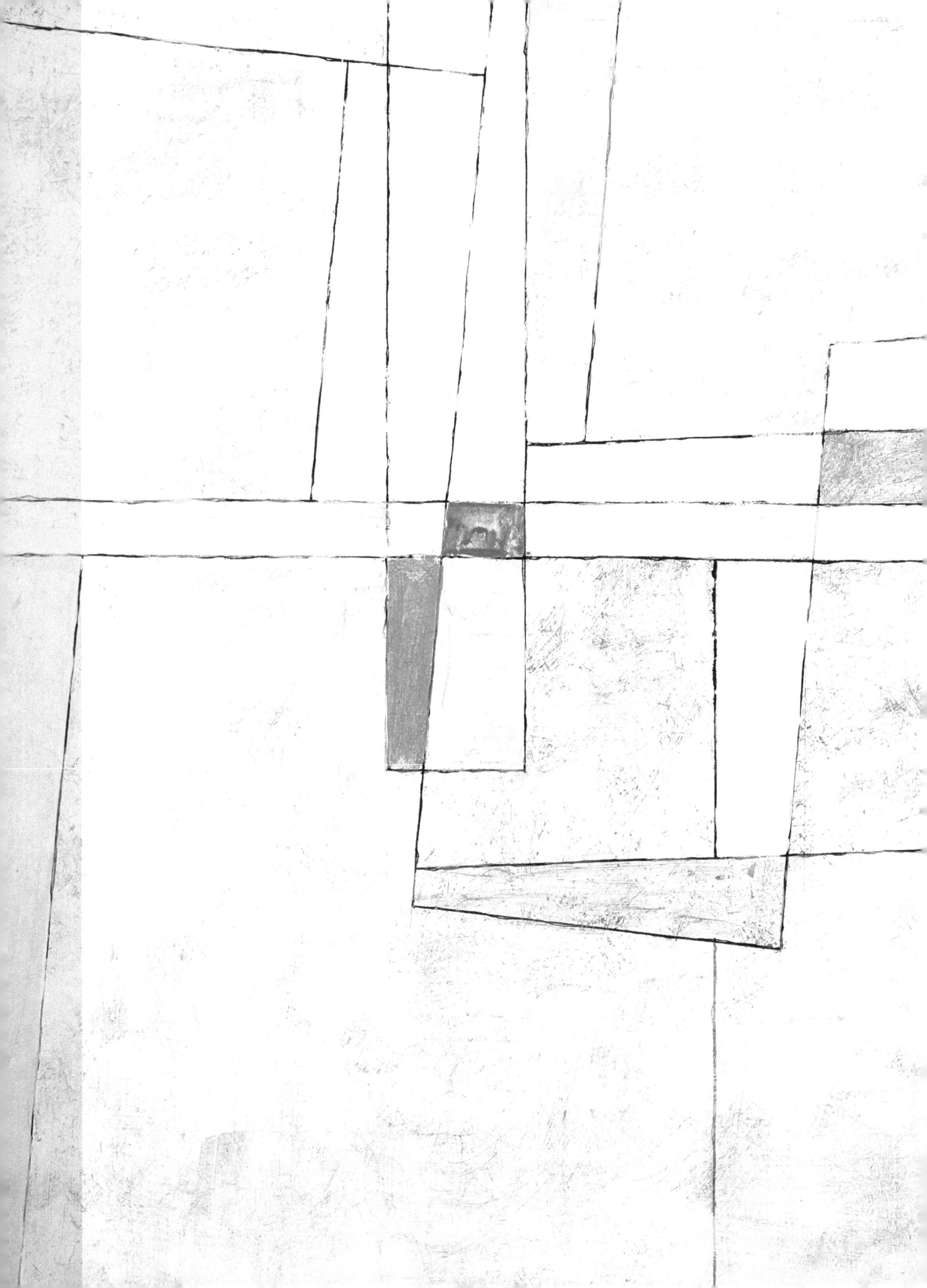

Gathering Information About Safety Concerns

Preparations for Exercise 9

1. Read the instructions in Chapter 2.

2. Download the Deliberate Practice Reaction Form and the Deliberate Practice Diary Form at https://www.apa.org/pubs/books/deliberate-practice-multicultural-therapy (see the "Clinician and Practitioner Resources" tab; also available in Appendixes A and B, respectively).

Skill Description

Skill Difficulty Level: Advanced

The goal of gathering information about safety concerns is to help clients thinking about their safety as it may relate to a variety of situations, including, but not limited to, self-harm, suicide, risky behaviors, legal issues, or substance use. The experience of racial, gender, and sexual identity–based microaggressions is associated with greater risk of suicidal ideation (Hollingsworth et al., 2017; O'Keefe et al., 2015; Parr & Howe, 2019). Intersectionality also plays an important role in suicide risk, substance use, risky sexual behaviors, and physical/sexual violence, with individuals who belong to multiple marginalized groups being at higher risk (Cramer & Plummer, 2009; Gattamorta et al., 2019; Shadick et al., 2015; Szlyk et al., 2019; Wiglesworth et al., 2022).

Often, clients may downplay or be unaware of the potential safety concerns. Although safety concerns commonly raise therapists' anxiety, it is important to remain calm and nonjudgmental while gathering more information and to consult with supervisors and make any necessary reports. In many ways, the initial steps in gathering information about safety concerns are the same across cultures and identities—the key is for the therapist to take a nonjudgmental and curious stance. Even when they are not explicitly

https://doi.org/10.1037/0000357-011

Deliberate Practice in Multicultural Therapy, by J. Harris, J. Jin, S. Hoffman, S. Phan, T. A. Prout, T. Rousmaniere, and A. Vaz

mentioned by clients, cultural identity factors are important to consider in assessing safety concerns. The therapist may be curious with the client about how cultural factors influence the client's experiences with risk and safety.

SKILL CRITERIA FOR EXERCISE 9

1. Acknowledge and validate the client's feelings, wants, or needs without judgment.
2. Using a calm and tentative tone, invite the client to elaborate on the safety concern.
3. If relevant, ask the client about or to comment on the potential role of identity in what they are describing.

Examples of Therapists Gathering Information About Safety Concerns

Note: Underlined text is to be read aloud by the person playing the client to provide context.

Example 1

The client has family members across three generations who struggle with alcohol abuse.

CLIENT: [*angry*] Last weekend, my parents, grandparents, a few aunts and uncles, and my two closest friends forced me into this unnecessary intervention about my [*gestures air quotes*] "drinking problem." So ridiculous and hypocritical!

THERAPIST: You seem really, really upset about this unnecessary intervention arranged by your family and closest friends. (Criterion 1) How would you describe your drinking? (Criterion 2)

Example 2

The client identifies as Catholic and is in an 18-year marriage.

CLIENT: [*defeated*] I've tried and done everything I can to prevent my marriage from falling apart. I really don't see the point to anything anymore.

THERAPIST: You have tried and did everything you could and still ended up here, where you never thought you would be. (Criterion 1) You have also shared how much your faith means to you. I wonder how that may be weighing on you at this time? (Criterion 3) Tell me more about what you mean when you say you "don't see the point to anything anymore." (Criterion 2)

Example 3

CLIENT: [*confident*] Since I'm going to rehab at the end of the week, I want to get high just one last time. Just one last time before I get clean again. It's not a big deal. Everyone has their one last hit before they go in.

THERAPIST: I'm glad you could tell me this. I'm hearing that you want to do this one last time before you enter rehab. (Criterion 1) Have you thought about how you will do this one last time? If so, could you tell me more? (Criterion 2)

INSTRUCTIONS FOR EXERCISE 9
Step 1: Role-Play and Feedback
• The client says the first beginner client statement. The therapist **improvises** a response based on the skill criteria.
• The trainer (or, if not available, the client) provides **brief** feedback based on the skill criteria.
• The client then repeats the same statement, and the therapist again improvises a response. The trainer (or client) again provides brief feedback.
Step 2: Repeat
• Repeat Step 1 for all the statements **in the current difficulty level** (beginner, intermediate, or advanced).
Step 3: Assess and Adjust Difficulty
• The therapist completes the Deliberate Practice Reaction Form (see Appendix A) and decides whether to make the exercise easier or harder or to repeat the same difficulty level.
Step 4: Repeat for Approximately 15 Minutes
• Repeat Steps 1 to 3 for at least 15 minutes.
• The trainees then switch therapist and client roles and start over.

Now it's your turn! Follow Steps 1 and 2 from the exercise instructions.

Remember: The goal of the role-play is for trainees to practice improvising responses to the client statements in a manner that (a) uses the skill criteria and (b) feels authentic for the trainee. **Example therapist responses for each client statement are provided at the end of this exercise. Trainees should attempt to improvise their own responses before reading the example responses.**

Note: Underlined text is to be read aloud by the person playing the client to provide context.

BEGINNER-LEVEL CLIENT STATEMENTS FOR EXERCISE 9
Beginner Client Statement 1
The client has family members across three generations who struggle with alcohol abuse. **[Angry]** Last weekend, my parents, grandparents, a few aunts and uncles, and my two closest friends forced me into this unnecessary intervention about my **[gestures air quotes]** "drinking problem." So ridiculous and hypocritical!
Beginner Client Statement 2
The client identifies as Catholic and is in an 18-year marriage. **[Defeated]** I've tried and done everything I can to prevent my marriage from falling apart. I really don't see the point to anything anymore.
Beginner Client Statement 3
The client struggles with chronic pain and disability due to a childhood accident. **[Confident]** Since I'm going to rehab at the end of the week, I want to get high just one last time. Just one last time before I get clean again. It's not a big deal. Everyone wants to get high one last time before they go in.
Beginner Client Statement 4
The client is in their mid-40s and is the only single person among their friends. **[Annoyed]** I'm single for the first time in years. It's so much fun meeting new people through the dating apps, but some people are gross and creepy and only want sex.
Beginner Client Statement 5
[Anxious] I can't wait to move out of here as soon as I can. There's been so much bad stuff going on in my neighborhood that I'm scared to go out after dark. I'm so tired of feeling scared all the time.

🛑 **Assess and adjust the difficulty before moving to the next difficulty level (see Step 3 in the exercise instructions).**

INTERMEDIATE-LEVEL CLIENT STATEMENTS FOR EXERCISE 9

Intermediate Client Statement 1

This is the first time you are hearing about the client's partner.

[Guilty] We got in a big fight that started over something really stupid. My partner accidentally hurt me and left a bruise on my arm. Afterward, they seemed worried, apologized, and said they didn't mean to. Anyway, the whole thing was my fault.

Intermediate Client Statement 2

The client is transgender and is in the process of gender transition.

[Embarrassed] I'm ashamed to even tell you this, but I started cutting again. Work has been stressful, and my partner and I fight all the time. When I cut, I feel so much better. I know that it can be unsafe, but it's hard to stop. I don't know what else to do.

Intermediate Client Statement 3

The client is Pakistani American in a college setting with predominantly White students.

[Sad] There is nobody on this campus who looks like me, talks like me, or understands me. I'm tired of feeling so alone. I bet that if I were to die tomorrow, nobody would even notice or miss me.

Intermediate Client Statement 4

[Eager] I've been having a hard time sleeping this week, so my friend gave me some of her Xanax. I've never slept better. I want to see if I can get my own prescription, but my family cannot know. They only believe in natural remedies and not Western medications and treatment.

Intermediate Client Statement 5

The client is formerly homeless.

[Casually] It's so weird. Sometimes when I'm waiting for the train on my way to work, I think about what it would be like to push someone in front of it. **[Laughs]** Wouldn't that just confirm all the stereotypes!

🛑 **Assess and adjust the difficulty before moving to the next difficulty level (see Step 3 in the exercise instructions).**

ADVANCED-LEVEL CLIENT STATEMENTS FOR EXERCISE 9

Advanced Client Statement 1

The client is a widow.

[Sad] Parents are supposed to go before their children. Not the other way around. At this point, I just want to be in heaven with my daughter. I've thought about jumping off the bridge near my home or the water tower a few miles north of my home.

Advanced Client Statement 2

The client is a Black cisgender man.

[Matter-of-fact] Look, everyone has different tolerance levels, and I know my own limits. I know just the right amount that works best for me and I'm fine to drive. Of course, I'm more likely than you are to get pulled over by the cops, even when I'm sober.

Advanced Client Statement 3

The client is a cisgender woman of color.

[Casually] Since taking these medications prescribed by my psychiatrist, I haven't felt like myself. They change my personality entirely. So last week, I decided to stop taking them, and I'm starting to feel like myself again.

Advanced Client Statement 4

The client is undocumented and does not have insurance.

[Scared, shaking] I've never told anyone this before, but when my partner gets upset, they hurt me. It used to be minor, like throwing stuff at the wall or breaking things, then throwing things at me . . . but now they're getting more and more physical with me. Last night, something happened again. This time was different and left me fearing for my life. I have no friends or family here and nowhere to go. I don't know what to do.

Advanced Client Statement 5

The client is in a wheelchair due to a debilitating accident that left them paralyzed from the waist down and has a history of incarceration.

[Angry] It's my life. If I want to get high, I'll get high. I don't care if I die. Nobody can tell me what to do or how to live my life—not my parents, and definitely not you.

🛑 **Assess and adjust the difficulty here (see Step 3 in the exercise instructions). If appropriate, follow the instructions to make the exercise even more challenging (see Appendix A).**

Example Therapist Responses: Gathering Information About Safety Concerns

Remember: Trainees should attempt to improvise their own responses before reading the example responses. **Do not read the following responses verbatim unless you are having trouble coming up with your own responses!**

EXAMPLE RESPONSES TO BEGINNER-LEVEL CLIENT STATEMENTS FOR EXERCISE 9
Example Response to Beginner Client Statement 1
You seem really, really upset about this intervention arranged by your family and closest friends. (Criterion 1) I'd like to know more about your drinking, (Criterion 2) but maybe first we can talk about how it feels to have this intervention given the long family history with alcohol? (Criterion 3)
Example Response to Beginner Client Statement 2
You have tried and did everything you could and still ended up here, where you never thought you'd be. (Criterion 1) You have also shared how much your faith means to you. I wonder how that may be weighing on you at this time. (Criterion 3) Tell me more about what you mean when you say you "don't see the point to anything anymore." (Criterion 2)
Example Response to Beginner Client Statement 3
I'm glad you could tell me this, and I'm proud of your recommitment to recovery and trying rehab again. I'm hearing that you want to get high just one last time. (Criterion 1) Can you tell me more about what you're planning? (Criterion 2) I'm also curious about how your experience of chronic pain may play a role in your path towards recovery. (Criterion 3)
Example Response to Beginner Client Statement 4
Part of you enjoys this different stage of your life, and there's a part that sounds a bit concerned about others' true intentions when it comes to dating. (Criterion 1) I also remember how you've talked about your identity as a single person and your sense that that has become a part of who you *are*. (Criterion 3) What are you looking for in a partner, and how do you navigate situations when you come across people that only want sex? (Criterion 2)
Example Response to Beginner Client Statement 5
You're feeling very unsafe in your neighborhood—it's scary! And you're working really hard to move away. (Criterion 1) Maybe there's a part of you that doesn't want to be identified with a neighborhood where people struggle with poverty and experience so much crime. (Criterion 3) Can you tell me about the most recent situation or event where you felt unsafe? What happened? (Criterion 2)

**EXAMPLE RESPONSES TO INTERMEDIATE-LEVEL
CLIENT STATEMENTS FOR EXERCISE 9**

Example Response to Intermediate Client Statement 1

Thank you for sharing this with me. It sounds like this fight may have gotten out of hand and you blame yourself for it. (Criterion 1) I'm realizing that I'm not sure if your partner is a man, woman, or nonbinary person. (Criterion 3) Has this ever happened before? If you can, tell me more about what happened before, during, and after the fight. (Criterion 2)

Example Response to Intermediate Client Statement 2

I'm glad you're telling me this, even though it's really hard to say aloud. There are a lot of stressors in your life right now, and cutting helps you feel better in the moment. (Criterion 1) I'd like to hear more about that—what is it about cutting that provides relief? (Criterion 2) Maybe we can also talk today about the stressors you mentioned and, if it's relevant, consider if trans identity in a world that can sometimes be really hostile adds to that stress. (Criterion 3)

Example Response to Intermediate Client Statement 3

You're feeling hopeless and alone right now. (Criterion 1) And maybe the things we've talked about around being Pakistani American in such an overwhelmingly White space sometimes makes you want to disappear as well. (Criterion 3) How long have you been feeling this way? Have you thought about killing yourself? (Criterion 2)

Example Response to Intermediate Client Statement 4

You have been having a lot of difficulty with sleep lately, and it seems you have found something that helps you. (Criterion 1) So you are thinking about getting your own prescription? (Criterion 2) I'm also curious how it feels to break away from your family's perspective on medication. (Criterion 3)

Example Response to Intermediate Client Statement 5

Thank you for sharing this with me. I want to better understand these thoughts you sometimes have. (Criterion 1) I'd like to know more about what feelings come up for you when you have these thoughts. (Criterion 2) You laughed at the end when you mentioned the idea that this would just "confirm all the stereotypes." I guess you're referencing your history of homelessness, and I can imagine there is a lot there to unpack. (Criterion 3)

EXAMPLE RESPONSES TO ADVANCED-LEVEL CLIENT STATEMENTS FOR EXERCISE 9

Example Response to Advanced Client Statement 1

I understand you have been feeling an overwhelming sense of pain and loss. Through all of this, I'm really glad you're here today and sharing this with me, as difficult as it may be. (Criterion 1) You've experienced loss in a multitude of ways, and it has shaped your identity. (Criterion 3) How long have you been thinking about these specific ways in which you can join your daughter? (Criterion 2)

Example Response to Advanced Client Statement 2

You sound certain about how well you know yourself and your limits when you drink. (Criterion 1) I'd like to know more about what the right amount means for you and how you know you're fine to drive? (Criterion 2) Also, you're highlighting a real difference between the two of us and the systemic issues that make you more likely to be targeted by police. I'm curious about how that factors into your decisions around drinking and driving. (Criterion 3)

Example Response to Advanced Client Statement 3

I'm hearing that your experience with this medication is causing you to feel worse and like a completely different person. I'm also glad that you're sharing this with me. (Criterion 1) Have you shared this with your psychiatrist? Tell me more about what feels different since you stopped taking the medication last week. (Criterion 2) It sounds like it made you feel like you were losing really important parts of yourself. (Criterion 3)

Example Response to Advanced Client Statement 4

I'm noticing how you were shaking as you're telling me this. It sounds like your relationship and sense of safety have come to a point where you're very scared and feeling hopeless about your options. (Criterion 1) I can imagine that being undocumented and relatively alone in this country adds an additional layer of pain. (Criterion 3) I'm wondering if you would be open to take a few deep breaths with me and slow things down. Going back to last night, can you tell me more about what happened before, during, and after the fight? (Criterion 2)

Example Response to Advanced Client Statement 5

You're right—it is your life. And I definitely do *not* want to be yet another person who is telling you how to live it. (Criterion 1) Maybe one place we could start is for me to get a much better understanding about how getting high serves you—what pressures it relieves, the benefits it provides. (Criterion 2) Your accident, being incarcerated . . . you've had a lot of freedoms taken from you. (Criterion 3) These experiences must make it even more important to be able to have a sense of agency—to make decisions that are truly your own.

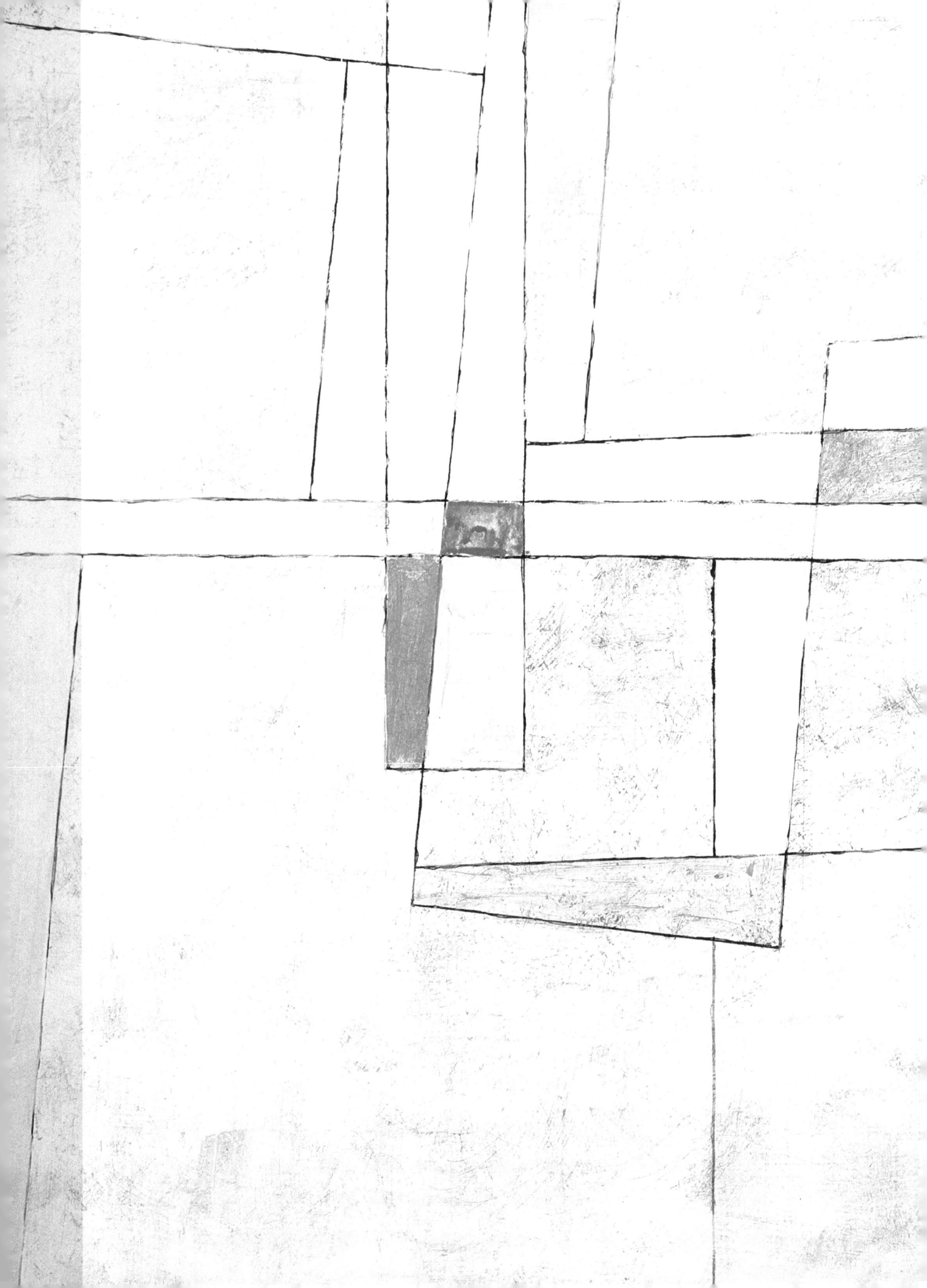

Talking About Sex and Success

Preparations for Exercise 10

1. Read the instructions in Chapter 2.

2. Download the Deliberate Practice Reaction Form and the Deliberate Practice Diary Form at https://www.apa.org/pubs/books/deliberate-practice-multicultural-therapy (see the "Clinician and Practitioner Resources" tab; also available in Appendixes A and B, respectively).

Skill Description

Skill Difficulty Level: Advanced

Skillfully discussing sex and success with clients is important because these topics are interdependent with one's cultural identities and values. When these topics are avoided, the unspoken message is that discussing sex and success is off limits or unimportant. Despite their centrality to the human experience, talking about sex and sexuality in therapy is often a difficult undertaking for therapists and clients and may lead to avoidance of the topic. Specifically, 42% of therapy clients report that they do not discuss the details of their sex life with their therapist, actively working to conceal these details (Love & Farber, 2019). Likewise, discussions surrounding success, professional or otherwise, are often equally difficult and shaped by cultural experiences. Take a moment to reflect on your own views, values, and attitudes about sex, sexual identity, and the meaning of success. Try "just asking" the tough questions and regularly checking in with your client if this is something they would like to discuss or explore further. Also, keep in mind that when clients view these topics as irrelevant to discuss in therapy, it may suggest their own unease surrounding the difficult topics. The skill criteria and prompts in this exercise will give you ample opportunity to practice.

https://doi.org/10.1037/0000357–012

Deliberate Practice in Multicultural Therapy, by J. Harris, J. Jin, S. Hoffman, S. Phan, T. A. Prout, T. Rousmaniere, and A. Vaz

SKILL CRITERIA FOR EXERCISE 10
1. Acknowledge the client's main concern, using the client's words.
2. Validate the client's statement.
3. Ask a question about the client's understanding of sex or success in the context of identity and values, using a tentative, nonjudgmental, and open tone.

Examples of Therapists Talking About Sex and Success

Example 1

CLIENT: [*upset*] My colleagues think I got promoted because I'm a woman of color and it will make the company look good.

THERAPIST: It sounds like your colleagues are not being supportive—even maybe bringing in their own biases to this situation—especially at a time when they should be celebrating your big achievement. (Criterion 1) I can understand how disappointed and even angry you might feel right now. (Criterion 2) Why do you think you were promoted? (Criterion 3)

Example 2

CLIENT: [*nervous*] I'm thinking about a career change. I guess I'm not as successful as I'd like to be. Am I crazy to think that I could go back to school and change careers at 57 years old?

THERAPIST: You are questioning whether it's crazy to pursue a career change at this stage of your life. (Criterion 1) There's something about the timing and perhaps even feelings you might have about age and success that is making you uncomfortable. Those are complex feelings that might feel hard to sort out. (Criterion 2) Can you tell me more about the conflict you see between your age and a decision to change careers? (Criterion 3)

Example 3

CLIENT: [*relieved*] It's easier for me to talk about sex here than it is to talk to my partner about it.

THERAPIST: Talking about sex with your partner is difficult for you. (Criterion 1) This can be a difficult topic for many folks to discuss. (Criterion 2) Was sex a topic that was discussed in your home or taught at school? What was that like? (Criterion 3)

INSTRUCTIONS FOR EXERCISE 10

Step 1: Role-Play and Feedback

- The client says the first beginner client statement. The therapist **improvises** a response based on the skill criteria.
- The trainer (or, if not available, the client) provides **brief** feedback based on the skill criteria.
- The client then repeats the same statement, and the therapist again improvises a response. The trainer (or client) again provides brief feedback.

Step 2: Repeat

- Repeat Step 1 for all the statements **in the current difficulty level** (beginner, intermediate, or advanced).

Step 3: Assess and Adjust Difficulty

- The therapist completes the Deliberate Practice Reaction Form (see Appendix A) and decides whether to make the exercise easier or harder or to repeat the same difficulty level.

Step 4: Repeat for Approximately 15 Minutes

- Repeat Steps 1 to 3 for at least 15 minutes.
- The trainees then switch therapist and client roles and start over.

Now it's your turn! Follow Steps 1 and 2 from the exercise instructions.

Remember: The goal of the role-play is for trainees to practice improvising responses to the client statements in a manner that (a) uses the skill criteria and (b) feels authentic for the trainee. **Example therapist responses for each client statement are provided at the end of this exercise. Trainees should attempt to improvise their own responses before reading the examples.**

Note: Underlined text is to be read aloud by the person playing the client to provide context.

BEGINNER-LEVEL CLIENT STATEMENTS FOR EXERCISE 10
Beginner Client Statement 1
[Upset] My colleagues think I got promoted because I'm a woman of color and it will make the company look good.
Beginner Client Statement 2
[Nervous] I am thinking about a career change. I guess I'm not as successful as I'd like to be. Am I crazy to think that I could go back to school and change careers at 57 years old?
Beginner Client Statement 3
[Relieved] It's easier for me to talk about sex here than it is to actually talk to my partner about it.
Beginner Client Statement 4
[Guilty] I want to save myself for marriage, but sometimes it's hard to hold back when I'm physically with my partner. Afterward, I feel so guilty for even having these thoughts and desires.
Beginner Client Statement 5
[Excited] I'm starting school soon! I'm the first person in my family to go to college.

Assess and adjust the difficulty before moving to the next difficulty level (see Step 3 in the exercise instructions).

INTERMEDIATE-LEVEL CLIENT STATEMENTS FOR EXERCISE 10

Intermediate Client Statement 1

The client is a cisgender woman.

[Matter-of-fact] I never really considered being with a woman. The only sex education I received only talked about heterosexual relationships. I didn't even know that women could have romantic relationships with other women until I went to college. It's kind of weird.

Intermediate Client Statement 2

[Sad] Last week, my partner suggested that we be in an open relationship. If I say yes, then she will probably find someone better and leave. If I say no, she will probably leave too. I don't know what to do.

Intermediate Client Statement 3

[Frustrated] My immigrant parents only care about my career and how much money I'm making. They think it is ridiculous that I'm only concerned about finding my passion and happiness. I'd rather be happy and pursue a career that I love than make a lot of money in a miserable job.

Intermediate Client Statement 4

The client uses a wheelchair.

[Sad] The doctors haven't been clear with me about whether I can have sex. Before my accident, I was proud to be a sex-positive individual. Now, I don't even know if I will ever be intimate with another person.

Intermediate Client Statement 5

[Sad] I closed the biggest deal on my team and was promoted last week. This is my greatest professional accomplishment, and yet I don't feel any happier.

Assess and adjust the difficulty before moving to the next difficulty level (see Step 3 in the exercise instructions).

ADVANCED-LEVEL CLIENT STATEMENTS FOR EXERCISE 10
Advanced Client Statement 1
[Frustrated] I've been in a four-way polyamorous relationship for going on 2 years now. But I can see from your ring that you're married, so I don't think you'll be able to really understand me.
Advanced Client Statement 2
[Dismissive] You're a professional, and you're probably successful. I pay a lot each week to see you. I'm sure my partner would be proud of me if I had a steady job like you.
Advanced Client Statement 3
[Sad] I wish I could connect with someone and have a romantic relationship that doesn't involve sex. I feel broken. What do you think is wrong with me?
Advanced Client Statement 4
[Frustrated] I worked my butt off in school growing up. But once I graduated from college, I was lost. I bet you think I'm a loser because I don't have a real job.
Advanced Client Statement 5
[Upset] You don't know how hard it is for someone like me to be successful or make enough money.

> **Assess and adjust the difficulty here (see Step 3 in the exercise instructions). If appropriate, follow the instructions to make the exercise even more challenging (see Appendix A).**

Example Therapist Responses: Talking About Sex and Success

Remember: Trainees should attempt to improvise their own responses before reading the example responses. **Do not read the following responses verbatim unless you are having trouble coming up with your own responses!**

EXAMPLE RESPONSES TO BEGINNER-LEVEL CLIENT STATEMENTS FOR EXERCISE 10
Example Response to Beginner Client Statement 1
It sounds like your colleagues are not being supportive—even maybe bringing in their own biases to this situation—especially at a time when they should be celebrating your big achievement. (Criterion 1) I can understand how disappointed and even angry you might feel right now. (Criterion 2) Why do you think you were promoted? (Criterion 3)
Example Response to Beginner Client Statement 2
You are questioning whether it is crazy to pursue a career change at this stage of your life. (Criterion 1) There's something about the timing and perhaps even feelings you might have about age and success that is making you uncomfortable. Those are complex feelings that might feel hard to sort out. (Criterion 2) Can you tell me more about the conflict you see between your age and a decision to change careers? (Criterion 3)
Example Response to Beginner Client Statement 3
Talking about sex with your partner is difficult for you. (Criterion 1) This can be a difficult topic for many folks to discuss. (Criterion 2) Was sex a topic that was discussed in your home or taught at school? What was that like? (Criterion 3)
Example Response to Beginner Client Statement 4
I can really understand that tension—the physical pull toward your partner and also wanting to save yourself for marriage. (Criterion 1) And it sounds like the guilt you feel about these desires, which are really natural and common, (Criterion 2) feels like a very heavy burden. Can you tell me more about the beliefs and values that inform your desire to "save yourself for marriage" and also add to the guilt you feel? (Criterion 3)
Example Response to Beginner Client Statement 5
Wow! Congrats—that's a huge accomplishment. (Criterion 2) Being the first person in your family to go to college can feel like an honor, a massive achievement, and even, for some people, like a lot of responsibility. (Criterion 1) Can you tell me more about what it means for you to be the first? (Criterion 3)

EXAMPLE RESPONSES TO INTERMEDIATE-LEVEL CLIENT STATEMENTS FOR EXERCISE 10
Example Response to Intermediate Client Statement 1
Your education about sex focused on romantic relationships between a man and woman. (Criterion 1) So learning about different types of romantic relationships for the first time in college was a weird experience for you. (Criterion 2) Can you tell me more about what you mean by "weird"? I'd also love to know more about your history of romantic relationships if you feel comfortable sharing. (Criterion 3)
Example Response to Intermediate Client Statement 2
You're concerned that the future of your relationship is riding on whether you say yes or no to being in an open relationship, (Criterion 1) and it sounds like you're feeling stuck between two impossible choices. (Criterion 2) What does your ideal relationship look like for you, in the context of your own values? (Criterion 3)
Example Response to Intermediate Client Statement 3
It sounds as though you and your parents hold very different views of success and happiness, (Criterion 1) and this really frustrates you. (Criterion 2) What does success look like for you? (Criterion 3)
Example Response to Intermediate Client Statement 4
You are wondering about the uncertainty of how this accident may change your identity and lifestyle. (Criterion 1) This accident has impacted you in unexpected ways. I can imagine how scary that must feel. (Criterion 2) Intimacy can look very different, depending on who you speak to. What does intimacy mean for you? (Criterion 3)
Example Response to Intermediate Client Statement 5
You seem sad, or even disappointed, that you are not feeling as happy as you expected. (Criterion 2) You were really hoping these professional accomplishments would make you feel better. (Criterion 1) How do your accomplishments align with your personal values and goals? (Criterion 3)

EXAMPLE RESPONSES TO ADVANCED-LEVEL CLIENT STATEMENTS FOR EXERCISE 10

Example Response to Advanced Client Statement 1

You are upset and concerned that I may not understand you and your relationship. (Criterion 2) It is true that you are in a polyamorous relationship and I am married. (Criterion 1) As much as you are comfortable in sharing, can you tell me more about what your relationship has meant to you? (Criterion 3)

Example Response to Advanced Client Statement 2

There is something about our relationship that reminds you of what it may mean to be successful or a professional. (Criterion 1) I see how defeated you must feel not to be where you wish to be in your career or even where you think your partner wants you to be. (Criterion 2) What do you hope to achieve professionally that would make you proud? (Criterion 3)

Example Response to Advanced Client Statement 3

You are longing for a relationship that doesn't involve sex (Criterion 2) and feel that there may be something wrong with you because of this. (Criterion 1) Relationships come in many forms. Can you tell me more about what you're looking for in a romantic relationship? (Criterion 3)

Example Response to Advanced Client Statement 4

You are frustrated that all your hard work may have been for nothing because you don't have a job that you think I and others would respect. (Criterion 1) How frustrating and scary to feel lost after all that work you put in! (Criterion 2) What is a "real" job for you? (Criterion 3)

Example Response to Advanced Client Statement 5

You are right in that our cultural differences have afforded us very different paths, experiences, and hurdles. (Criterion 2) I do not know how hard it must be for you and what you have had to overcome, but I will try to understand. (Criterion 1) As much as you are comfortable sharing, can you tell me more about what you mean when you say how hard it is for "someone like you"? (Criterion 3)

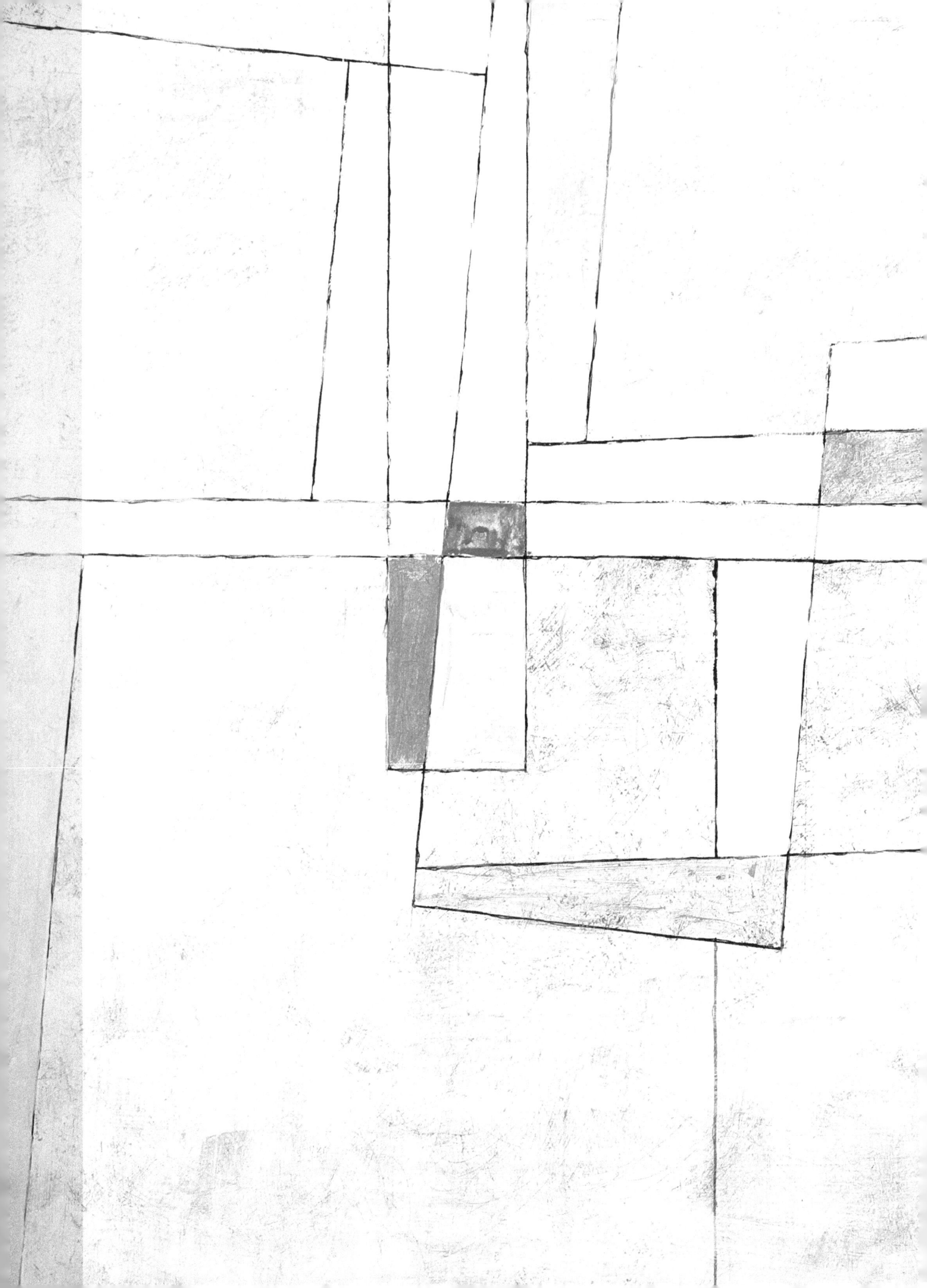

Responding to Resistance and Ambivalence

Preparations for Exercise 11

1. Read the instructions in Chapter 2.

2. Download the Deliberate Practice Reaction Form and the Deliberate Practice Diary Form at https://www.apa.org/pubs/books/deliberate-practice-multicultural-therapy (see the "Clinician and Practitioner Resources" tab; also available in Appendixes A and B, respectively).

Skill Description

Skill Difficulty Level: Advanced

In this exercise, you will practice responding to moments of resistance or ambivalence that have either an explicit or implicit relationship to the intersectional identity of the client. Keep in mind that "competency" in this skill is never fully achieved; rather, we view this as an ongoing and aspirational project. It is crucial to remember that the work of therapy and the interpersonal coconstruction of the therapeutic relationship exist within the structures of oppression, historic marginalization, purposeful and political pathologizing, and unequal access to services and supports. These factors naturally give rise to a variety of valid treatment resistances and ambivalence in clients. It is also important to acknowledge our own intersectional identities, relationship to marginalization, and proximity to or direct access to power and privilege. We do this at the same time that we acknowledge a client's sometimes necessary, protective, and important resistance and ambivalence to therapy. Within a multicultural framework, how do we hold space for resistance nondefensively? How do we hold space for the liberatory possibilities of therapy while respecting the realities of experiences of therapy and mental health systems as often oppressive, carceral, antiliberatory, and unhelpful? We do our

https://doi.org/10.1037/0000357–013

Deliberate Practice in Multicultural Therapy, by J. Harris, J. Jin, S. Hoffman, S. Phan, T. A. Prout, T. Rousmaniere, and A. Vaz

best and start by developing a practice of cultural humility. We develop a "way of being" that invites all of these complex dynamics into the room. In this way we can honor, work with, and move through clients' ambivalence and resistance nondefensively and respectfully.

SKILL CRITERIA FOR EXERCISE 11
1. Acknowledge the validity of the client's statement given their historical identity or cultural context.
2. Ask the client to elaborate on their statement.
3. Maintain a warm, nondefensive stance.

Examples of Therapists Responding to Resistance and Ambivalence

Example 1

CLIENT: [*hostile*] I've been mandated to be in therapy before, and it doesn't work. I'm not going to tell you anything.

THERAPIST: It makes sense that you'd feel that way. Sounds like your previous experience in therapy was a bad one. (Criterion 1) Will you tell me more about it? (Criterion 2)

Example 2

CLIENT: [*hopeless*] There is no way someone like you can help me. We're just too different.

THERAPIST: I'd really like to try, but I get that it doesn't even seem possible right now. (Criterion 1) Can we explore what "someone like me" means for you? (Criterion 2)

Example 3

CLIENT: [*frustrated*] When you suggest things, it makes me feel like you don't understand how my family works. It's not like that for people from my culture . . .

THERAPIST: It sounds like I've been getting something wrong, maybe misunderstanding and letting my own experiences in the world get in the way of listening to what might work for you. (Criterion 1) Can we reset and see if you can tell me more about what I got wrong just then? (Criterion 2)

INSTRUCTIONS FOR EXERCISE 11

Step 1: Role-Play and Feedback

- The client says the first beginner client statement. The therapist **improvises** a response based on the skill criteria.
- The trainer (or, if not available, the client) provides **brief** feedback based on the skill criteria.
- The client then repeats the same statement, and the therapist again improvises a response. The trainer (or client) again provides brief feedback.

Step 2: Repeat

- Repeat Step 1 for all the statements **in the current difficulty level** (beginner, intermediate, or advanced).

Step 3: Assess and Adjust Difficulty

- The therapist completes the Deliberate Practice Reaction Form (see Appendix A) and decides whether to make the exercise easier or harder or to repeat the same difficulty level.

Step 4: Repeat for Approximately 15 Minutes

- Repeat Steps 1 to 3 for at least 15 minutes.
- The trainees then switch therapist and client roles and start over.

Now it's your turn! Follow Steps 1 and 2 from the exercise instructions.

Remember: The goal of the role-play is for trainees to practice improvising responses to the client statements in a manner that (a) uses the skill criteria and (b) feels authentic for the trainee. **Example therapist responses for each client statement are provided at the end of this exercise. Trainees should attempt to improvise their own responses before reading the example responses.**

BEGINNER-LEVEL CLIENT STATEMENTS FOR EXERCISE 11
Beginner Client Statement 1
[Hostile] I've been mandated to be in therapy before, and it doesn't work. I'm not going to tell you anything.
Beginner Client Statement 2
[Hopeless] There is no way someone like you can help me. We're just too different.
Beginner Client Statement 3
[Matter-of-fact] I'm not sure I really believe in therapy; I mean I'm not sure it's for people like me. I've tried getting help in a lot of different ways, and I was constantly reminded of this systematic oppression against people like me. How can I trust therapy after that, you know?
Beginner Client Statement 4
[Hurried and frustrated] Sorry I'm late again. Sessions at this time are just so hard because I am the one who makes dinner and gets the kids' homework done. There's so much to do. I'm just not sure I have time for this.
Beginner Client Statement 5
[Wistful] I don't always have the right words. You want the words so much, sometimes it's just a feeling.
Beginner Client Statement 6
[Frustrated] Never mind, I don't want to talk to you about that. You wouldn't understand that. I'll save that story for someone who knows what I'm talking about—who's more like me.

🛑 **Assess and adjust the difficulty before moving to the next difficulty level (see Step 3 in the exercise instructions).**

INTERMEDIATE-LEVEL CLIENT STATEMENTS FOR EXERCISE 11

Intermediate Client Statement 1

[Resigned] I wanted to see a [insert an identity not held by the trainee playing the therapist (e.g., Black, gay, trans, Korean)] therapist, but I couldn't find one that would take my insurance. But I know I need to talk to someone, so I guess I'm here with you.

Intermediate Client Statement 2

[Matter-of-fact] I've been seeing you for a while, and the more I feel like I'm understanding my sexuality as "not quite straight," the more I feel like you're not the right therapist for me.

Intermediate Client Statement 3

[Anxious] I don't think my parents considered it abuse, but I think some people might. People like you might.

Intermediate Client Statement 4

[Laughing] I told my parents I've been seeing a therapist, and they were horrified. Like, in their minds it's only for crazy people.

Intermediate Client Statement 5

[Uneasy] I don't think you'd judge me. I think I feel like it's wrong. Not for other people, but for me. My parents would never say anything overtly homophobic, but I know it would be hard for them to accept. So, I don't really want to explore it.

Intermediate Client Statement 6

[Apologetic] I don't think it has anything to do with English being my second language. I think it's just me. I'm not really one for talking about feelings.

🛑 **Assess and adjust the difficulty before moving to the next difficulty level (see Step 3 in the exercise instructions).**

ADVANCED-LEVEL CLIENT STATEMENTS FOR EXERCISE 11
Advanced Client Statement 1
[Angry adolescent] I wanted to see a **[insert identity not held by the trainee playing the therapist]** therapist. But my mom said we just needed to see "the best" one. So I guess you're the best, huh?
Advanced Client Statement 2
[Agitated] Honestly, you don't seem like a person that has ever done anything bad in your life. Why would I tell you all the things I've done?
Advanced Client Statement 3
[Uncertain] My husband thinks I should be seeing our pastor for therapy. That's what he does. I think it would make sense for both of us to see him because he knows us and what we are going through.
Advanced Client Statement 4
[Disappointed] When you suggest things, it makes me feel like you don't understand how my family works. It's not like that for people from my culture . . .
Advanced Client Statement 5
[Irritable] My mom says therapy is for White people.
Advanced Client Statement 6
[Exasperated] That isn't the way we parent. It may be the way that people like you parent, but it's not the way I was raised and not the way I'm raising my kids.
Advanced Client Statement 7
[Amused] When you ask me that many questions in a row you sound like a cop interrogating me.

Assess and adjust the difficulty here (see Step 3 in the exercise instructions). If appropriate, follow the instructions to make the exercise even more challenging (see Appendix A).

Example Therapist Responses: Responding to Resistance and Ambivalence

Remember: Trainees should attempt to improvise their own responses before reading the example responses. **Do not read the following responses verbatim unless you are having trouble coming up with your own responses!**

EXAMPLE RESPONSES TO BEGINNER-LEVEL CLIENT STATEMENTS FOR EXERCISE 11
Example Response to Beginner Client Statement 1
It makes sense that you'd feel that way. Sounds like your previous experience in therapy was a bad one. (Criterion 1) Will you tell me more about it? (Criterion 2)
Example Response to Beginner Client Statement 2
I'd really like to try, but I get that it doesn't even seem possible right now. (Criterion 1) Can we explore what "someone like me" means for you? (Criterion 2)
Example Response to Beginner Client Statement 3
Yeah, you've tried a lot of different things already to try and feel better. And it sounds like therapy isn't something that was designed to help "people like you." In a lot of ways therapy has not historically been accessible or tailored to meet the needs of people who have experienced systemic oppression. (Criterion 1) Can you tell me more about who people like you are? (Criterion 2)
Example Response to Beginner Client Statement 4
It sounds like you have a lot going on right now and there are so many pressures on you as a parent. (Criterion 1) I'm wondering if you can tell me more about your life so I can understand and maybe help you think through it. (Criterion 2)
Example Response to Beginner Client Statement 5
Words are sometimes really inadequate to describe the hard things you've been through. (Criterion 1) Can you tell me more about how you would prefer to express yourself? (Criterion 2)
Example Response to Beginner Client Statement 6
It makes sense that a part of you would prefer to talk to someone else. There may be things I can't know from your perspective—that's true—but I'd like to try to understand. (Criterion 1) Would you be willing to tell me about someone who might be "more like you"? (Criterion 2)

EXAMPLE RESPONSES TO INTERMEDIATE-LEVEL CLIENT STATEMENTS FOR EXERCISE 11
Example Response to Intermediate Client Statement 1
Sounds like you had a frustrating time finding the kind of therapist you were looking for. I'm really sorry to hear that. (Criterion 1) Will you tell me a little about what felt important about working with someone who is **[insert identity]**? (Criterion 2)
Example Response to Intermediate Client Statement 2
I'm wondering if we can make space for that possibly being true (Criterion 1) but also some space to explore why you feel that way? Maybe there are specific ways you think I'm not able to fully understand or affirm your experience? (Criterion 2)
Example Response to Intermediate Client Statement 3
There are so many different perspectives on the kind of things you're describing and many of those perspectives are influenced by culture and values. (Criterion 1) Would you tell me a little more about what you mean by "people like me"? (Criterion 2)
Example Response to Intermediate Client Statement 4
Horrified, huh? Folks from different family backgrounds have a really wide range of thoughts and feelings about therapy. (Criterion 1) Do you think it's only for crazy people? (Criterion 2)
Example Response to Intermediate Client Statement 5
You don't really want to explore it right now—that's OK. (Criterion 1) Maybe we can explore the why of not wanting to go a little deeper? (Criterion 2)
Example Response to Intermediate Client Statement 6
That's OK—a lot of people have difficulty talking about their feelings, especially at first. (Criterion 1) Can you tell me more about your previous experiences of talking, or not being able to talk, about your feelings? (Criterion 2)

EXAMPLE RESPONSES TO ADVANCED-LEVEL
CLIENT STATEMENTS FOR EXERCISE 11

Example Response to Advanced Client Statement 1

A lot of people want to see a therapist who has the same identity as they do, so that makes a lot of sense to me. It sounds like your mom had a different idea than you do about all this. (Criterion 1) I'm not so sure I'm the best, but I'd like to be at least a "good" one for you. I wonder what the "best one" means for you? (Criterion 2)

Example Response to Advanced Client Statement 2

All of us have done a lot of things in our lives—I may not have the exact same experience, but I am interested in hearing about your experiences. (Criterion 1) What would a person who does "bad things" seem like? (Criterion 2)

Example Response to Advanced Client Statement 3

Faith is clearly important to your relationship. (Criterion 1) Maybe we can explore some of the pros and cons of making that switch for you? (Criterion 2)

Example Response to Advanced Client Statement 4

It sounds like I've made some suggestions that didn't quite land for you. And there are some pretty important cultural considerations I need to be more aware of. (Criterion 1) Can we rewind a little and talk about where I went wrong? (Criterion 2)

Example Response to Advanced Client Statement 5

I'd really like to understand more about what that means for her or for you. And, honestly, I kind of get it . . . therapy hasn't typically been available or tailored to the needs of **[insert the client's racial/ethnic background]** folks. (Criterion 1) Do you think therapy is for White people? (Criterion 2)

Example Response to Advanced Client Statement 6

It isn't the way you parent. It sounds like maybe I made some assumptions there. And those assumptions might come from my own cultural background. (Criterion 1) Will you tell me a little more about what I missed? (Criterion 2)

Example Response to Advanced Client Statement 7

Well, that sounds awful. Like I'm just another part of the system that doesn't have your interests in mind. (Criterion 1) Let's reset and see if we can find a better way to move through the session together in a way that helps you feel understood and safe. (Criterion 2)

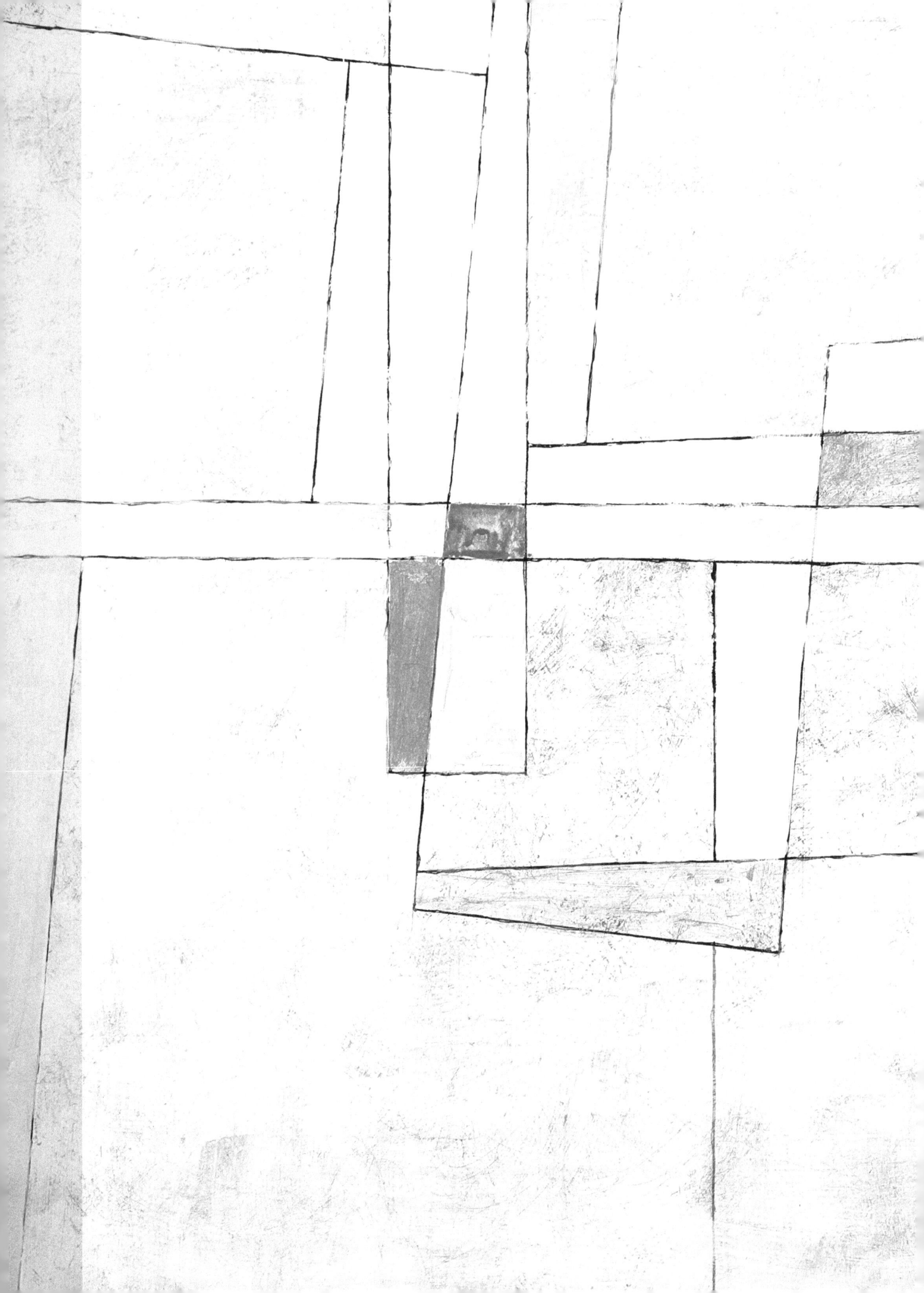

Repairing Ruptures
Due to Microaggressions

Preparations for Exercise 12

1. Read the instructions in Chapter 2.

2. Download the Deliberate Practice Reaction Form and the Deliberate Practice Diary Form at https://www.apa.org/pubs/books/deliberate-practice-multicultural-therapy (see the "Clinician and Practitioner Resources" tab; also available in Appendixes A and B, respectively).

Skill Description

Skill Difficulty Level: Advanced

In this exercise, you will practice repairing ruptures that occur as a result of micro-aggressions. Historically, *microaggressions* have been defined as subtle, daily, and often unintentional slights committed against members of racial groups (Sue, 2017). While the term initially focused on racial microaggressions, more recent authors have expanded the definition to include other aspects of identity, including gender and sexual orientation (Capodilupo et al., 2010; Weber et al., 2018). These incidents of "othering"—indirect, subtle, and often unintentional forms of discrimination—also occur in therapy, with at least 50% of clients reporting having experienced a microaggression from their therapist (Owen et al., 2017).

When microaggressions occur in therapy, they are considered a form of alliance rupture and are important to address and repair (Owen et al., 2014; M. T. Williams et al., 2021). There is evidence that when therapists specifically attend to issues of difference and diversity in the therapeutic dyad, this can be associated with better psychotherapy outcomes for traditionally marginalized clients (Davis et al., 2018). Whenever there is a break in the therapeutic bond, we suggest that the responsibility lies with the therapist

https://doi.org/10.1037/0000357-014

Deliberate Practice in Multicultural Therapy, by J. Harris, J. Jin, S. Hoffman, S. Phan, T. A. Prout, T. Rousmaniere, and A. Vaz

to repair the rupture. This becomes increasingly important because it is probable that experiencing a microaggression from the therapist may lead to cultural concealment—that is, the hiding of cultural information relevant to the client's problem, which in turn leads to poor client outcomes (Drinane et al., 2018) and a poorer therapeutic alliance (Yeo & Torres-Harding, 2021). The following statements are all examples of ruptures clients might bring into therapy that involve some aspect of intersectionality.

SKILL CRITERIA FOR EXERCISE 12

1. Using the client's words, acknowledge their core concern.
2. Invite the client to tell you more about the emotional impact of your words or actions.
3. Reiterate your personal commitment to repairing the rupture.

Examples of Therapists Repairing Ruptures Due to Microaggressions

Example 1

CLIENT: [irritated] You know, that thing you said about the police, well, they don't protect everyone, you know. They disproportionately antagonize people of color.

THERAPIST: Yes, for many people of color, the police aren't safe. That's so true. (Criterion 1) Can you tell me more about how what I said impacted you? (Criterion 2) It's really important that I understand this part of you. (Criterion 3)

Example 2

CLIENT: [concerned] I just wanted to bring up something you said last week. About vaccines. It really worried me.

THERAPIST: I'm so glad you brought up how my statements about vaccines worried you. (Criterion 1) Can you tell me how it impacted you? (Criterion 2) This is really important that I understand how this worried you. (Criterion 3)

Example 3

CLIENT: [frustrated] Do I have kids? No! Just because I'm a woman doesn't mean I love kids.

THERAPIST: You're right. It's wrong to assume that just because you're a woman you love kids. (Criterion 1) Can we explore this? (Criterion 2) I really need to understand how the phrasing of my question sent that message. (Criterion 3)

INSTRUCTIONS FOR EXERCISE 12
Step 1: Role-Play and Feedback
• The client says the first beginner client statement. The therapist **improvises** a response based on the skill criteria.
• The trainer (or, if not available, the client) provides **brief** feedback based on the skill criteria.
• The client then repeats the same statement, and the therapist again improvises a response. The trainer (or client) again provides brief feedback.
Step 2: Repeat
• Repeat Step 1 for all the statements **in the current difficulty level** (beginner, intermediate, or advanced).
Step 3: Assess and Adjust Difficulty
• The therapist completes the Deliberate Practice Reaction Form (see Appendix A) and decides whether to make the exercise easier or harder or to repeat the same difficulty level.
Step 4: Repeat for Approximately 15 Minutes
• Repeat Steps 1 to 3 for at least 15 minutes.
• The trainees then switch therapist and client roles and start over.

Now it's your turn! Follow Steps 1 and 2 from the exercise instructions.

Remember: The goal of the role-play is for trainees to practice improvising responses to the client statements in a manner that (a) uses the skill criteria and (b) feels authentic for the trainee. **Example therapist responses for each client statement are provided at the end of this exercise. Trainees should attempt to improvise their own responses before reading the example responses.**

BEGINNER-LEVEL CLIENT STATEMENTS FOR EXERCISE 12
Beginner Client Statement 1
[Irritated] I'm young, but I'm not that young, and that doesn't mean I don't know what I'm doing or I don't have something to offer.
Beginner Client Statement 2
[Insistent] I know this is about my age. People my age can't just quit their jobs. I need you to believe that.
Beginner Client Statement 3
[Skeptical] There's a Buddha on your side table. Are you into that stuff? I'm not really here for that.
Beginner Client Statement 4
[Matter-of-fact] We immigrated, but that doesn't mean we have money. Everyone thinks that because we came to the States, we have lots of money. It's expensive to live here.
Beginner Client Statement 5
[Angry] Just because I don't show my emotions doesn't mean I don't have feelings. I'm so tired of this strong woman trope.

Assess and adjust the difficulty before moving to the next difficulty level (see Step 3 in the exercise instructions).

INTERMEDIATE-LEVEL CLIENT STATEMENTS FOR EXERCISE 12
Intermediate Client Statement 1
[Tired] "Once an addict, always an addict"? The entire narrative around that is steeped in racism.
Intermediate Client Statement 2
[Sad] I don't feel like you get it. You don't know what it's like to have a kid who's disabled.
Intermediate Client Statement 3
[Defensively] Well, I mean I could go back to work if I wanted. I choose to take some time off to be with my kids while they are young. I have my master's. I could get a job anywhere.
Intermediate Client Statement 4
[Defensively] You keep asking these questions. No! My boss was racist. He was! I'm so tired of having to prove everything.
Intermediate Client Statement 5
[Anxious] When I showed you a picture of my kids, you said one of them didn't look like me. That's a sensitive issue for me—for my whole family. It's hard marrying a White man and having biracial children.

🛑 **Assess and adjust the difficulty before moving to the next difficulty level (see Step 3 in the exercise instructions).**

ADVANCED-LEVEL CLIENT STATEMENTS FOR EXERCISE 12
Advanced Client Statement 1
[Annoyed] Hey, you used the wrong pronouns just then. I prefer zhim or zhey. Please get this right.
Advanced Client Statement 2
[Angry] So remember when I said my husband never washes dishes, and you asked me, "Why should he wash the dishes?" That really offended me. You may not have meant it that way, but that's how I perceived it.
Advanced Client Statement 3
[Irritated] Last week, your coffee mug said "queen." It felt like a dig. I know you didn't even think about it, but because I'm gay, it kinda made me feel weird.
Advanced Client Statement 4
[Worried] When you asked if I was suicidal, it was triggering. My last therapist sent me to an inpatient unit and thought I was crazy.
Advanced Client Statement 5
[Sad] When you used my dead name, it really triggered me.

Assess and adjust the difficulty here (see Step 3 in the exercise instructions). If appropriate, follow the instructions to make the exercise even more challenging (see Appendix A).

Example Therapist Responses: Repairing Ruptures Due to Microaggressions

Remember: Trainees should attempt to improvise their own responses before reading the example responses. **Do not read the following responses verbatim unless you are having trouble coming up with your own responses!**

EXAMPLE RESPONSES TO BEGINNER-LEVEL CLIENT STATEMENTS FOR EXERCISE 12
Example Response to Beginner Client Statement 1
Yes. You are young and have a lot to offer. Your age doesn't take away from how much you have to offer. (Criterion 1) Can you help me understand this? (Criterion 2) It seems like you got the message that I don't think you have a lot to offer because of your age. It's important to me that I understand this. (Criterion 3)
Example Response to Beginner Client Statement 2
I'm sure they look down on you because of your age. (Criterion 1) What else here do I need to understand? (Criterion 2) I don't want to move on too quickly and miss how important this is to you. (Criterion 3)
Example Response to Beginner Client Statement 3
Hey, I'm not going to push anything on you. This is a place for you and your growth. (Criterion 1) Can you tell me what you think it means about the work we'll do here because I have a Buddha? (Criterion 2) I really want to understand what this means to you. (Criterion 3)
Example Response to Beginner Client Statement 4
Yes, immigrant life is hard. I don't want to make any assumptions here. (Criterion 1) How did my statements impact you? (Criterion 2) It's really important for me to understand this and take ownership for my statements. (Criterion 3)
Example Response to Beginner Client Statement 5
Oh my goodness. I agree. This trope is worn thin. I see that. (Criterion 1) Can you clarify how my comment hurt you? (Criterion 2) I don't want to gloss over how my comment struck you. (Criterion 3)

EXAMPLE RESPONSES TO INTERMEDIATE-LEVEL CLIENT STATEMENTS FOR EXERCISE 12
Example Response to Intermediate Client Statement 1
Yeah. There's a long history of racism in our stories about drugs. (Criterion 1) Can we talk about how my saying that impacted you? (Criterion 2) This is really important for me to understand. (Criterion 3)
Example Response to Intermediate Client Statement 2
Yeah, you wonder if I can understand you. That's a valid concern. (Criterion 1) Can you tell me what it would mean if I couldn't understand you here? (Criterion 2) It's really important that I understand how this is hitting you. (Criterion 3)
Example Response to Intermediate Client Statement 3
Of course. The decision to stay home with the kids was your decision. I support that. (Criterion 1) Can we talk about this? It seems like you got the message that I looked down on you for your decision. (Criterion 2) I don't. It's really important to me that I understand how upsetting my words were. (Criterion 3)
Example Response to Intermediate Client Statement 4
Right, you really need me to get that he is a racist. I believe you. He's a racist. I don't want to invalidate your truth. (Criterion 1) Can we explore this? (Criterion 2) It's important for me to understand how my questions sent that message that I don't believe you. (Criterion 3)
Example Response to Intermediate Client Statement 5
I can totally see how that was off. I own that. (Criterion 1) What else do I need to understand about this? About how what I said hurt? (Criterion 2) I want to make sure this is a safe place for you. (Criterion 3)

EXAMPLE RESPONSES TO ADVANCED-LEVEL CLIENT STATEMENTS FOR EXERCISE 12

Example Response to Advanced Client Statement 1

Oh, I'm so sorry. You deserve to have your pronouns respected, and getting your pronouns right is important. (Criterion 1) Can you tell me the message you just got from me, maybe that I don't respect you? (Criterion 2) It's important that I get this right. (Criterion 3)

Example Response to Advanced Client Statement 2

Yeah, relationships should be an equal partnership. I totally agree with that. (Criterion 1) Can you tell me how what I said offended you? What's the message you felt I was saying? (Criterion 2) The last thing I want to do is offend you. (Criterion 3)

Example Response to Advanced Client Statement 3

Wow. I didn't think about it. Still, it makes total sense that would be a trigger. (Criterion 1) How specifically did that land for you? (Criterion 2) I want to make sure I really hear you here. (Criterion 3)

Example Response to Advanced Client Statement 4

Oh, that sounds like it was really hard. Traumatizing even. (Criterion 1) It sounds like you got the message that I thought you were crazy just like your last therapist? Can we talk about that? (Criterion 2) It's a big deal that I really hear your pain. (Criterion 3)

Example Response to Advanced Client Statement 5

Yep. Of course. First, I apologize. That shouldn't have happened. (Criterion 1) What about this do I need to get? What's the message about therapy you received when I used your dead name? (Criterion 2) It's a big deal to me that we repair this. (Criterion 3)

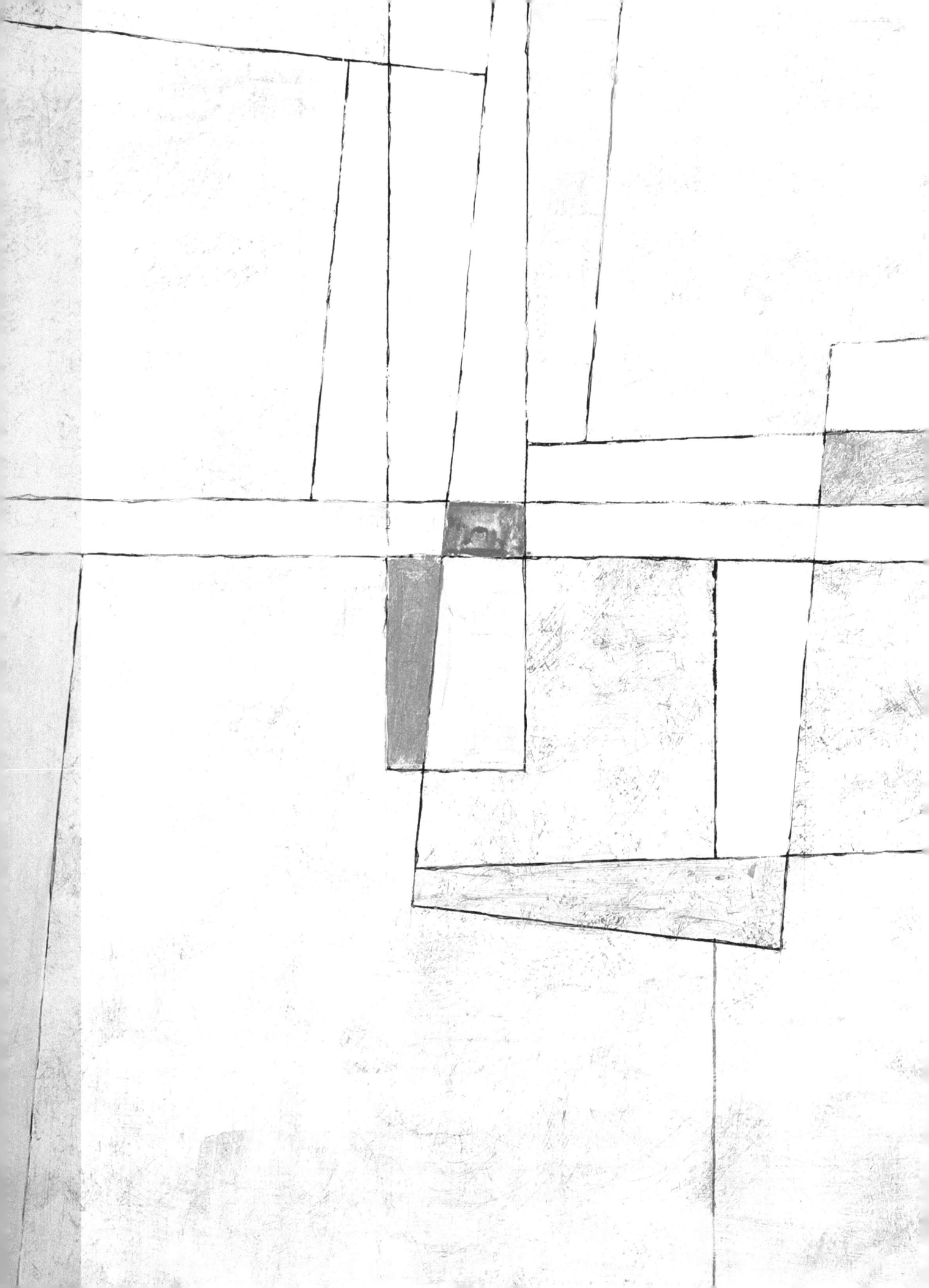

EXERCISE

13

Mock Multicultural Therapy Sessions

In contrast to highly structured and repetitive deliberate practice exercises, a mock multi Like a jazz rehearsal, mock sessions let you practice the art and science of *appropriate responsiveness* (Hatcher, 2015; Stiles & Horvath, 2017), putting your psychotherapy skills together in a way that is helpful to your mock client. This exercise outlines the procedure for conducting a mock multicultural therapy session. It offers different client profiles you may choose to adopt when playing the client role.

Mock sessions are an opportunity for trainees to practice the following:

- using psychotherapy skills responsively
- navigating challenging choice-points in therapy
- choosing which interventions to use
- tracking the arc of a therapy session and the overall big-picture therapy treatment
- guiding treatment in the context of the client's preferences
- determining realistic goals for therapy in the context of the client's capacities
- knowing how to proceed when the therapist is unsure, lost, or confused
- recognizing and recovering from therapeutic errors
- discovering your personal therapeutic style
- building endurance for working with real clients

Mock Multicultural Therapy Session Overview

For the mock session, **you will perform a role-play of an initial therapy session**. As is true with the exercises to build individual skills, the role-play involves three people: One trainee role-plays the therapist, another trainee role-plays the client, and a trainer (a professor or a supervisor) observes and provides feedback. This is an open-ended role-play, as is commonly done in training. However, this differs in two important ways from the role-plays used in more traditional training. First, the therapist will use their hand to indicate

https://doi.org/10.1037/0000357-015

Deliberate Practice in Multicultural Therapy, by J. Harris, J. Jin, S. Hoffman, S. Phan, T. A. Prout, T. Rousmaniere, and A. Vaz

how difficult the role-play feels. Second, the client will attempt to make the role-play easier or harder to ensure the therapist is practicing at the right difficulty level.

Preparation

1. Download the Deliberate Practice Reaction Form and the Deliberate Practice Diary Form from the "Clinician and Practitioner Resources" tab at https://www.apa.org/pubs/books/deliberate-practice-multicultural-therapy (also available in Appendixes A and B, respectively). Every student will need their own copy of the Deliberate Practice Reaction Form on a separate piece of paper so they can access it quickly.

2. Designate one student to role-play the therapist and one student to role-play the client. The trainer will observe and provide corrective feedback.

Mock Multicultural Therapy Session Procedure

1. The trainees will role-play an initial (first) therapy session. The trainee role-playing the client selects a client profile from the end of this exercise.

2. Before beginning the role-play, the therapist raises their hand to their side, at the level of their chair seat (see Figure E13.1). They will use this hand throughout the whole role-play to indicate how challenging it feels to them to help the client. Their starting hand level (chair seat) indicates that the role-play feels easy. By raising their hand, the

FIGURE E13.1. Ongoing Difficulty Assessment Through Hand Level

Note. Left: Start of role-play. Right: Role-play is too difficult. From *Deliberate Practice in Emotion-Focused Therapy* (p. 156), by R. N. Goldman, A. Vaz, and T. Rousmaniere, 2021, American Psychological Association (https://doi.org/10.1037/0000227-000). Copyright 2021 by the American Psychological Association.

therapist indicates that the difficulty is rising. If their hand rises above their neck level, it indicates that the role-play is too difficult.

3. The therapist begins the role-play. The therapist and client should engage in the role-play in an improvised manner, as they would engage in a real therapy session. The therapist keeps their hand out at their side throughout this process. (This may feel strange at first!)

4. Whenever the therapist feels that the difficulty of the role-play has changed significantly, they should move their hand up if it feels more difficult, down if it feels easier. If the therapist's hand drops below the seat of their chair, the client should make the role-play more challenging; if the therapist's hand rises above their neck level, the client should make the role-play easier. Instructions for adjusting the difficulty of the role-play are described in the "Varying the Level of Challenge" section.

Note to Therapists

Remember to be aware of your vocal quality. Match your tone to the client's presentation. Thus, if the clients present vulnerable, soft emotions behind their words, soften your tone to be soothing and calm. If, on the other hand, clients are aggressive and angry, match your tone to be firm and solid. If you choose responses that are prompting client exploration, such as working with emotions in context (Exercise 5), remember to adopt a more querying, exploratory tone of voice.

5. The role-play continues for at least 15 minutes. The trainer may provide corrective feedback during this process if the therapist gets significantly off-track. However, trainers should exercise restraint and keep feedback as short and tight as possible, as this will reduce the therapist's opportunity for experiential training.

6. After the role-play is finished, the therapist and client switch roles and begin a new mock session.

7. After both trainees have completed the mock session as a therapist, the trainees and the trainer discuss the experience.

Varying the Level of Challenge

If the therapist indicates that the mock session is too easy, the person enacting the role of the client can use the following modifications to make it more challenging (see also Appendix A):

- The client can improvise with topics that are more evocative or make the therapist uncomfortable, such as expressing currently held strong feelings (see Figure A.2).
- The client can use a distressed voice (e.g., angry, sad, sarcastic) or unpleasant facial expression. This increases the emotional tone.
- Blend complex mixtures of opposing feelings (for example, love and rage).
- Become confrontational, questioning the purpose of therapy or the therapist's fitness for the role.

If the therapist indicates that the mock session is too hard:

- The client can be guided by Figure A.2 to
  - present topics that are less evocative,
  - present material on any topic but without expressing feelings, or
  - present material concerning the future or the past or events outside therapy.

- The client can ask the questions in a soft voice or with a smile. This softens the emotional stimulus.

- The therapist can take short breaks during the role-play.

- The trainer can expand the "feedback phase" by discussing multicultural therapy or psychotherapy theory more generally.

Mock Session Client Profiles

Following are six client profiles for trainees to use during mock sessions, presented in order of difficulty. The choice of client profile may be determined by the trainee playing the therapist, the trainee playing the client, or assigned by the trainer.

The most important aspect of role-plays is for trainees to convey the emotional tone indicated by the client profile (for example, "angry" or "sad"). The demographics of the client (e.g., age, gender) and specific content of the client profiles are not important. Thus, trainees should adjust the client profile to be most comfortable and easy for the trainee to role-play. For example, a trainee may change the client profile from female to male, from 45 to 22 years old, and so on.

Beginner Profile: Building Rapport With a Client at the Beginning of Treatment

Jo is a 30-year-old White nonbinary person living in a large northeastern city. They have a stable, professional office job and stable housing and finances. They recently came out to their family of origin as nonbinary, and this has caused strain in a previously close relationship. They report that when they came out as gay in their late teens, they did not experience the same rupture as when expressing their desire to be addressed with a name different than the one their parents gave them at birth as well as a change in their pronouns. This disturbance in their relationship with their mother and sister has caused significant strain on their current romantic relationship, causing increased conflict with their partner of 1 year.

- **Symptoms:** Excessive worry, sleep disturbance, distractibility, and increased interpersonal conflict with their romantic partner

- **Client's goals for therapy:** Jo's relationship with their family of origin has changed since coming out as nonbinary. Jo would like to process these feelings, reduce feelings of excessive worry, and gain more insight into the impact this is having on their current romantic relationship.

- **Attitude toward therapy:** Jo has very positive associations with therapy but is hesitant at first working with a new therapist whom they worry will not be able to understand the nuances of their gender identity. You were the only therapist they could find who took their insurance and was accepting new clients.

- **Strengths:** Jo is very invested in therapy and has positive associations with it. They have a strong social network and community. They also have a fairly high level of understanding of the psychotherapeutic process based on previous experience.

Beginner Profile: Addressing Emotions and Issues of Success With a Client Trying Therapy for the First Time

Jamal is a 33-year-old African American man who recently returned to the area to be more involved in the life of his two sons. He is coming to therapy because he feels himself "pulling back." Previously he was able to make a decent living flipping houses, but since returning to the area, he has struggled making local contacts. The stress of wanting to provide for his sons without a secure financial future is causing him to bounce between being engaged with his kids and emotionally withdrawing. This pattern of at times being engaged and at times distancing has caused his kids' mother to mistrust him.

- **Symptoms:** Numbness, emotional withdrawal, and feelings of shame
- **Client's goals for therapy:** "I want to be able to be there for my kids, even when I feel like I can't provide."
- **Attitude toward therapy:** Jamal has not been to therapy before and is uncertain about the process. However, he states, "I'm willing to give therapy a try if I can learn coping skills to stop pulling back."
- **Strengths:** Jamal is highly intelligent and a self-starter. He's generally able to acquire new skills quickly. Also, although he currently does not have income, he has substantial savings from the sale of his last house.

Intermediate Profile: Navigating Hopelessness With an Ambivalent Client

Riley is a 20-year-old Puerto Rican trans male who recently became homeless with his 4-year-old daughter. This led Riley to feel hopeless, depressed, stuck, and alone. He is overwhelmed by the various steps to obtain a housing voucher and enroll his daughter in preschool. Although he has family and friends nearby, he does not want to be a burden. Riley is coming to therapy to become more motivated to get back on track with his life and take care of himself and his daughter.

- **Symptoms:** Loneliness, sadness, and hopelessness
- **Client's goals for therapy:** Riley wants to increase his motivation to obtain safe housing and enroll his daughter in school.
- **Attitude toward therapy:** Riley is ambivalent about starting therapy because he is concerned about whether a therapist will understand him.
- **Strengths:** Riley is self-aware, insightful, and resilient.

Intermediate Profile: Helping a Sarcastic and Avoidant Client

Anh is a 35-year-old Vietnamese American cisgender woman who has lived in the United States for nearly 20 years to attend university. She has been struggling to pursue a career as a comedian, which has led to estrangement with her family. Recently, Anh's manager recommended that she seek professional help because of her irritability and angry outbursts as well as drinking and substance use. Anh cites that she drinks and uses a typical amount and that it helps with her creativity. However, she agreed to try therapy for one month.

- **Symptoms:** Anger, drinking, and substance use
- **Client's goals for therapy:** Anh wants to manage her irritability and anger.
- **Attitude toward therapy:** Anh has never been in therapy before and is embarrassed about it. She is trying it to appease her manager.
- **Strengths:** Anh is smart, funny, and resourceful.

Advanced Profile: Addressing Loneliness With a Motivated Client

Nathan is a 64-year-old Mexican American cisgender man who is contemplating a divorce after a recent health scare. Although he identifies as gay, Nathan married his wife and had a family because of his religious values and family's expectations. After recovering from a serious case of pneumonia, Nathan is contemplating a divorce and living his life more authentically. He is afraid of how his family and religious community will respond and having to start his life over.

- **Symptoms:** Anxiety and sadness

- **Client's goals for therapy:** Nathan wants to live his life more authentically.

- **Attitude toward therapy:** Nathan has never been in therapy before but has friends who have had positive experiences. He is open and hopeful.

- **Strengths:** Nathan is hopeful and has strong social support. He is well liked in his community.

Advanced Profile: Helping a Client With Mood Lability and Self-Harm

Peter is a 19-year-old Korean American cisgender man and a college student who is distressed about his suicidal ideations. He has never attempted suicide but has started to drink alcohol more to numb his thoughts. He moved to the midwestern region of the United States from South Korea for college as an international student. His parents are pressuring him to become a dentist and sent him to this country to receive a "Christian education." Peter is unsure he can meet the demands of his academic studies or satisfy his parents' expectations. He barely knows what he wants for his own life. He knows how much they are paying to support his education, but the transition has been hard.

- **Symptoms:** Perfectionism, depression, suicidal ideation, and alcohol use

- **Client's goals for therapy:** Peter wants to focus more on his studies.

- **Attitude toward therapy:** Peter has never received professional mental health services before. He has received support and pastoral counseling in the past, which reminded him that he needs to be a better son. He is skeptical that you (his new therapist) will understand his situation and is interested in a "quick fix" so he can improve his study habits.

- **Strengths:** Peter is empathic, caring, and respectful, with strong religious commitment.

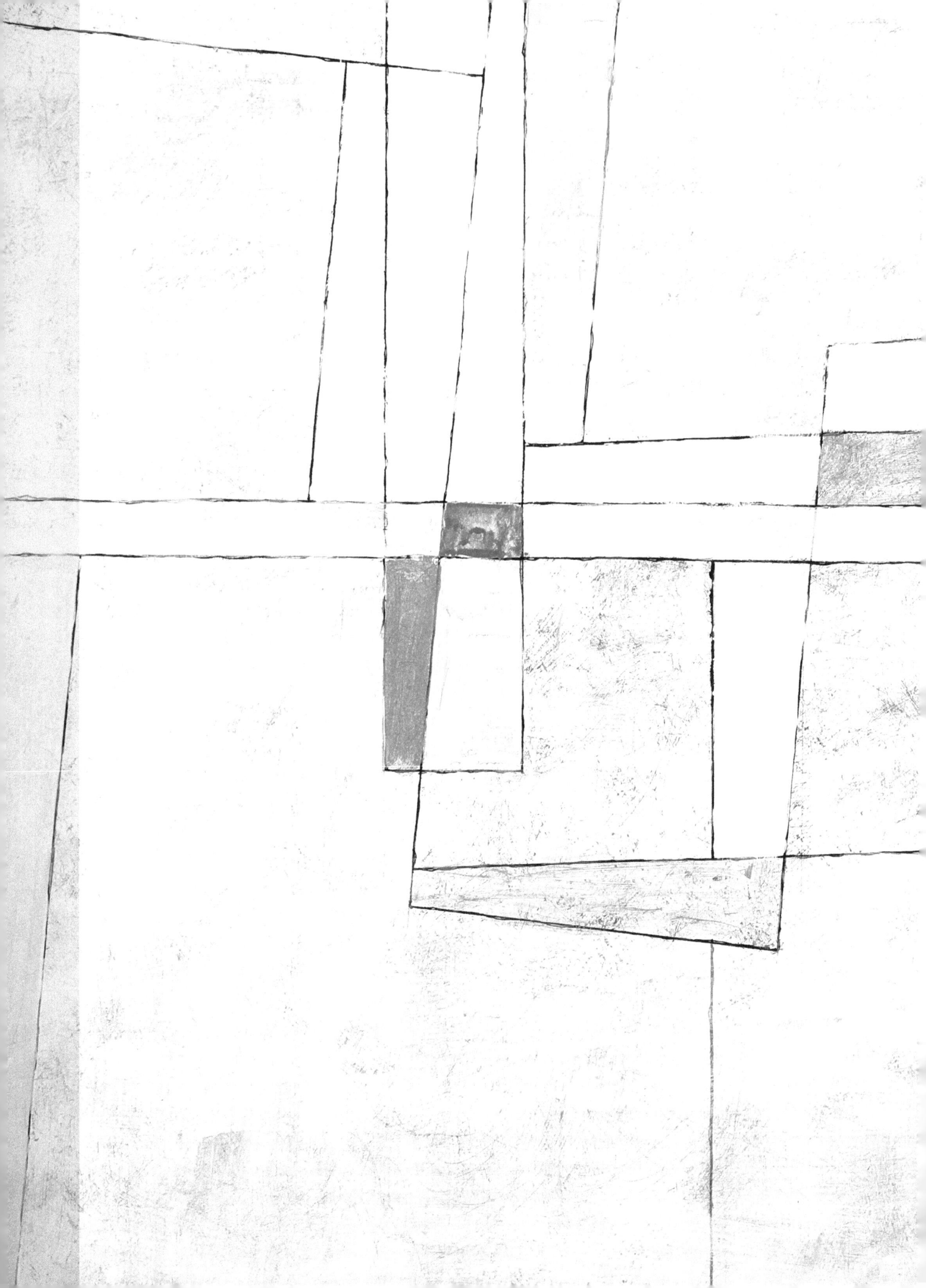

Strategies for Enhancing the Deliberate Practice Exercises

PART

III

Part III consists of one chapter, Chapter 3, that provides additional advice and instructions for trainers and trainees so that they can reap more benefits from the deliberate practice exercises in Part II. Chapter 3 offers six key points for getting the most out of deliberate practice, guidelines for practicing appropriately responsive treatment, evaluation strategies, methods for ensuring trainee well-being and respecting their privacy, and advice for monitoring the trainer–trainee relationship.

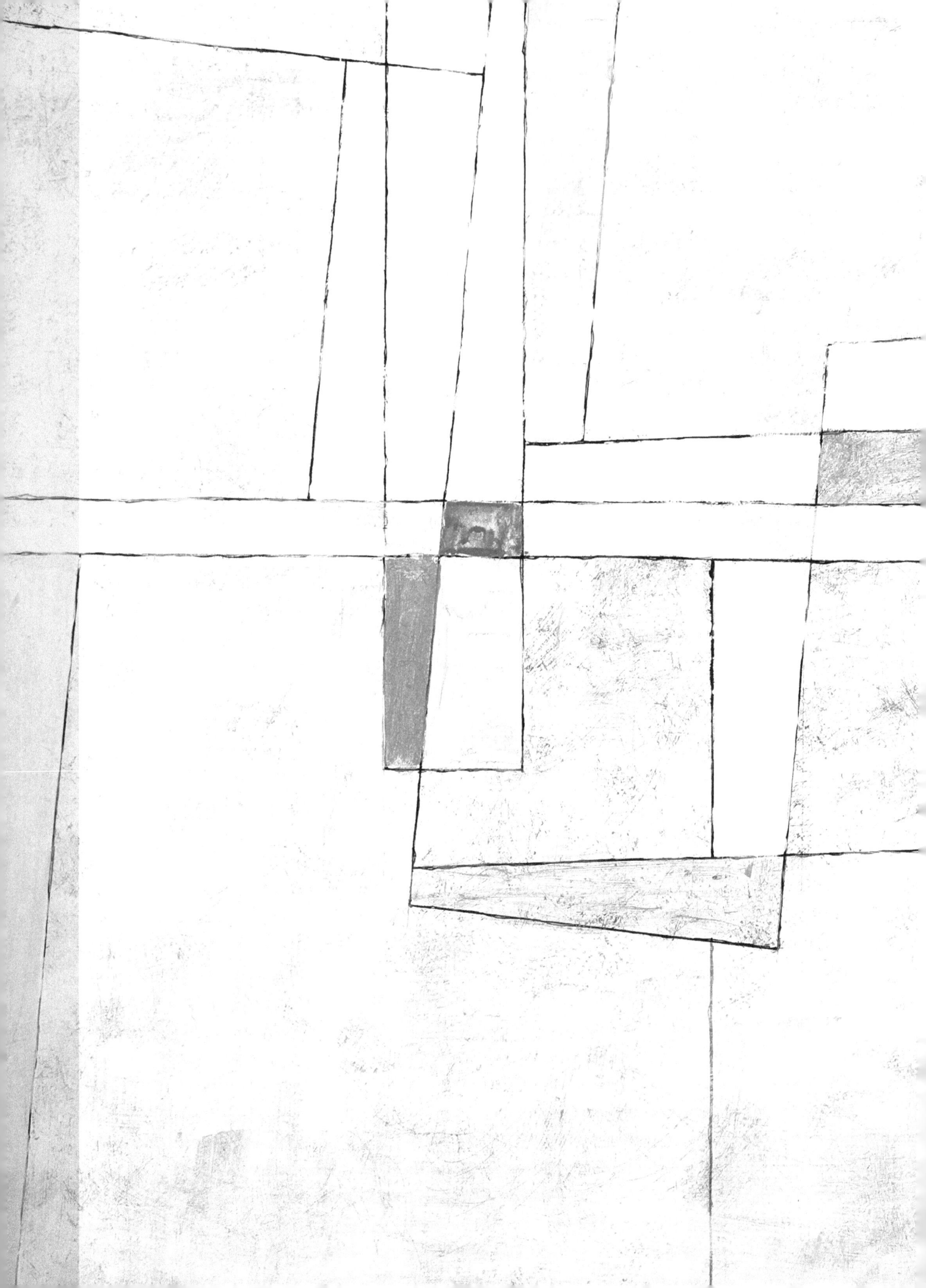

How to Get the Most Out of Deliberate Practice: Additional Guidance for Trainers and Trainees

In Chapter 2, and in the exercises themselves, we provide instructions for completing this book's deliberate practice exercises. This chapter provides guidance on big-picture topics that trainers will need to integrate deliberate practice successfully into their training program. This guidance is based on relevant research and the experiences and feedback from trainers at more than a dozen psychotherapy training programs. We cover topics including evaluation, getting the most from deliberate practice, trainee well-being, respecting trainee privacy, trainer self-evaluation, responsive treatment, and the trainee–trainer alliance.

Six Key Points for Getting the Most From Deliberate Practice

Following are six key points of advice for trainers and trainees to get the most benefit from the multicultural therapy deliberate practice exercises. The following advice is gleaned from experiences vetting and practicing the exercises, sometimes in different languages, with many trainees, across many countries.

Key Point 1: Create Realistic Emotional Stimuli

A key component of deliberate practice is using stimuli that provoke similar reactions to challenging real-life work settings. For example, pilots train with flight simulators that present mechanical failures and dangerous weather conditions; surgeons practice with surgical simulators that present medical complications with only seconds to respond. Training with challenging stimuli will increase trainees' capacity to perform therapy effectively under stress—for example, with clients they find challenging. The stimuli used for multicultural therapy deliberate practice exercises are role-plays of challenging client statements in therapy. **It is important that the trainee who is role-playing the client perform the script with appropriate emotional expression and maintain eye contact with the therapist.** For example, if the client statement calls for sad emotion,

https://doi.org/10.1037/0000357-016

Deliberate Practice in Multicultural Therapy, by J. Harris, J. Jin, S. Hoffman, S. Phan, T. A. Prout, T. Rousmaniere, and A. Vaz

the trainee should try to express sadness eye-to-eye with the therapist. We offer the following suggestions regarding emotional expressiveness:

1. The emotional tone of the role-play matters more than the exact words of each script. Trainees role-playing the client should feel free to improvise and change the words if it will help them be more emotionally expressive. Trainees do not need to stick 100% exactly to the script. In fact, to read from the script during the exercise can sound flat and prohibit eye contact. Rather, trainees in the client role should first read the client statement silently to themselves, then, when ready, say it in an emotional manner while looking directly at the trainee playing the therapist. This will help the experience feel more real and engaging for the therapist.

2. Trainees whose first language isn't English may particularly benefit from reviewing and changing the words in the client statement script before each role-play so they can find words that feel congruent and facilitate emotional expression.

3. Trainees role-playing the client should try to use tonal and nonverbal expressions of feelings. For example, if a script calls for anger, the trainee can speak with an angry voice and make fists with their hands; if a script calls for shame or guilt, the trainee could hunch over and wince; if a script calls for sadness, the trainee could speak in a soft or deflated voice.

4. If trainees are having persistent difficulties acting believably when following a particular script in the role of client, it may help to first do a "demo round" by reading directly from paper, and then, immediately after, dropping the paper to make eye contact and repeating the same client statement from memory. Some trainees reported this helped them "become available as a real client" and made the role-play feel less artificial. Some trainees did three for four "demo rounds" to get fully into their role as a client.

5. Taking on the role of a client who has historically been marginalized may feel uncomfortable at times. While trainees are encouraged to be emotionally expressive in their role-plays, we encourage trainees to avoid use of accents, speech patterns, or other behaviors that might be seen as stereotypical of a particular identity or group. There is no need to attempt to act out the part of a particular intersectional identity because this is likely to be inauthentic or even offensive. Simply describe the client's cultural/identity background where indicated and embrace an emotionally expressive tone that is congruent with the client statement.

Key Point 2: Customize the Exercises to Fit Your Unique Training Circumstances

Deliberate practice is less about adhering to specific rules than it is about using training principles. Every trainer has their own individual teaching style, and every trainee their own learning process. Thus, the exercises in this book are designed to be flexibly customized by trainers across different training contexts within different cultures. Trainees and trainers are encouraged to adjust exercises continually to optimize their practice. The most effective training will occur when deliberate practice exercises are customized to fit the learning needs of each trainee and culture of each training site. In our experience with numerous trainers and trainees across many countries, we found that everyone spontaneously customized the exercises for their unique training circumstances. No two trainers followed the exact same procedure. The following are a few examples.

• One supervisor used the exercises with a trainee who found all the client statements to be too hard, including the "beginner" stimuli. This trainee had multiple reactions in the "too hard" category, including nausea, severe shame, and self-doubt. The trainee disclosed to the supervisor that she had experienced extremely harsh learning environments earlier in her life and found the role-plays to be highly evocative. To help, the supervisor followed the suggestions offered in Appendix A to make the stimuli progressively easier until the trainee reported feeling "good challenge" on the Deliberate Practice Reaction Form. Over many weeks of practice, the trainee developed a sense of safety and was able to practice with more difficult client statements. (Note that if the supervisor had proceeded at the too hard difficulty level, the trainee might have complied while hiding her negative reactions, become emotionally flooded and overwhelmed, leading to withdrawal and thus prohibiting her skill development and risking dropout from training.)

- Supervisors of trainees for whom English was not their first language adjusted the client statements to their own primary language.

- One supervisor used the exercises with a trainee who found all the stimuli to be too easy, including the advanced client statements. This supervisor quickly moved to improvising more challenging client statements from scratch by following the instructions in Appendix A on how to make client statements more challenging.

Key Point 3: Discover Your Own Unique Personal Therapeutic Style

Deliberate practice in psychotherapy can be likened to the process of learning to play jazz music. Every jazz musician prides themselves in their skillful improvisations, and the process of "finding your own voice" is a prerequisite for expertise in jazz musicianship. Yet improvisations are not a collection of random notes but the culmination of extensive deliberate practice over time. Indeed, the ability to improvise is built on many hours of dedicated practice of scales, melodies, harmonies, and so on. Much in the same way, psychotherapy trainees are encouraged to experience the scripted interventions in this book not as ends in themselves but as a means to promote skill in a systematic fashion. Over time, effective therapeutic creativity can be aided, instead of constrained, by dedicated practice in these therapeutic "melodies."

Key Point 4: Engage in a Sufficient Amount of Rehearsal

Deliberate practice uses rehearsal to move skills into procedural memory, which helps trainees maintain access to skills even when working with challenging clients. This only works if trainees engage in many repetitions of the exercises. Think of a challenging sport or musical instrument you learned: How many rehearsals would a professional need to feel confident performing a new skill? Psychotherapy is no easier than those other fields!

Key Point 5: Continually Adjust Difficulty

A crucial element of deliberate practice is training at an optimal difficulty level: neither too easy nor too hard. To achieve this, do difficulty assessments and adjustments with the Deliberate Practice Reaction Form in Appendix A. **Do not skip this step!** If trainees don't feel any of the "good challenge" reactions at the bottom of the Deliberate Practice Reaction Form, then the exercise is probably too easy; if they feel any of the "too hard" reactions then the exercise could be too difficult for the trainee to benefit. Advanced trainees and therapists may find all the client statements too easy. If so, they should follow the instructions in Appendix A on making client statements harder to make the role-plays sufficiently challenging.

Key Point 6: Putting It All Together With the Mock Therapy Sessions

Some trainees may feel a further need for greater contextualization of the individual therapy responses associated with each skill, feeling the need to integrate the disparate pieces of their training in a more coherent manner, with a simulation that mimics a real therapy session. The mock therapy sessions in Exercise 13 give trainees this opportunity, allowing them to practice delivering different responses sequentially in a more realistic therapeutic encounter.

Responsive Treatment

The exercises in this book are designed to help trainees to not only acquire specific skills of multicultural therapy but also to use them in ways that are responsive to each individual client (Arredondo, 2019; Hays, 2022; Hays & Iwamasa, 2006; Liu & Herndon, 2022; Tummala-Narra, 2015). Across the psychotherapy literature, this stance has been referred to as *appropriate responsiveness*, wherein the therapists exercise flexible judgment, based in their perception of the client's emotional state, needs, and goals, and integrate techniques and other interpersonal skills in pursuit of optimal client outcomes (Hatcher, 2015; Stiles et al., 1998). The effective therapist is responsive to the emerging context. As Stiles and Horvath (2017) argued, a therapist is effective because they are appropriately responsive. Doing the "right thing" may be different each time and means providing each client with an individually tailored response.

Appropriate responsiveness counters a misconception that deliberate practice rehearsal is designed to promote robotic repetition of therapy techniques. Psychotherapy researchers have shown that overadherence to a particular model while neglecting client preferences reduces therapy effectiveness (e.g., Castonguay et al., 1996; Henry et al., 1993; Owen & Hilsenroth, 2014). Therapist flexibility, on the other hand, has been shown to improve outcomes (e.g., Bugatti & Boswell, 2016; Kendall & Beidas, 2007; Kendall & Frank, 2018). It is important, therefore, that trainees practice their newly learned skills in a manner that is flexible and responsive to the unique needs of a diverse range of clients (Bernal et al., 2009; Bochicchio et al., 2022; Soto et al., 2019).

Supervisors can also adopt a multicultural orientation to supervision, supporting supervisees with cultural humility, cultural comfort, and by seizing opportunities to discuss issues of culture and intersectionality in the psychotherapy process and the parallel process of supervision itself (Watkins et al., 2019). In addition to the typical didactic feedback offered by culturally responsive supervisors, supervisees report that supervisor empathy, awareness of power and privilege, acknowledgment of their own blind spots, and nonjudgmental stance are all helpful aspects of clinical supervision (Wilcox, Winkeljohn Black, et al., 2022). Supervisors are encouraged not only to attend to the client's cultural context but to also consider and prioritize the therapist's own intersectional identity (Wilcox, Drinane, et al., 2022). Although multicultural orientation in supervision does not necessarily predict supervisees' development of culturally responsive psychotherapy skills, factors such as cultural humility and cultural opportunities are associated with supervisees' level of comfort and satisfaction in supervision (King et al., 2020).

It is also important that deliberate practice occur within a context of wider multicultural therapy learning. As noted in Chapter 1, training should be combined with supervision of actual therapy recordings, theoretical learning, observation of competent multicultural therapy psychotherapists, and personal therapeutic work. When the trainer or trainee determine that the trainee is having difficulty acquiring multicultural therapy skills, it is important to assess carefully what is missing or needed. Assessment of multicultural therapy skills, self-reflection, and close process analysis should then lead to the appropriate remedy, as the trainer and trainee collaboratively determine what is needed.

Being Mindful of Trainee Well-Being

Although negative effects that some clients experience in psychotherapy, as a result of therapist microaggressions or lack of cultural humility and missed cultural opportunities, have been well documented (Kelley, 2015; Kuo et al., 2021; Owen et al., 2010, 2011, 2014), the literature on negative effects of training and supervision on trainees has only recently begun to grow (Adams et al., 2022; Wilcox, Drinane, et al., 2022; Wilcox, Winkeljohn Black, et al., 2022). Multicultural therapy supervision is rooted in the long history of creating safe and supportive space for the process to unfold. In keeping with this tradition, the supervisory and training relationship is built on warmth, empathy, cultural humility, cultural opportunities, and cultural comfort. Supervisees want supervisors to discuss the "client's cultural or ethnic background as it relates to clinical presentation or client perspective of challenges" and to explore "how aspects of diversity, power, privilege could influence the therapy relationship" (Adams et al., 2022, pp. 3–4). The supervisor must maintain an empathic, open, nonjudgmental stance and stay rooted in awareness of their own privilege and power (Wilcox, Winkeljohn Black, et al., 2022). This includes discussion of their own blind spots and a humble approach to issues of difference and diversity; supervisors should be careful about putting supervisees on the spot or implicitly communicating that there is a "correct" answer when it comes to the complexities of self-reflection and personal growth of the therapist (Wilcox, Winkeljohn Black, et al., 2022). Supervisors who comfortably initiate discussion of cultural issues, intersectionality, and vectors of oppression set the tone for a solid multicultural orientation framework in the supervisory relationship.

To support strong self-efficacy, trainers must ensure that trainees are practicing at a correct difficulty level. The exercises in this book feature guidance for frequently assessing and adjusting the difficulty level so that trainees can rehearse at a level that precisely targets their personal skill threshold. Trainers and supervisors must be mindful to provide an appropriate challenge. One risk to trainees that is particularly pertinent to this book occurs when using role-plays that are too difficult. The Deliberate Practice Reaction Form in Appendix A is provided to help trainers ensure that role-plays are done at an appropriate challenge level. Trainers or trainees may be tempted to skip the difficulty assessments and adjustments, out of their motivation to focus on rehearsal to make fast progress and quickly acquire skills. But across all our test sites, we found that skipping the difficulty assessments and adjustments caused more problems and hindered skill acquisition more than any other error. Thus, trainers are advised to remember that **one of their most important responsibilities is to remind trainees to do the difficulty assessments and adjustments.**

Additionally, the Reaction Form serves a dual purpose of helping trainees develop the important skills of self-monitoring and self-awareness (Bennett-Levy, 2019). This will help trainees adopt a positive and empowered stance regarding their own self-care and should facilitate career-long professional development.

Respecting Trainee Privacy

The deliberate practice exercises in this book may stir up complex or uncomfortable personal reactions within trainees, including, for example, memories of past traumas. Exploring psychological and emotional reactions may make some trainees feel vulnerable. Therapists at every career stage, from trainees to seasoned therapists with decades of experience, commonly experience shame, embarrassment, and self-doubt in this process. Although these experiences can be valuable for building trainees' self-awareness, it is important that training remain focused on professional skill development and not blur into personal therapy (e.g., Ellis et al., 2014). Therefore, one trainer role is to remind trainees to maintain appropriate boundaries.

Trainees must have the final say about what to disclose or not disclose to their trainer. Trainees should keep in mind that the goal is for the trainee to expand their own self-awareness and psychological capacity to stay active and helpful while experiencing uncomfortable reactions. The trainer does not need to know the specific details about the trainee's inner world for this to happen.

Trainees should be instructed to share only personal information that they feel comfortable sharing. The Deliberate Practice Reaction Form and difficulty assessment process is designed to help trainees build their self-awareness while retaining control over their privacy. Trainees can be reminded that the goal is for them to learn about their own inner world. They do not necessarily have to share that information with trainers or peers (Bennett-Levy & Finlay-Jones, 2018). Likewise, trainees should be instructed to respect the confidentiality of their peers.

Trainer Self-Evaluation

The exercises in this book were tested at a wide range of training sites around the world, including graduate courses, practicum sites, and private practice offices. Although trainers reported that the exercises were highly effective for training, some also said that they felt disoriented by how different deliberate practice feels compared with their traditional methods of clinical education. Many felt comfortable evaluating their trainees' performance but were less sure about their own performance as trainers.

The most common concern we heard from trainers was, "My trainees are doing great, but I'm not sure if I am doing this correctly!" To address this concern, we recommend trainers perform periodic self-evaluations along the following five criteria:

1. Observe trainees' work performance.
2. Provide continual corrective feedback.
3. Ensure rehearsal of specific skills is just beyond the trainees' current ability.
4. Ensure that the trainee is practicing at the right difficulty level (neither too easy nor too challenging).
5. Continuously assess trainee performance with real clients.

Criterion 1: Observe Trainees' Work Performance

Determining how well we are doing as trainers means first having valid information about how well trainees are responding to training. This requires that we directly observe trainees practicing skills to provide corrective feedback and evaluation. One risk of deliberate practice is that trainees gain competence in performing therapy skills in role-plays, but those skills do not transfer to trainees' work with real clients. Thus, trainers will ideally also have the opportunity to observe samples of trainees' work with real clients, either live or via recorded video. Supervisors and consultants rely heavily—and, too often, exclusively—on supervisees' and consultees' narrative accounts of their work with clients (Goodyear & Nelson, 1997). Haggerty and Hilsenroth (2011) described this challenge:

> Suppose a loved one has to undergo surgery and you need to choose between two surgeons, one of whom has never been directly observed by an experienced surgeon while performing any surgery. He or she would perform the surgery and return to his or her attending physician and try to recall, sometimes incompletely or inaccurately, the intricate steps of the surgery they just performed. It is hard to imagine that anyone, given a choice, would prefer this over a professional who has been routinely observed in the practice of their craft. (p. 193)

Criterion 2: Provide Continual Corrective Feedback

Trainees need corrective feedback to learn what they are doing well, what they are doing poorly, and how to improve their skills. Feedback should be as specific and incremental as possible. Examples of specific feedback are: "Your voice sounds rushed. Try slowing down by pausing for a few seconds between your statements to the client" and "You are making excellent eye contact with the client." Examples of vague and nonspecific feedback are "Try to build better rapport with the client" and "Try to be more open to the client's feelings."

Criterion 3: Specific Skill Rehearsal Just Beyond the Trainees' Current Ability (Zone of Proximal Development)

Deliberate practice emphasizes skill acquisition via behavioral rehearsal. Trainers should endeavor not to get caught up in client conceptualization at the expense of focusing on skills. For many trainers, this requires significant discipline and self-restraint. It is simply more enjoyable to talk about psychotherapy theory (e.g., case conceptualization, treatment planning, nuances of psychotherapy models, similar cases the supervisor has had) than watch trainees rehearse skills. Trainees have many questions, and supervisors have an abundance of experience; the allotted supervision time can easily be filled sharing knowledge. The supervisor gets to sound smart, while the trainee doesn't have to struggle with acquiring skills at their learning edge. Although answering questions is important, trainees' intellectual knowledge about psychotherapy can quickly surpass their procedural ability to perform psychotherapy, particularly with clients they find challenging. Here's a simple rule of thumb: The trainer provides the knowledge, but the behavioral rehearsal provides the skill (Rousmaniere, 2019).

Criterion 4: Practice at the Right Difficulty Level (Neither Too Easy nor Too Challenging)

Deliberate practice involves *optimal strain*: practicing skills just beyond the trainee's current skill threshold so that they can learn incrementally without becoming overwhelmed (Ericsson, 2006).

Trainers should use difficulty assessments and adjustments throughout deliberate practice to ensure that trainees are practicing at the right difficulty level. Note that some trainees are surprised by their unpleasant reactions to exercises (e.g., disassociation, nausea, blanking out) and may be tempted to "push through" exercises that are too hard. This can happen out of fear of failing a course, fear of being judged as incompetent, or negative self-impressions by the trainee (e.g., "This shouldn't be so hard"). Trainers should normalize the fact that there will be wide variation in perceived difficulty of the exercises and encourage trainees to respect their own personal training process.

Criterion 5: Continuously Assess Trainee Performance With Real Clients

The goal of deliberately practicing psychotherapy skills is to improve trainees' effectiveness at helping real clients. One of the risks in deliberate practice training is that the benefits will not generalize: Trainees' acquired competence in specific skills may not translate into work with real clients. Thus, it is important that trainers assess the impact of deliberate practice on trainees' work with real clients. Ideally, this is done through triangulation of multiple data points:

- client data (verbal self-report and routine outcome monitoring data)
- supervisor's report
- trainee's self-report

If the trainee's effectiveness with real clients is not improving after deliberate practice, the trainer should do a careful assessment of the difficulty. If the supervisor or trainer feels it is a skill acquisition issues, they may want to consider adjusting the deliberate practice routine to better suit the trainee's learning needs or style.

Therapists have traditionally been evaluated from a lens of *process accountability* (Markman & Tetlock, 2000; see also Goodyear, 2015), which focuses on demonstrating specific behaviors (e.g., fidelity to a treatment model) without regard to the impact on clients. We propose that clinical effectiveness is better assessed through a lens tightly focused on client outcomes and that learning objectives shift from performing behaviors that experts have decided are effective (i.e., the competence model) to highly individualized behavioral goals tailored to each trainee's zone of proximal development and performance feedback. This model of assessment has been termed *outcome accountability* (Goodyear, 2015), which focuses on client changes, rather than therapist competence, independent of how the therapist might be performing expected tasks.

Guidance for Trainees

The central theme of this book has been that skill rehearsal is not automatically helpful. Deliberate practice must be done well for trainees to benefit (Ericsson & Pool, 2016). In this chapter and in the exercises, we offer guidance for effective deliberate practice. We would also like to provide additional advice specifically for trainees. This advice is drawn from what we have learned at our volunteer deliberate practice test sites around the world. We cover how to discover your own training process, active effort, playfulness, and taking breaks during deliberate practice; your right to control your self-disclosure to trainers; monitoring training results; monitoring complex reactions toward the trainer; and your own personal therapy.

Individualized Multicultural Therapy Training: Finding Your Zone of Proximal Development

Deliberate practice works best when training targets each trainee's personal skill thresholds. Also termed the *zone of proximal development*, a term first coined by

Vygotsky in reference to developmental learning theory (Zaretskii, 2009), this is the area just beyond the trainee's current ability but that is possible to reach with the assistance of a teacher or coach (Wass & Golding, 2014). **If a deliberate practice exercise is either too easy or too hard, the trainee will not benefit.** To maximize training productivity, elite performers follow a "challenging but not overwhelming" principle: Tasks that are too far beyond their capacity will prove ineffective and even harmful; it is equally true that mindlessly repeating what they already can do confidently will prove equally fruitless. Because of this, deliberate practice requires ongoing assessment of the trainee's current skill and concurrent difficulty adjustment to consistently target a "good enough" challenge. Thus, if you are practicing Exercise 7, "Inquiring About Cultural Implications of the Problem," and it just feels too difficult, consider moving back to a more comfortable skill such as "Maintaining a Not-Knowing Stance" (Exercise 6) or "Reflecting Content Through a Cultural Lens" (Exercise 3) that you feel you have already mastered.

Active Effort

It is important for trainees to maintain an active and sustained effort while doing the deliberate practice exercises in this book. Deliberate practice really helps when trainees push themselves up to and past their current ability. This is best achieved when trainees take ownership of their own practice by guiding their training partners to adjust role-plays to be as high on the difficulty scale as possible without hurting themselves. This will look different for every trainee. Although it can feel uncomfortable or even frightening, this is the zone of proximal development where the most gains can be made. Simply reading and repeating the written scripts will provide little or no benefit. Trainees are advised to remember that their effort from training should lead to more confidence and comfort in session with real clients.

Stay the Course: Effort Versus Flow

Deliberate practice only works if trainees push themselves hard enough to break out of their old patterns of performance, which then permits growth of new skills (Ericsson & Pool, 2016). Because deliberate practice constantly focuses on the current edge of one's performance capacity, it is inevitably a straining endeavor. Indeed, professionals are unlikely to make lasting performance improvements unless there is sufficient engagement in tasks that are just at the edge of one's current capacity (Ericsson, 2003, 2006). From athletics or fitness training, many of us are familiar with this process of being pushed out of our comfort zones followed by adaptation. The same process applies to our mental and emotional abilities.

Many trainees are surprised to discover that deliberate practice for multicultural therapy feels harder than psychotherapy with a real client. This may be because when working with a real client a therapist can get into a state of *flow* (Csikszentmihalyi, 1997), where work feels effortless. As a young therapist in training, instructed to not ask questions (something she felt she knew how to do well) but only focus on cultural opportunities (something she did not feel proficient at), one author of this text often felt exhausted after psychotherapy sessions. Therapists training in multicultural therapy skills may find it difficult to focus continually on seizing cultural opportunities, feeling they are just repeating themselves or have captured the experience as best as they can and are ready to move forward. In such cases, therapists may want to move back to offering response formats with which they are more familiar and feel more proficient and try those for a short time, in part to increase a sense of confidence and mastery.

Discover Your Own Training Process

The effectiveness of deliberate practice is directly related to the effort and ownership trainees exert while doing the exercises. Trainers can provide guidance, but it is important for trainees to learn about their own idiosyncratic training processes over time. This will let them become masters of their own training and prepare for a career-long process of professional development. The following are a few examples of personal training processes trainees discovered while engaging in deliberate practice:

- One trainee noticed that she was good at persisting while an exercise is challenging, but also that she required more rehearsal than other trainees to feel comfortable with a new skill. This trainee focused on developing patience with her own pace of progress.

- One trainee noticed that he could acquire new skills rather quickly, with only a few repetitions. However, he also noticed that his reactions to evocative client statements could jump quickly and unpredictably from the "good challenge" to "too hard" categories, so he needed to attend carefully to the reactions listed in the Deliberate Practice Reaction Form.

- One trainee described herself as "perfectionistic" and felt a strong urge to "push through" an exercise even when she had anxiety reactions in the "too hard" category, such as nausea and disassociation. Such reactions caused the trainee not to benefit from the exercises and to risk getting demoralized. This trainee focused on going slower, developing self-compassion regarding her anxiety reactions, and asking her training partners to make role-plays less challenging.

- Another trainee reported having difficulty with client statements that reflected her own personal intersectional identity or microaggressions that she had experienced herself. She noticed that she became overwhelmed and distressed in these exercises. When encountering these client statements, she first completed the skill criteria from Exercise 1 ("Therapist Self-Awareness") before moving on to the skill criteria for the current exercise. Trainees are encouraged to reflect deeply on their own experiences using the exercises to learn the most about themselves and their personal learning processes.

Being Playful and Taking Breaks

Psychotherapy is serious work that often involves painful feelings. However, practicing psychotherapy can be playful and fun (Scott Miller, personal communication, 2017). Trainees should remember that one of the main goals of deliberate practice is to experiment with different approaches and styles of therapy. If deliberate practice ever feels rote, boring, or routine, it probably isn't going to help advance trainees' skill. In this case, trainees should try to liven it up. A good way to do this is to introduce an atmosphere of playfulness. For example, trainees can try the following:

- Use different vocal tones, speech pacing, body gestures, or other languages. This can expand trainees' communication range.

- Practice with your eyes closed or, when using video, with the sound off. This can increase sensitivity in the other senses.

- Practice while standing up or walking around outside. This can help trainees gain new perspectives on the process of therapy.

The supervisor can also ask trainees if they would like to take a 5- to 10-minute break between questions, particularly if the trainees are dealing with difficult emotions and are feeling stressed out.

Additional Deliberate Practice Opportunities

This book focuses on deliberate practice methods that involve active, live engagement between trainees and a supervisor. Importantly, deliberate practice can extend beyond these focused training sessions as be used for homework. For example, a trainee might read the client stimuli quietly or aloud and practice their responses independently between sessions with a supervisor. In such cases, it is important for the trainee to say their therapist responses aloud, rather than rehearse silently in one's head. Alternatively, two trainees can practice as a pair, without the supervisor. Although the absence of a supervisor limits one source of feedback, the peer trainee who is playing the client can serve this role, as they can when a supervisor is present. These additional deliberate practice opportunities are intended to take place between focused training sessions with a supervisor. To optimize the quality of the deliberate practice when conducted independently or without a supervisor, we have developed a Deliberate Practice Diary Form that can be found in Appendix B or downloaded from https://www.apa.org/pubs/books/deliberate-practice-multicultural-therapy (see the "Clinician and Practitioner Resources" tab). This form provides a template for the trainee to record their experience of the deliberate practice activity, and, ideally, it will aid in the consolidation of learning. This form can be used as part of the evaluation process with the supervisor but is not necessarily intended for that purpose, and trainees are certainly welcome to bring their experience with the independent practice into the next meeting with the supervisor.

Monitoring Training Results

While trainers will evaluate trainees using a competency-focused model, trainees are also encouraged to take ownership of their own training process and look for results of deliberate practice themselves. Trainees should experience the results of deliberate practice within a few training sessions. A lack of results can be demoralizing for trainees and result in trainees applying less effort and focus in deliberate practice. Trainees who are not seeing results should openly discuss this problem with their trainer and experiment with adjusting their deliberate practice process. Results can include client outcomes and improving the trainee's own work as a therapist, their personal development, and their overall training.

Client Outcomes

The most important result of deliberate practice is an improvement in trainees' client outcomes. This can be assessed via routine outcome measurement (Lambert, 2010; Prescott et al., 2017), qualitative data (McLeod, 2017), and informal discussions with clients. However, trainees should note that an improvement in client outcome due to deliberate practice can sometimes be challenging to achieve quickly, given that the largest amount of variance in client outcome is due to client variables (Bohart & Wade, 2013). For example, a client with severe chronic symptoms may not respond quickly to any treatment, regardless of how effectively a trainee practices. For some clients, an increase in patience and self-compassion regarding their symptoms may be a sign of progress rather than an immediate decrease in symptoms. Thus, trainees are advised to keep their expectations for client change realistic in the context of their client's symptoms, history, and presentation. It is important that trainees do not try to force their clients to improve in therapy in order for the trainee to feel like they are making progress in their training (Rousmaniere, 2016).

Trainee's Work as a Therapist

One important result of deliberate practice is change within the trainee regarding their work with clients. For example, trainees at test sites reported feeling more comfortable sitting with evocative clients, more confident addressing uncomfortable topics in therapy, and more responsive to a broader range of clients.

Trainees' Personal Development

Another important result of deliberate practice is personal growth within the trainee. For example, trainees at test sites reported becoming more in touch with their own feelings, increased self-compassion, and enhanced motivation to work with a broader range of clients.

Trainee's Training Process

Another valuable result of deliberate practice is improvement in the trainees' training process. For example, trainees at test sites reported becoming more aware of their personal training style, preferences, strengths, and challenges. Over time, trainees should grow to feel more ownership of their training process. It is also recommended that training to be a psychotherapist is a complex process that occurs over many years. Experienced, expert therapists still report continuing to grow well beyond their graduate school years (Orlinsky et al., 2005). Furthermore, training is not a linear process. We may feel we are diligently studying, engaging in thoughtful self-reflection, and developing a wide array of multicultural therapy skills; however, this does not automatically translate into clients experiencing healing and relief from their distress. As described in Chapter 1, developing a multicultural orientation is a lifelong process of learning and humility without a clear endpoint. It requires constant growth, open-mindedness, curiosity, and responsiveness. Remember, be easy on yourself!

The Trainee–Trainer Alliance: Monitoring Complex Reactions Toward the Trainer

Trainees who engage in hard deliberate practice often report experiencing complex feelings toward their trainer. For example, one trainee said, "I know this is helping, but I also don't look forward to it!" Another trainee reported feeling both appreciation and frustration toward her trainer simultaneously. Trainees are advised to remember intensive training they have done in other fields, such as athletics or music. When a coach pushes a trainee to the edge of their ability, it is common for trainees to have complex reactions toward them.

This does not necessarily mean that the trainer is doing anything wrong. In fact, intensive training inevitably stirs up reactions toward the trainer, such as frustration, annoyance, disappointment, or anger that coexist with the appreciations they feel. In fact, if trainees do not experience complex reactions, it is worth considering whether the deliberate practice is sufficiently challenging. But what we asserted earlier about rights to privacy apply here as well. Because professional mental health training is hierarchical and evaluative, trainers should not require or even expect trainees to share complex reactions they may be experiencing toward them. Trainers should stay open to their sharing, but the choice always remains with the trainee.

Trainee's Own Therapy

When engaging in deliberate practice, many trainees discover aspects of their inner world that may benefit from attending their own psychotherapy. For example, one trainee discovered that her clients' anger stirred up her own painful memories of abuse, another trainee found himself dissociating while practicing empathy skills, and another trainee experienced overwhelming shame and self-judgment when she couldn't master skills after just a few repetitions.

Although these discoveries were unnerving at first, they were ultimately very beneficial because they motivated the trainees to seek out their own therapy. Many therapists attend their own therapy. In fact, in their review of 17 studies, Norcross and Guy (2005) found that about 75% of the more than 8,000 therapist-participants had attended their own therapy. Orlinsky et al. (2005) found that more than 90% of therapists who attended their own therapy reported it as helpful.

QUESTIONS FOR TRAINEES
1. Are you balancing the effort to improve your skills with patience and self-compassion for your learning process?
2. Are you attending to any shame or self-judgment that arising from training?
3. Are you being mindful of your personal boundaries and also respecting any complex feelings you may have toward your trainers?

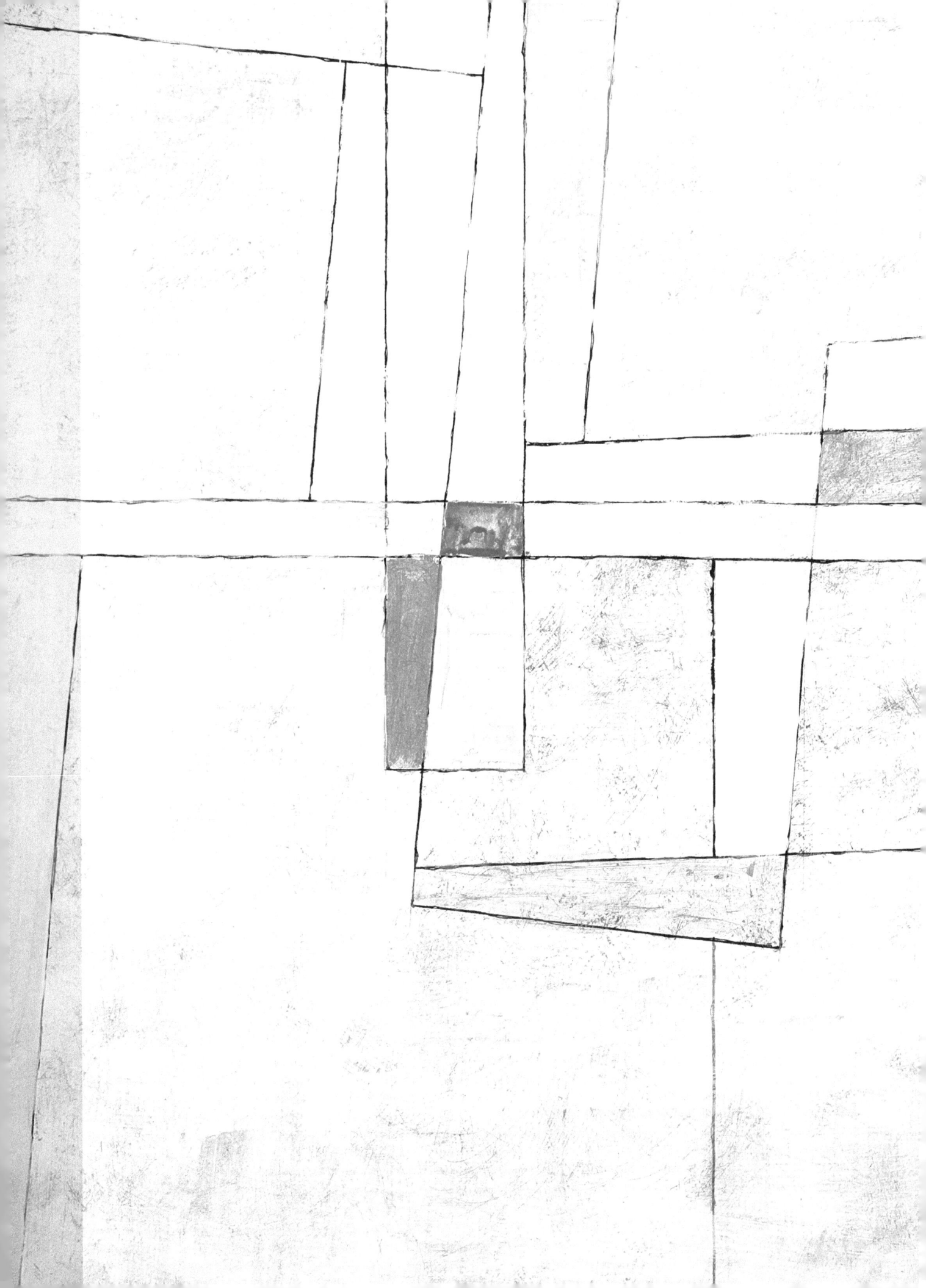

Difficulty Assessments and Adjustments

Deliberate practice works best if the exercises are performed at a good level of challenge that is neither too hard nor too easy. To ensure that trainees are practicing at the correct difficulty, they should do a difficulty assessment and adjustment after each level of client statement is completed (beginner, intermediate, and advanced). To do this, use the following instructions and the Deliberate Practice Reaction Form (Figure A.1), which is also available in the "Clinician and Practitioner Resources" tab online (https://www.apa.org/pubs/books/deliberate-practice-multicultural-therapy). **Do not skip this process!**

How to Assess Difficulty

The therapist completes the Deliberate Practice Reaction Form (Figure A.1). If they

- rate the difficulty of the exercise above an 8 or had any of the reactions in the "Too Hard" column, follow the instructions to make the exercise easier;

- rate the difficulty of the exercise below a 4 or didn't have any of the reactions in the "Good Challenge" column, proceed to the next level of harder client statements or follow the instructions to make exercise harder; or

- rate the difficulty of the exercise between 4 and 8 and have at least one reaction in the "Good Challenge" column, do not proceed to the harder client statements but rather repeat the same level.

Making Client Statements Easier

If the therapist ever rates the difficulty of the exercise above an 8 or has any of the reactions in the "Too Hard" column, use the next level easier client statements (e.g., if you were using advanced client statements, switch to intermediate). But if you already were using beginner client statements, use the following methods to make the client statements even easier:

- The person playing the client can use the same beginner client statements but this time in a softer, calmer voice and with a smile. This softens the emotional tone.

FIGURE A.1. Deliberate Practice Reaction Form

Question 1: How challenging was it to fulfill the skill criteria for this exercise?

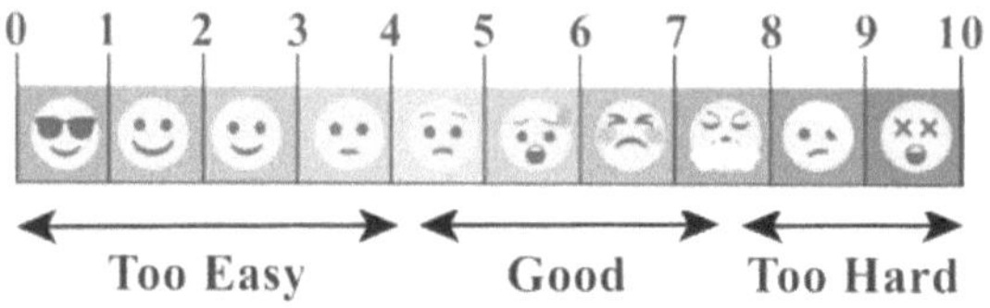

Question 2: Did you have any reactions in "good challenge" or "too hard" categories? (yes/no)

Good Challenge			Too Hard		
Emotions and Thoughts	**Body Reactions**	**Urges**	**Emotions and Thoughts**	**Body Reactions**	**Urges**
Manageable shame, self-judgment, irritation, anger, sadness, etc.	Body tension, sighs, shallow breathing, increased heart rate, warmth, dry mouth	Looking away, withdrawing, changing focus	Severe or overwhelming shame, self-judgment, rage, grief, guilt, etc.	Migraines, dizziness, foggy thinking, diarrhea, disassociation, numbness, blanking out, nausea, etc.	Shutting down, giving up

Too Easy	Good Challenge	Too Hard
⬇	⬇	⬇
Proceed to next difficulty level	Repeat the same difficulty level	Go back to previous difficulty level

Note. From *Deliberate Practice in Emotion-Focused Therapy* (p. 180), by R. N. Goldman, A. Vaz, and T. Rousmaniere, 2021, American Psychological Association (https://doi.org/10.1037/0000227-000). Copyright 2021 by the American Psychological Association.

- The client can improvise with topics that are less evocative or make the therapist more comfortable, such as talking about topics without expressing feelings, the future or past (avoiding the here and now), or any topic outside therapy (see Figure A.2).
- The therapist can take a short break (5–10 minutes) between questions.
- The trainer can expand the "feedback phase" by discussing principles of multicultural therapy or psychotherapy theory and research. This should shift the trainees' focus toward more detached or intellectual topics and reduce the emotional intensity.

Making Client Statements Harder

If the therapist rates the difficulty of the exercise below a 4 or didn't have any of the reactions in the "Good Challenge" column, proceed to next-level, harder client statements. If you were already using the advanced client statements, the client should make the exercise harder, using the following guidelines:

FIGURE A.2. How to Make Client Statements Easier or Harder in Role-Plays

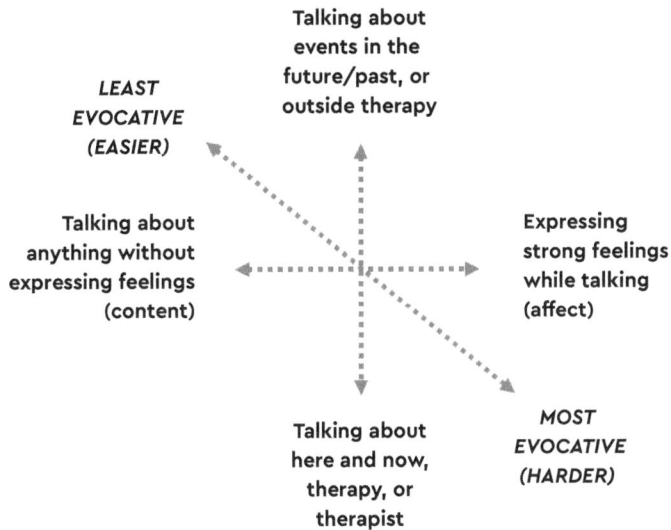

LEAST EVOCATIVE (EASIER)

Talking about events in the future/past, or outside therapy

Talking about anything without expressing feelings (content)

Expressing strong feelings while talking (affect)

Talking about here and now, therapy, or therapist

MOST EVOCATIVE (HARDER)

Note. Figure created by Jason Whipple, PhD.

- The person playing the client can use the advanced client statements again with a more distressed voice (e.g., very angry, sad, sarcastic) or unpleasant facial expression. This should increase the emotional tone.

- The client can improvise new client statements with topics that are more evocative or make the therapist uncomfortable, such as expressing strong feelings or talking about the here and now, therapy, or the therapist (see Figure A.2).

Note. The purpose of a deliberate practice session is not to get through all the client statements and therapist responses but rather to spend as much time as possible practicing at the correct difficulty level. This may mean that trainees repeat the same statements and responses many times, which is OK, as long as the difficulty remains in the "Good Challenge" level.

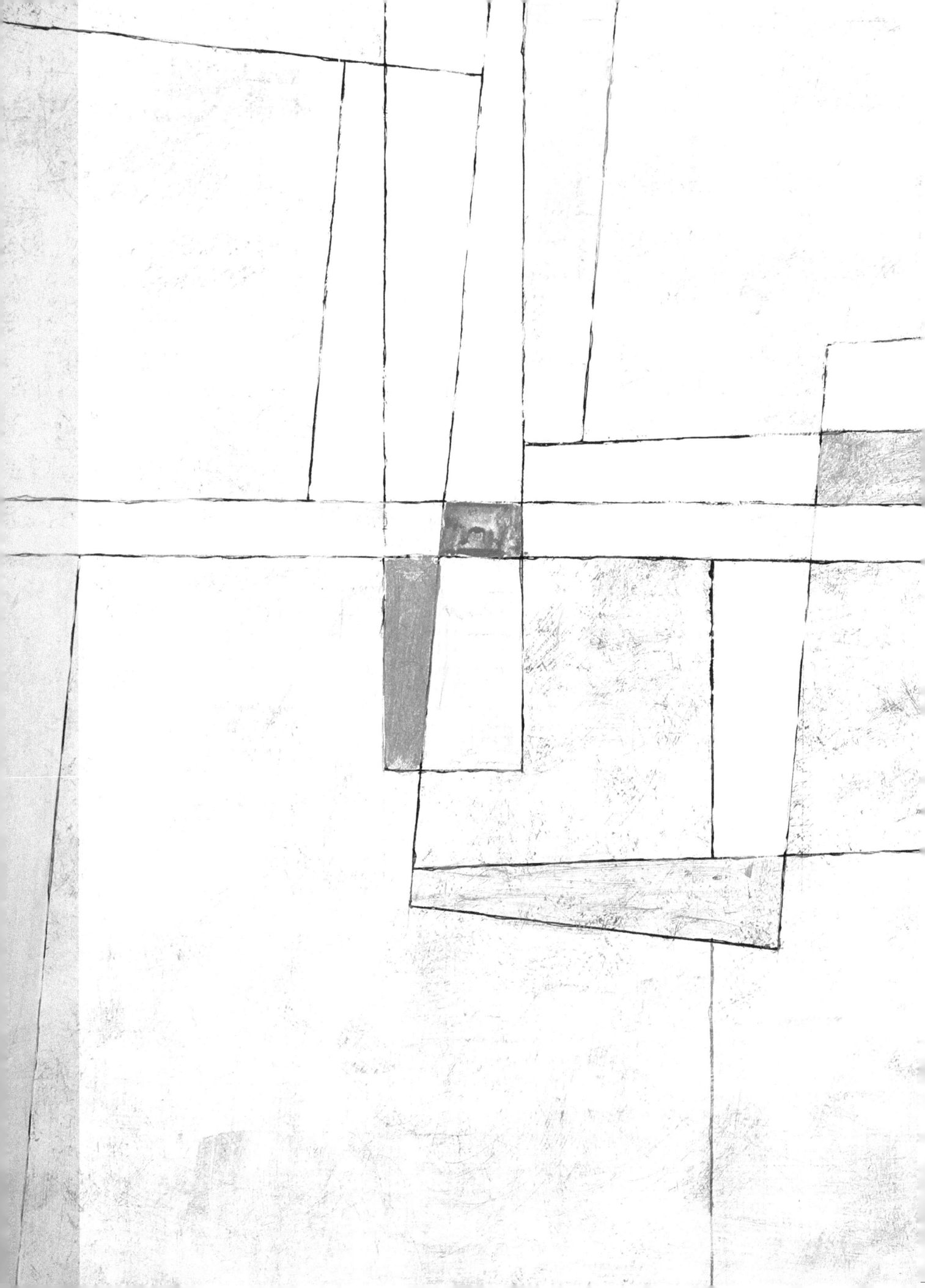

Deliberate Practice Diary Form

This book focuses on deliberate practice methods that involve active, live engagement between trainees and a supervisor. Importantly, deliberate practice can extend beyond these focused training sessions. For example, a trainee might read the client stimuli quietly or aloud and practice their responses independently between sessions with a supervisor. In such cases, it is important for the trainee to speak aloud rather than rehearse silently in one's head. Alternatively, two trainees can practice without the supervisor. Although the absence of a supervisor limits one source of feedback, the peer trainee who is playing the client can serve this role, as they can when a supervisor is present. Importantly, these additional deliberate practice opportunities are intended to take place between focused training sessions with a supervisor. To optimize the quality of the deliberate practice when conducted independently or without a supervisor, we have developed a Deliberate Practice Diary Form that can also be downloaded from the "Clinician and Practitioner Resources" tab online (https://www.apa.org/pubs/books/deliberate-practice-multicultural-therapy). This form provides a template for the trainee to record their experience of the deliberate practice activity and, ideally, will aid in the consolidation of learning. This form can also be used as part of the evaluation process with the supervisor but is not necessarily intended for that purpose, and trainees are certainly welcome to bring their experience with the independent practice into the next meeting with the supervisor.

Deliberate Practice Diary Form

Use this form to consolidate learnings from the deliberate practice exercises. Please protect your personal boundaries by only sharing information that you are comfortable disclosing.

Name: _____ Date: _____

Exercise: _____

Question 1. What was helpful or worked well this deliberate practice session? In what way?

Question 2. What was unhelpful or didn't go well this deliberate practice session? In what way?

Question 3. What did you learn about yourself, your current skills, and skills you'd like to keep improving? Feel free to share any details, but only those you are comfortable disclosing.

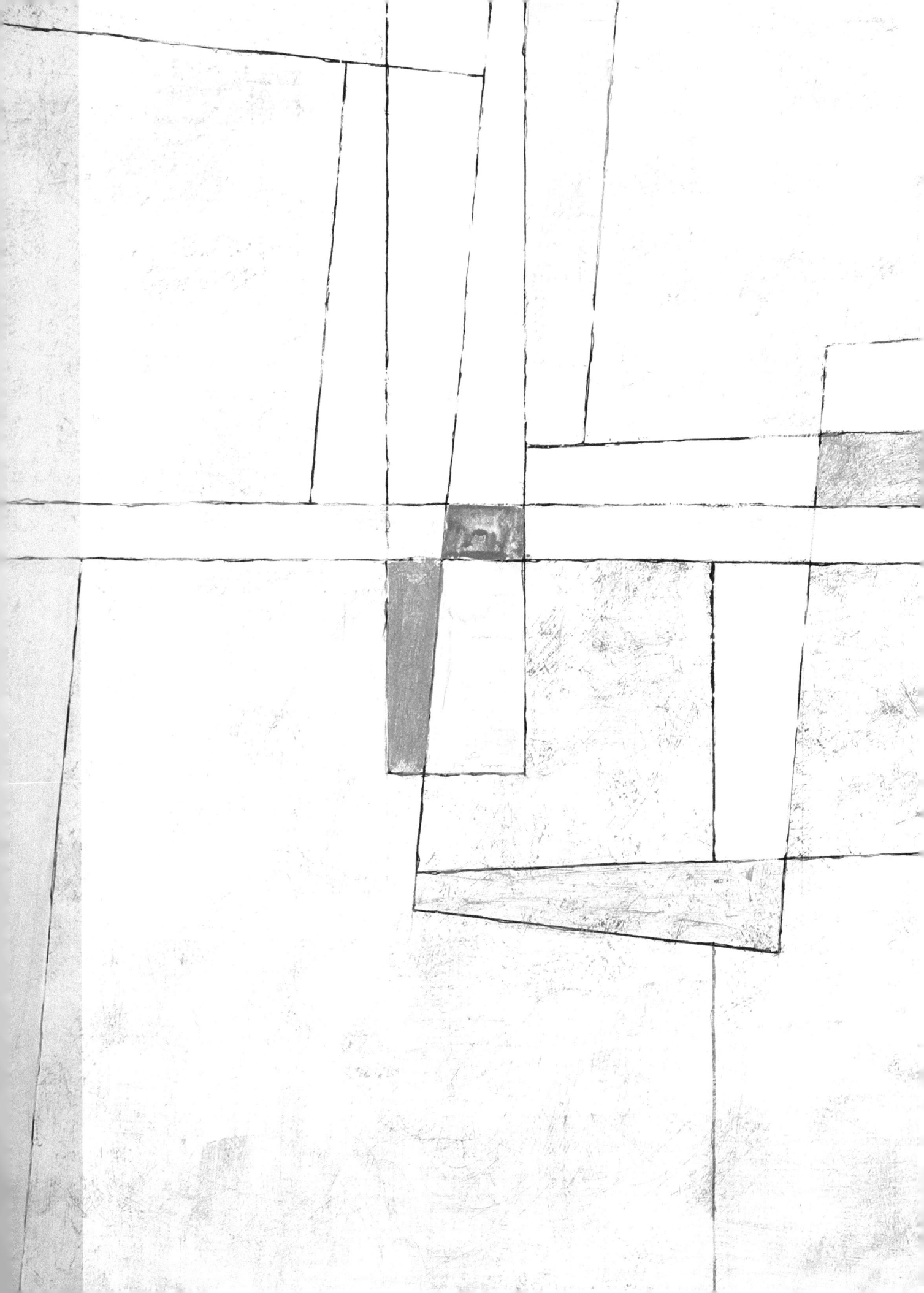

Sample Multicultural Therapy Syllabus With Embedded Deliberate Practice Exercises

This appendix provides a sample one-semester, three-unit course dedicated to teaching multicultural therapy. This course is appropriate for graduate students (master's and doctoral) at all levels of training, including first-year students who have not yet worked with clients. We present it as a model that can be adopted to a specific program's contexts and needs. For example, instructors may borrow portions of it to use in other courses, practica, didactic training events at externships and internships, workshops, and continuing education for postgraduate therapists.

Course Title: Integrating Multiculturalism Into Clinical Practice

Course Description

This course represents an introduction to developing multicultural humility and sensitivity in the context of psychotherapy. It focuses on the ways that class, race, gender, sexual orientation, and other historically marginalized identities of both clinician and client interact with systems of power and privilege. This class will require students to reflect on their own identities and relationship to structures of power and privilege and asks students to reflect on their own biases and prejudices. The class seeks to begin students' journey toward being actively antiracist and antioppressive mental health practitioners.

This class will also use a mindful approach to the work of cultural humility. We will approach this work as building an ongoing, reflective practice that pulls on both our theoretical knowledge as well as our own knowledge of ourselves and the communities we serve as mental health practitioners. One of the important aspects of deliberate practice as well as a cultural humility approach to clinical work is that rehearsal and reflection can make us better clinicians.

Course Objectives

Students who complete this course will be able to do the following:

1. Develop personal awareness, sensitivity to, and self-reflection of their attitudes toward others, including the ways in which their own identities (social, cultural, political, economic) influence interactions

2. Acknowledge and recognize power and privilege, including social systems that reinforce power differentials

3. Understand the many ways in which power, privilege, and oppression influence individuals and systems

4. Become aware of and able to identify strategies that orient psychological practice and research toward social justice

5. Explain the importance of cultural humility, particularly as it pertains to research and practice in psychology

6. Practice clinical skills with peers to further develop cultural humility as a practice in our clinical work

7. Develop ways to address systems of power and privilege in a therapeutic context

8. Reflect on the development of these skills through ongoing deliberate practice

Course Requirements and Assignments

- Instructors can insert their preferred text here.

Grading and Academic Integrity

- Instructors can insert their preferred text here.

Course Model for Discussion

As a class, we will seek to adhere to the Anti-Oppression Resource & Training Alliance (AORTA; https://aorta.coop/) model of antioppressive facilitation for a democratic process, as it applies to the class setting. Please review the guidelines before our first meeting.

A Note About Respect for Diversity

Much of what we consider science aims to be objective but is in many ways subjective. The field of psychology has been built on theories and ideas developed by people, often from a narrow set of cultural backgrounds and identities, who received support and funding from various institutions and systems. I have attempted to include in this syllabus readings that will focus discussion on systemic oppression and social justice in the context of psychotherapy. I have also made an effort to include the voices of authors from diverse identities and backgrounds. However, I acknowledge the possibility that there may be both overt and covert biases in the material due to the lens with which it was written. Integrating a diverse set of experiences is important for a more comprehensive understanding of science. Please contact me or submit anonymous feedback on course evaluations if you have any suggestions to improve the quality of the course materials.

Furthermore, I would like to create a learning environment for students that supports a diversity of perspectives and experiences and honors your identities. I believe trust and respect are central to creating spaces where there can be an open discussion, mutual learning, and growth. It is expected that some of the material in this course may evoke strong emotions; please be respectful of others' emotions and be mindful of your own.

I (like many people) am still in the process of learning about diverse perspectives and identities. Please let me know if something said or done in the classroom by either myself or other students is particularly troubling or causes discomfort or offense. Although our intention may not be to cause discomfort or offense, the impact of what happens

Date	Lecture and Discussion	Skills Lab	Homework (for next class)
Week 1	Class overview/introduction to multicultural orientation	Review syllabus with emphasis on antioppressive facilitation for a democratic process; introduce multicultural orientation in contrast to multicultural competency **Watch & Discuss** *Multicultural Orientation (MCO) Deliberate Practice Webinar* (Sentio Therapist Training, 2020)	**Watch** *Juliana Mosley, PhD: Cultural Humility* (TED, 2017); *Cultural Humility* (Chavez, 2013); *Cultural Humility in Mental Health: A Move Away From Competence* (Velasquez, 2020) **Read** Harris et al. (2024, Chapters 1 & 2); Hicks et al. (2022); Hook et al. (2013); Roberts-Crews (2020); Sue & Sue (2016, Chapters 3 & 4) If you are not already participating in the antiracism training provided by Academics for Black Survival and Wellness (2020), I highly suggest and encourage everyone to engage in it.
Week 2	What is cultural humility? How do we develop a practice? The intrapsychic and the interpersonal	Exercise 1: Therapist Self-Awareness: Cultural Humility I	**Read** Bor et al. (2018); Breland-Noble (2020, Introduction & Chapter 7); Fukuyama et al. (2014); Sue & Sue (2016, Chapters 9 & 10)
Week 3	How do we assess client expectations in the context of intersectional identities?	Exercise 2: Assessing Client Expectations	**Watch** *The Urgency of Intersectionality* (Crenshaw, 2016) **Read** Crenshaw (1989); López et al. (2022); Rosenthal (2016)
Week 4	Intersectionality: introduction to Pamela Hays's ADDRESSING model	Exercise 3: Reflecting Content Through a Cultural Lens **Review & Discuss** *The ADDRESSING Model* (Ohio University, n.d.)	**Read** Sue et al. (2010); Sue & Sue (2016, Chapters 11 & 12); Tatum (2017, Chapters 6 & 7)
Week 5	Power and privilege	Exercise 4: Inquiring About Identity: Cultural Opportunities I **Identity Exercise** *Social Justice Standards: Unpacking Identity* (Learning for Justice, n.d.)	**Read** Gushue & Constantine (2007); Lukianoff & Haidt (2015)
Week 6	Examining bias and understanding bias	Exercise 5: Working With Emotions in Context	**Watch** *Helping a Patient With Racial Stress & Working With the Trauma of Racism* (National Institute for the Clinical Application of Behavioral Medicine, 2020a, 2020b) **Read** Abe (2020); Benkert et al. (2006); Bryant-Davis (2019); Comas-Díaz et al. (2019); Dolan (2015); Drustrup (2020)
Week 7	Working with the trauma of racism	Exercise 6: Maintaining a Not-Knowing Stance: Cultural Humility II	**Watch** *Moving From Cultural Competence to Antiracism* (Bryant-Davis, n.d.) **Read** Comas-Díaz et al. (2019); Helms et al. (2012)
Week 8	Antiracism in clinical work	Exercise 7: Inquiring About Cultural Implications of the Problem: Cultural Opportunities II	**Read** Adames et al. (2018); McGeorge et al. (2021); dickey & Singh (2020)
Week 9	Affirmative practice for LGBTQIA people	Exercise 8: Acknowledging Therapist Limitations	**Read** Artman & Daniels (2010); Dávila (2015); Shelton & Delgado-Romero (2011)
Week 10	Disability and ableism in the therapy room	Exercise 9: Gathering Information About Safety Concerns	**Watch** *Psychology and Disability: Minimizing Ableism in the Counselling Room* (CAMH Professionals Videos, 2016) **Read** Disability Visibility Project (n.d.); Heredia & Rider (2020); Kattari et al. (2018)
Week 11	Midterm paper due, self-evaluation, skill coaching feedback	Exercise 10: Talking About Sex and Success	**Read** Goodwin et al. (2018)
Week 12	Cultivating a social justice–oriented practice	Exercise 11: Responding to Resistance and Ambivalence	**Watch** *Handling Microaggressions in Therapy* (Psychotherapy Networker, 2019) **Read** Akoury et al. (2019); Delapp & Williams (2015); Nadal et al. (2015); Sue & Sue (2016, Chapters 6 & 7); M. T. Williams (2020)
Week 13	Identifying and responding to therapeutic alliance ruptures due to microaggressions	Exercise 12: Repairing Ruptures Due to Microaggressions	**Watch** *The Trauma of Systematic Racism Is Killing Black women. A First Step Toward Change* (Dixon & Garrison, 2017); *How Racism Makes Us Sick* (D. R. Williams, 2016) **Read** Owen et al. (2014)
Week 14	Wrap-up/creating an antiracist professional identity	Exercise 13: Mock Multicultural Therapy Sessions	**Watch** *Jessica Dere: Challenges and Rewards of a Culturally-Informed Approach to Mental Health* (TED, 2015) **Read** Carter (2007); F. Taylor (2019)
Week 15	Annotated session due, final exam, self-evaluation, skill coaching feedback	Exercise 13: Mock Multicultural Therapy Sessions	**Watch** Sue et al. (2019, short videos 2.3–2.6) **Review Survey** UConn Racial/Ethnic Stress & Trauma Survey (UnRESTS; n.d.)

throughout the course is not to be ignored and is something that I consider to be especially important and deserving of attention. If this occurs, please consider one of the following ways to address what you experienced and, I hope, somewhat alleviate distress:

- Discuss the situation privately with me. I am always open to listening to students' experiences and want to work with you to find acceptable ways to process and address the issue.

- Discuss the situation with the class. Chances are that there is at least one other student who had a similar response to the material or statements. Discussion enhances the ability of all class participants to understand fully the context and impact of course material and class discussions.

- Please notify me of the issue through another source, such as your academic advisor, a trusted faculty member, or a peer. If for any reason you do not feel comfortable discussing the issue directly with me, I encourage you to seek out another, more comfortable avenue to address the issue. If you are unsure who to speak with, Dr. X and Dr. Y are two faculty members whom I will look to for feedback on my course.

Required Texts and Resources

Abe, J. (2020). Beyond cultural competence, toward social transformation: Liberation psychologies and the practice of cultural humility. *Journal of Social Work Education, 56*(4), 696–707. https://doi.org/10.1080/10437797.2019.1661911

Academics for Black Survival and Wellness. (2020). *Academics for Black Survival and Wellness anti-racism training.* https://www.academics4blacklives.com/anti-racism-training

Adames, H. Y., Chavez-Dueñas, N. Y., Sharma, S., & La Roche, M. J. (2018). Intersectionality in psychotherapy: The experiences of an AfroLatinx queer immigrant. *Psychotherapy, 55*(1), 73–79. https://doi.org/10.1037/pst0000152

Akoury, L. M., Schafer, K. J., & Warren, C. S. (2019). Fat women's experiences in therapy: "You can't see beyond . . . unless I share it with you." *Women & Therapy, 42*(1–2), 93–115. https://doi.org/10.1080/02703149.2018.1524063

Artman, L., & Daniels, J. A. (2010). Disability and psychotherapy practice: Cultural competence and practical tips. *Professional Psychology: Research and Practice, 41*(5), 442–448. https://doi.org/10.1037/a0020864

Benkert, R., Peters, R. M., Clark, R., & Keves-Foster, K. (2006). Effects of perceived racism, cultural mistrust and trust in providers on satisfaction with care. *Journal of the National Medical Association, 98*(9), 1532–1540. https://www.ncbi.nlm.nih.gov/pmc/articles/PMC2569718/pdf/jnma00196-0134.pdf

Bor, J., Venkataramani, A. S., Williams, D. R., & Tsai, A. C. (2018). Police killings and their spillover effects on the mental health of Black Americans: A population-based, quasi-experimental study. *The Lancet, 392*(10144), 302–310. https://doi.org/10.1016/s0140-6736(18)31130-9

Breland-Noble, A. M. (Ed.). (2020). *Community mental health engagement with racially diverse populations.* Academic Press.

Bryant-Davis, T. (n.d.). *Moving from cultural competence to antiracism* [Video]. National Institute for the Clinical Application of Behavioral Medicine. https://www.nicabm.com/moving-from-cultural-competence-to-antiracism/

Bryant-Davis, T. (2019). The cultural context of trauma recovery: Considering the posttraumatic stress disorder practice guideline and intersectionality. *Psychotherapy, 56*(3), 400–408. https://doi.org/10.1037/pst0000241

CAMH Professionals Videos. (2016). *Psychology and disability: Minimizing ableism in the counselling room* [Video]. YouTube. https://www.youtube.com/watch?v=wZ_a4N1IekQ&t=2s

Carter, R. T. (2007). Racism and psychological and emotional injury: Recognizing and assessing race-based traumatic stress. *The Counseling Psychologist, 35*(1), 13–105. https://doi.org/10.1177/0011000006292033

Chavez, V. (2013). *Cultural humility* [Video]. YouTube. https://www.youtube.com/watch?v=SaSHLbS1V4w

Comas-Díaz, L., Hall, G. N., & Neville, H. A. (2019). Racial trauma: Theory, research, and healing: Introduction to the special issue. *American Psychologist, 74*(1), 1–5. https://doi.org/10.1037/amp0000442

Crenshaw, K. (1989). Demarginalizing the intersection of race and sex: A Black feminist critique of antidiscrimination doctrine, feminist theory, and antiracist politics. *University of Chicago Legal Forum, 140*, 139–167.

Crenshaw, K. (2016). *The urgency of intersectionality* [Video]. TED Conferences. https://www.ted.com/talks/kimberle_crenshaw_the_urgency_of_intersectionality

Dávila, B. (2015). Critical race theory, disability microaggressions and Latina/o student experiences in special education. *Race Ethnicity and Education, 18*(4), 443–468. https://doi.org/10.1080/13613324.2014.885422

Delapp, R. C., & Williams, M. T. (2015). Professional challenges facing African American psychologists: The presence and impact of racial microaggressions. *The Behavior Therapist, 38*(4), 101–105.

dickey, l. m., & Singh, A. A. (2020). Evidence-based relationship variables: Working with trans and gender nonbinary clients. *Practice Innovations, 5*(3), 189–201. https://doi.org/10.1037/pri0000116

Disability Visibility Project. (n.d.) https://disabilityvisibilityproject.com/

Dixon, T. M., & Garrison, V. (2017). *The trauma of systematic racism is killing Black women. A first step toward change* [Video]. TED Conferences. https://www.ted.com/talks/t_morgan_dixon_and_vanessa_garrison_the_trauma_of_systematic_racism_is_killing_black_women_a_first_step_toward_change?language=en

Dolan, K. A. (2015). *Why White people downplay their individual racial privileges*. Insights by Stanford Business. https://www.gsb.stanford.edu/insights/why-whites-downplay-their-individual-racial-privileges

Drustrup, D. (2020). White therapists addressing racism in psychotherapy: An ethical and clinical model for practice. *Ethics & Behavior, 30*(3), 181–196. https://doi.org/10.1080/10508422.2019.1588732

Fukuyama, M., Puig, A., Wolf, C. P., & Baggs, A. (2014). Exploring the intersections of religion and spirituality with race-ethnicity and gender in counseling. In M. L. Miville & A. D. Ferguson (Eds.), *Handbook of race-ethnicity and gender in psychology* (pp. 23–43). Springer.

Goodwin, B. J., Coyne, A. E., & Constantino, M. J. (2018). Extending the context-responsive psychotherapy integration framework to cultural processes in psychotherapy. *Psychotherapy, 55*(1), 3–8. https://doi.org/10.1037/pst0000143

Gushue, G. V., & Constantine, M. G. (2007). Color-blind racial attitudes and White racial identity attitudes in psychology trainees. *Professional Psychology: Research & Practice, 38*(3), 321–328. https://doi.org/10.1037/0735-7028.38.3.321

Harris, J., Jin, J., Hoffman, S., Phan, S., Prout, T. A., Rousmaniere, T., & Vaz, A. (2024). *Deliberate practice in multicultural therapy*. American Psychological Association. https://doi.org/10.1037/0000357-000

Helms, J. E., Nicolas, G., & Green, C. E. (2012). Racism and ethnoviolence as trauma: Enhancing professional and research training. *Traumatology, 18*(1), 65–74. https://doi.org/10.1177/1534765610396728

Heredia, D., Jr., & Rider, G. N. (2020). Intersectionality in sex therapy: Opportunities for promoting sexual wellness among queer people of color. *Current Sexual Health Reports, 12*(3), 195–201.

Hicks, E. T., de la Caridad Alvarez, M., & Domenech Rodríguez, M. M. (2022). Impact of difficult dialogues on social justice attitudes during a multicultural psychology course. *Teaching of Psychology*. Advance online publication. https://journals.sagepub.com/doi/full/10.1177/00986283221104057

Hook, J. N., Davis, D. E., Owen, J., Worthington, E. L., Jr., & Utsey, S. O. (2013). Cultural humility: Measuring openness to culturally diverse clients. *Journal of Counseling Psychology, 60*(3), 353–366. https://doi.org/10.1037/a0032595

Kattari, S. K., Olzman, M., & Hanna, M. D. (2018). "You look fine!" Ableist experiences by people with invisible disabilities. *Affilia*, 33(4), 477–492. https://doi.org/10.1177/0886109918778073

Learning for Justice. (n.d.). *Social justice standards: Unpacking identity.* https://www.learningforjustice.org/professional-development/social-justice-standards-unpacking-identity

López, D. J., Yuan, Y., Booth, J., Wei, K., & Friedman, M. R. (2022). Discrimination and rejection: The effects of ethnic and sexuality-based discrimination against Latino gay and bisexual men. *Journal of Homosexuality.* Advance online publication. https://doi.org/10.1080/00918369.2022.2081105

Lukianoff, G., & Haidt, J. (2015, September). The coddling of the American mind. *The Atlantic.* https://www.theatlantic.com/magazine/archive/2015/09/the-coddling-of-the-american-mind/399356/

McGeorge, C. R., Coburn, K. O., & Walsdorf, A. A. (2021). Deconstructing cissexism: The journey of becoming an affirmative family therapist for transgender and nonbinary clients. *Journal of Marital and Family Therapy*, 47(3), 785–802. https://doi.org/10.1111/jmft.12481

Nadal, K. L., Davidoff, K. C., Davis, L. S., Wong, Y., Marshall, D., & McKenzie, V. (2015). A qualitative approach to intersectional microaggressions: Understanding, influences of race, ethnicity, gender, sexuality, and religion. *Qualitative Psychology*, 2(2), 147–163. https://doi.org/10.1037/qup0000026

National Institute for the Clinical Application of Behavioral Medicine. (2020a). *Helping a patient with racial stress* [Video]. YouTube. https://www.youtube.com/watch?v=lBxYs2a2Ibo

National Institute for the Clinical Application of Behavioral Medicine. (2020b). *Working with the trauma of racism* [Video]. YouTube. https://www.youtube.com/watch?v=egr2279UiAI

Ohio University. (n.d.). *The ADDRESSING model.* https://www.ohio.edu/cas/psychology/diversity/addressing-model

Owen, J., Tao, K. W., Imel, Z. E., Wampold, B. E., & Rodolfa, E. (2014). Addressing racial and ethnic microaggressions in therapy. *Professional Psychology: Research and Practice*, 45(4), 283–290. https://doi.org/10.1037/a0037420

Psychotherapy Networker. (2019). *Handling microaggressions in therapy* [Video]. YouTube. https://www.youtube.com/watch?v=-4kODpuhngo

Roberts-Crews, J. (2020, June 8). *White academia: Do better.* https://medium.com/the-faculty/white-academia-do-better-fa96cede1fc5

Rosenthal, L. (2016). Incorporating intersectionality into psychology: An opportunity to promote social justice and equity. *American Psychologist*, 71(6), 474–485. https://doi.org/10.1037/a0040323

Sentio Therapist Training. (2020). *Multicultural orientation (MCO) deliberate practice webinar* [Video]. YouTube. https://www.youtube.com/watch?v=IJ1cWH88RI0&t=1622s

Shelton, K., & Delgado-Romero, E. A. (2011). Sexual orientation microaggressions: The experience of lesbian, gay, bisexual, and queer clients in psychotherapy. *Journal of Counseling Psychology*, 58(2), 210–221. https://doi.org/10.1037/a0022251

Sue, D. W., Rivera, D. P., Capodilupo, C. M., Lin, A. I., & Torino, G. C. (2010). Racial dialogues and White trainee fears: Implications for education and training. *Cultural Diversity and Ethnic Minority Psychology*, 16(2), 206–214. https://doi.org/10.1037/a0016112

Sue, D. W., & Sue, D. (2016). *Counseling the culturally diverse: Theory and practice* (7th ed.). John Wiley & Sons.

Sue, D. W., Sue, D., Neville, H. A., & Smith, L. (2019). *Counseling the culturally diverse: Theory and practice* (8th ed.). John Wiley & Sons. Videos to accompany chapter 2 available at https://higheredbcs.wiley.com/legacy/college/sue/1119448247/vss/ch02.html?newwindow=true

Tatum, B. D. (2017). *Why are all the Black kids sitting together in the cafeteria? And other conversations about race.* Basic Books.

Taylor, F. (2019). As much space as we can imagine. *Therapy Today*, 30(8). https://www.bacp.co.uk/bacp-journals/therapy-today/2019/october-2019/as-much-space-as-we-can-imagine/

TED. (2015, April 20). *Jessica Dere: Challenges and rewards of a culturally-informed approach to mental health* [Video]. YouTube. https://www.youtube.com/watch?v=VrYmQDiunSc

TED. (2017, December 1). *Juliana Mosley, PhD: Cultural humility* [Video]. YouTube. https://www.youtube.com/watch?v=Ww_ml21L7Ns

UConn Racial/Ethnic Stress & Trauma Survey (UnRESTS). (n.d.). https://www.mentalhealthdisparities.org/docs/UnRESTS_0716_English.pdf

Velasquez, M. (2020, June 12). *Cultural humility in mental health: A move away from competence* [Video]. YouTube. https://www.youtube.com/watch?v=WXRGPSjMjWE

Williams, D. R. (2016). *How racism makes us sick* [Video]. TED Conferences. https://www.ted.com/talks/david_r_williams_how_racism_makes_us_sick?language=en

Williams, M. T. (2020). Psychology cannot afford to ignore the many harms caused by microaggressions. *Perspectives on Psychological Science, 15*(1), 38–43. https://doi.org/10.1177/1745691619893362

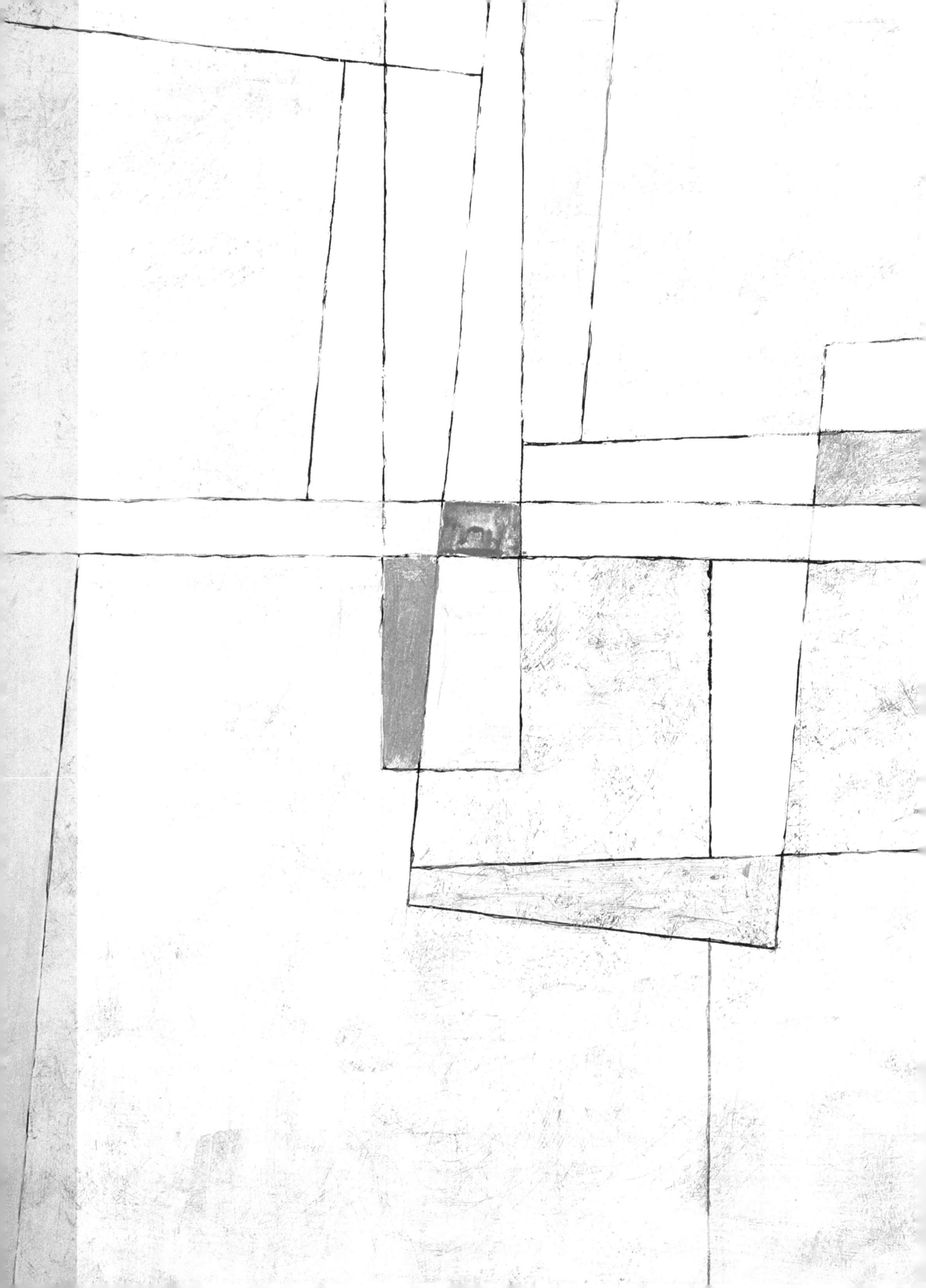

References

Abe, J. (2020). Beyond cultural competence, toward social transformation: Liberation psychologies and the practice of cultural humility. *Journal of Social Work Education, 56*(4), 696–707. https://doi.org/10.1080/10437797.2019.1661911

Academics for Black Survival and Wellness. (2020). *Academics for Black Survival and Wellness anti-racism training.* https://www.academics4blacklives.com/anti-racism-training

Adames, H. Y., Chavez-Dueñas, N. Y., Sharma, S., & La Roche, M. J. (2018). Intersectionality in psychotherapy: The experiences of an AfroLatinx queer immigrant. *Psychotherapy, 55*(1), 73–79. https://doi.org/10.1037/pst0000152

Adams, L. J., MacLean, R. R., Portnoy, G. A., Beauvais, J., & Stacy, M. A. (2022). Psychology trainee and supervisor perspectives of multicultural supervision. *Psychological Services.* Advance online publication. https://doi.org/10.1037/ser0000643

Akoury, L. M., Schafer, K. J., & Warren, C. S. (2019). Fat women's experiences in therapy: "You can't see beyond . . . unless I share it with you." *Women & Therapy, 42*(1–2), 93–115. https://doi.org/10.1080/02703149.2018.1524063

American Psychological Association. (2003). Guidelines on multicultural education, training, research, practice, and organizational change for Psychologists. *American Psychologist, 58*(5), 377–402. https://doi.org/10.1037/0003-066X.58.5.377

American Psychological Association. (2017). *Multicultural guidelines: An ecological approach to context, identity, and intersectionality.* https://www.apa.org/about/policy/multicultural-guidelines.pdf

Anders, C., Kivlighan, D. M., III, Porter, E., Lee, D., & Owen, J. (2021). Attending to the intersectionality and saliency of clients' identities: A further investigation of therapists' multicultural orientation. *Journal of Counseling Psychology, 68*(2), 139–148. https://doi.org/10.1037/cou0000447

Anderson, K. N., Bautista, C. L., & Hope, D. A. (2019). Therapeutic alliance, cultural competence and minority status in premature termination of psychotherapy. *American Journal of Orthopsychiatry, 89*(1), 104–114. https://doi.org/10.1037/ort0000342

Anderson, T., Ogles, B. M., Patterson, C. L., Lambert, M. J., & Vermeersch, D. A. (2009). Therapist effects: Facilitative interpersonal skills as a predictor of therapist success. *Journal of Clinical Psychology, 65*(7), 755–768. https://doi.org/10.1002/jclp.20583

Anderson, T., & Perlman, M. R. (2022). Therapist and client facilitative interpersonal skills in psychotherapy. In J. N. Fuertes (Ed.), *The other side of psychotherapy: Understanding clients' experiences and contributions in treatment* (pp. 99–124). American Psychological Association. https://doi.org/10.1037/0000303-005

APA PsycTherapy. (2005). A culturally competent approach to working with mixed-race clients (client 2) [Online streaming video]. American Psychological Association. https://doi.org/10.1037/v00117-001

APA PsycTherapy. (2011). Being sensitive to socioeconomic class in psychotherapy [Online streaming video]. American Psychological Association. https://doi.org/10.1037/v00471-001

Arredondo, P. (2019). *Eliminating race-based mental health disparities: Promoting equity and culturally responsive care across settings.* New Harbinger Publications.

Artman, L., & Daniels, J. A. (2010). Disability and psychotherapy practice: Cultural competence and practical tips. *Professional Psychology: Research and Practice, 41*(5), 442–448. https://doi.org/10.1037/a0020864

Bailey, R. J., & Ogles, B. M. (2019). Common factors as a therapeutic approach: What is required? *Practice Innovations, 4*(4), 241–254. https://doi.org/10.1037/pri0000100

Bartholomew, T. T., Pérez-Rojas, A. E., Lockard, A. J., Joy, E. E., Robbins, K. A., Kang, E., & Maldonado-Aguiñiga, S. (2021). Therapists' cultural comfort and clients' distress: An initial exploration. *Psychotherapy, 58*(2), 275–281. https://doi.org/10.1037/pst0000331

Benkert, R., Peters, R. M., Clark, R., & Keves-Foster, K. (2006). Effects of perceived racism, cultural mistrust and trust in providers on satisfaction with care. *Journal of the National Medical Association, 98*(9), 1532–1540. https://www.ncbi.nlm.nih.gov/pmc/articles/PMC2569718/pdf/jnma00196-0134.pdf

Bennett-Levy, J. (2019). Why therapists should walk the talk: The theoretical and empirical case for personal practice in therapist training and professional development. *Journal of Behavior Therapy and Experimental Psychiatry, 62*, 133–145. https://doi.org/10.1016/j.jbtep.2018.08.004

Bennett-Levy, J., & Finlay-Jones, A. (2018). The role of personal practice in therapist skill development: A model to guide therapists, educators, supervisors and researchers. *Cognitive Behaviour Therapy, 47*(3), 185–205. https://doi.org/10.1080/16506073.2018.1434678

Benuto, L. T., Casas, J., & O'Donohue, W. T. (2018). Training culturally competent psychologists: A systematic review of the training outcome literature. *Training and Education in Professional Psychology, 12*(3), 125–134. https://doi.org/10.1037/tep0000190

Bernal, G., Jiménez-Chafey, M. I., & Domenech Rodríguez, M. M. (2009). Cultural adaptation of treatments: A resource for considering culture in evidence-based practice. *Professional Psychology, Research and Practice, 40*(4), 361–368. https://doi.org/10.1037/a0016401

Berzoff, J., Flanagan, L. M., & Hertz, P. (Eds.). (2022). *Inside out and outside in: Psychodynamic clinical theory and psychopathology in contemporary multicultural contexts* (5th ed.). Rowman & Littlefield.

Bochicchio, L., Reeder, K., Ivanoff, A., Pope, H., & Stefancic, A. (2022). Psychotherapeutic interventions for LGBTQ+ youth: A systematic review. *Journal of LGBT Youth, 19*(2), 152–179. https://doi.org/10.1080/19361653.2020.1766393

Bohart, A. C., & Wade, A. G. (2013). The client in psychotherapy. In M. J. Lambert (Ed.), *Bergin and Garfield's handbook of psychotherapy and behavior change* (5th ed., pp. 219–257). John Wiley & Sons.

Boiger, M., Ceulemans, E., De Leersnyder, J., Uchida, Y., Norasakkunkit, V., & Mesquita, B. (2018). Beyond essentialism: Cultural differences in emotions revisited. *Emotion, 18*(8), 1142–1162. https://doi.org/10.1037/emo0000390

Bor, J., Venkataramani, A. S., Williams, D. R., & Tsai, A. C. (2018). Police killings and their spillover effects on the mental health of Black Americans: A population-based, quasi-experimental study. *The Lancet, 392*(10144), 302–310. https://doi.org/10.1016/s0140-6736(18)31130-9

Bordin, E. S. (1979). The generalizability of the psychoanalytic concept of the working alliance. *Psychotherapy, 16*(3), 252–260. https://doi.org/10.1037/h0085885

Breland-Noble, A. M. (Ed.). (2020). *Community mental health engagement with racially diverse populations.* Academic Press.

Bryant-Davis, T. (n.d.). *Moving from cultural competence to antiracism* [Video]. National Institute for the Clinical Application of Behavioral Medicine. https://www.nicabm.com/moving-from-cultural-competence-to-antiracism/

Bryant-Davis, T. (2019). The cultural context of trauma recovery: Considering the posttraumatic stress disorder practice guideline and intersectionality. *Psychotherapy, 56*(3), 400–408. https://doi.org/10.1037/pst0000241

Bugatti, M., & Boswell, J. F. (2016). Clinical errors as a lack of context responsiveness. *Psychotherapy, 53*(3), 262–267. https://doi.org/10.1037/pst0000080

Cabral, R. R., & Smith, T. B. (2011). Racial/ethnic matching of clients and therapists in mental health services: A meta-analytic review of preferences, perceptions, and outcomes. *Journal of Counseling Psychology, 58*(4), 537–554. https://doi.org/10.1037/a0025266

CAMH Professionals Videos. (2016). *Psychology and disability: Minimizing ableism in the counselling room* [Video]. YouTube. https://www.youtube.com/watch?v=wZ_a4N1IekQ

Capodilupo, C. M., Nadal, K. L., Corman, L., Hamit, S., Lyons, O. B., & Weinberg, A. (2010). The manifestation of gender microaggressions. In D. W. Sue (Ed.), *Microaggressions and marginality: Manifestation, dynamics, and impact* (pp. 193–216). John Wiley & Sons.

Carter, R. T. (2007). Racism and psychological and emotional injury: Recognizing and assessing race-based traumatic stress. *The Counseling Psychologist, 35*(1), 13–105. https://doi.org/10.1177/0011000006292033

Castonguay, L. G., Goldfried, M. R., Wiser, S., Raue, P. J., & Hayes, A. M. (1996). Predicting the effect of cognitive therapy for depression: A study of unique and common factors. *Journal of Consulting and Clinical Psychology, 64*(3), 497–504. https://doi.org/10.1037/0022-006X.64.3.497

Chavez, V. (2013). *Cultural humility* [Video]. YouTube. https://www.youtube.com/watch?v=SaSHLbS1V4w

Cheng, C., Cheung, S. F., Chio, J. H., & Chan, M.-P. S. (2013). Cultural meaning of perceived control: A meta-analysis of locus of control and psychological symptoms across 18 cultural regions. *Psychological Bulletin, 139*(1), 152–188. https://doi.org/10.1037/a0028596

Chung, R. C.-Y. (2021). *Culturally informed teletherapy with a client experiencing COVID-related racism and stress* [Video]. APA PsycTherapy. https://doi.org/10.1037/v00715-001

Clauss-Ehlers, C. S., Chiriboga, D. A., Hunter, S. J., Roysircar, G., & Tummala-Narra, P. (2019). APA Multicultural Guidelines executive summary: Ecological approach to context, identity, and intersectionality. *American Psychologist, 74*(2), 232–244. https://doi.org/10.1037/amp0000382

Coker, J. (1990). *How to practice jazz.* Jamey Aebersold.

Comas-Díaz, L. (2011). Multicultural approaches to psychotherapy. In J. C. Norcross, G. R. VandenBos, & D. K. Freedheim (Eds.), *History of psychotherapy: Continuity and change* (2nd ed., pp. 243–267). American Psychological Association. https://doi.org/10.1037/12353-008

Comas-Díaz, L. (2015). *Focusing on strengths through multicultural counseling* [Video]. APA PsycTherapy. https://doi.org/10.1037/v00481-001

Comas-Díaz, L., Hall, G. N., & Neville, H. A. (2019). Racial trauma: Theory, research, and healing: Introduction to the special issue. *American Psychologist, 74*(1), 1–5. https://doi.org/10.1037/amp0000442

Consedine, N. S., Chentsova-Dutton, Y. E., & Krivoshekova, Y. S. (2014). Emotional acculturation predicts better somatic health: Experiential and expressive acculturation among immigrant women from four ethnic groups. *Journal of Social and Clinical Psychology, 33*(10), 867–889. https://doi.org/10.1521/jscp.2014.33.10.867

Cook, R. (2005). *It's about that time: Miles Davis on and off record.* Atlantic Books.

Cornish, J. A. E., Schreier, B. A., Nadkarni, L. I., Metzger, L. H., & Rodolfa, E. R. (Eds.). (2010). *Handbook of multicultural counseling competencies.* John Wiley & Sons.

Cramer, E. P., & Plummer, S. B. (2009). People of color with disabilities: Intersectionality as a framework for analyzing intimate partner violence in social, historical, and political contexts. *Journal of Aggression, Maltreatment & Trauma, 18*(2), 162–181. https://doi.org/10.1080/10926770802675635

Crenshaw, K. (1989). Demarginalizing the intersection of race and sex: A Black feminist critique of antidiscrimination doctrine, feminist theory, and antiracist politics. *University of Chicago Legal Forum, 140*, 139–167.

Crenshaw, K. (2016). *The urgency of intersectionality* [Video]. TED Conferences. https://www.ted.com/talks/kimberle_crenshaw_the_urgency_of_intersectionality

Csikszentmihalyi, M. (1997). *Finding flow: The psychology of engagement with everyday life.* HarperCollins.

Dávila, B. (2015). Critical race theory, disability microaggressions and Latina/o student experiences in special education. *Race Ethnicity and Education, 18*(4), 443–468. https://doi.org/10.1080/13613324.2014.885422

Davis, D., DeBlaere, C., Hook, J. N., & Owen, J. (2020). *Mindfulness-based practices in therapy: A cultural humility approach*. American Psychological Association. https://doi.org/10.1037/0000156-000

Davis, D. E., DeBlaere, C., Owen, J., Hook, J. N., Rivera, D. P., Choe, E., Van Tongeren, D. R., Worthington, E. L., Jr., & Placeres, V. (2018). The multicultural orientation framework: A narrative review. *Psychotherapy, 55*(1), 89–100. https://doi.org/10.1037/pst0000160

Davis, D. E., Hook, J. N., Worthington, E. L., Jr., Van Tongeren, D. R., Gartner, A. L., Jennings, D. J., II, & Emmons, R. A. (2011). Relational humility: Conceptualizing and measuring humility as a personality judgment. *Journal of Personality Assessment, 93*(3), 225–234. https://doi.org/10.1080/00223891.2011.558871

DeBlaere, C., & Owen, J. (2020). *Cultural humility in therapy* [Video]. APA PsycTherapy.

Delapp, R. C., & Williams, M. T. (2015). Professional challenges facing African American psychologists: The presence and impact of racial microaggressions. *The Behavior Therapist, 38*(4), 101–105.

De Leersnyder, J. (2017). Emotional acculturation: A first review. *Current Opinion in Psychology, 17*, 67–73. https://doi.org/10.1016/j.copsyc.2017.06.007

De Leersnyder, J., Kim, H. S., & Mesquita, B. (2020). My emotions belong here and there: Extending the phenomenon of emotional acculturation to heritage culture fit. *Cognition and Emotion, 34*(8), 1573–1590. https://doi.org/10.1080/02699931.2020.1781063

Díaz-Lázaro, C. M., & Cohen, B. B. (2001). Cross-cultural contact in counseling training. *Journal of Multicultural Counseling and Development, 29*(1), 41–56. https://doi.org/10.1002/j.2161-1912.2001.tb00502.x

dickey, l. m. (2018). *Affirmative therapy with a gender nonbinary client* [Video]. APA PsychTherapy. https://doi.org/10.1037/v00620-001

dickey, l. m., & Singh, A. A. (2020). Evidence-based relationship variables: Working with trans and gender nonbinary clients. *Practice Innovations, 5*(3), 189–201. https://doi.org/10.1037/pri0000116

Disability Visibility Project. (n.d.) https://disabilityvisibilityproject.com/

Dixon, T. M., & Garrison, V. (2017). *The trauma of systematic racism is killing Black women. A first step toward change* [Video]. TED Conferences. https://www.ted.com/talks/t_morgan_dixon_and_vanessa_garrison_the_trauma_of_systematic_racism_is_killing_black_women_a_first_step_toward_change?language=en

Dolan, K. A. (2015). *Why White people downplay their individual racial privileges*. Insights by Stanford Business. https://www.gsb.stanford.edu/insights/why-whites-downplay-their-individual-racial-privileges

Drinane, J. M., Owen, J., & Tao, K. W. (2018). Cultural concealment and therapy outcomes. *Journal of Counseling Psychology, 65*(2), 239–246. https://doi.org/10.1037/cou0000246

Drustrup, D. (2020). White therapists addressing racism in psychotherapy: An ethical and clinical model for practice. *Ethics & Behavior, 30*(3), 181–196. https://doi.org/10.1080/10508422.2019.1588732

Ellis, M. V., Berger, L., Hanus, A. E., Ayala, E. E., Swords, B. A., & Siembor, M. (2014). Inadequate and harmful clinical supervision: Testing a revised framework and assessing occurrence. *The Counseling Psychologist, 42*(4), 434–472. https://doi.org/10.1177/0011000013508656

Ericsson, K. A. (2003). Development of elite performance and deliberate practice: An update from the perspective of the expert performance approach. In J. L. Starkes & K. A. Ericsson (Eds.), *Expert performance in sports: Advances in research on sport expertise* (pp. 49–83). Human Kinetics.

Ericsson, K. A. (2004). Deliberate practice and the acquisition and maintenance of expert performance in medicine and related domains: Invited address. *Academic Medicine, 79*(10, Suppl.), S70–S81. https://doi.org/10.1097/00001888-200410001-00022

Ericsson, K. A. (2006). The influence of experience and deliberate practice on the development of superior expert performance. In K. A. Ericsson, N. Charness, P. J. Feltovich, & R. R. Hoffman (Eds.), *The Cambridge handbook of expertise and expert performance* (pp. 683–703). Cambridge University Press. https://doi.org/10.1017/CBO9780511816796.038

Ericsson, K. A., Hoffman, R. R., Kozbelt, A., & Williams, A. M. (Eds.). (2018). *The Cambridge handbook of expertise and expert performance* (2nd ed.). Cambridge University Press. https://doi.org/10.1017/9781316480748

Ericsson, K. A., Krampe, R. T., & Tesch-Römer, C. (1993). The role of deliberate practice in the acquisition of expert performance. *Psychological Review, 100*(3), 363–406. https://doi.org/10.1037/0033-295X.100.3.363

Ericsson, K. A., & Pool, R. (2016). *Peak: Secrets from the new science of expertise.* Houghton Mifflin Harcourt.

Fisher, R. P., & Craik, F. I. M. (1977). Interaction between encoding and retrieval operations in cued recall. *Journal of Experimental Psychology: Human Learning and Memory, 3*(6), 701–711. https://doi.org/10.1037/0278-7393.3.6.701

Flückiger, C., Del Re, A. C., Wampold, B. E., & Horvath, A. O. (2018). The alliance in adult psychotherapy: A meta-analytic synthesis. *Psychotherapy, 55*(4), 316–340. https://doi.org/10.1037/pst0000172

Fukuyama, M., Puig, A., Wolf, C. P., & Baggs, A. (2014). Exploring the intersections of religion and spirituality with race-ethnicity and gender in counseling. In M. L. Miville & A. D. Ferguson (Eds.), *Handbook of race-ethnicity and gender in psychology* (pp. 23–43). Springer.

Gattamorta, K. A., Salerno, J. P., & Castro, A. J. (2019). Intersectionality and health behaviors among US high school students: Examining race/ethnicity, sexual identity, and sex. *The Journal of School Health, 89*(10), 800–808. https://doi.org/10.1111/josh.12817

Gladwell, M. (2008). *Outliers: The story of success.* Little, Brown & Company.

Goldberg, S. B., Babins-Wagner, R., Rousmaniere, T., Berzins, S., Hoyt, W. T., Whipple, J. L., Miller, S. D., & Wampold, B. E. (2016). Creating a climate for therapist improvement: A case study of an agency focused on outcomes and deliberate practice. *Psychotherapy, 53*(3), 367–375. https://doi.org/10.1037/pst0000060

Goldberg, S. B., Rousmaniere, T., Miller, S. D., Whipple, J., Nielsen, S. L., Hoyt, W. T., & Wampold, B. E. (2016). Do psychotherapists improve with time and experience? A longitudinal analysis of outcomes in a clinical setting. *Journal of Counseling Psychology, 63*(1), 1–11. https://doi.org/10.1037/cou0000131

Goldman, R. N., Vaz, A., & Rousmaniere, T. (2021). *Deliberate practice in emotion-focused therapy.* American Psychological Association. https://doi.org/10.1037/0000227-000

Goodmann, D. R., Daouk, S., Sullivan, M., Cabrera, J., Liu, N. H., Barakat, S., Muñoz, R. F., & Leykin, Y. (2021). Factor analysis of depression symptoms across five broad cultural groups. *Journal of Affective Disorders, 282*, 227–235. https://doi.org/10.1016/j.jad.2020.12.159

Goodwin, B. J., Coyne, A. E., & Constantino, M. J. (2018). Extending the context-responsive psychotherapy integration framework to cultural processes in psychotherapy. *Psychotherapy, 55*(1), 3–8. https://doi.org/10.1037/pst0000143

Goodyear, R. K. (2015). Using accountability mechanisms more intentionally: A framework and its implications for training professional psychologists. *American Psychologist, 70*(8), 736–743. https://doi.org/10.1037/a0039828

Goodyear, R. K., & Nelson, M. L. (1997). The major formats of psychotherapy supervision. In C. E. Watkins, Jr. (Ed.), *Handbook of psychotherapy supervision* (pp. 328–344). John Wiley & Sons.

Gregus, S. J., Stevens, K. T., Seivert, N. P., Tucker, R. P., & Callahan, J. L. (2020). Student perceptions of multicultural training and program climate in clinical psychology doctoral programs. *Training and Education in Professional Psychology, 14*(4), 293–307. https://doi.org/10.1037/tep0000289

Gundel, B. E., Bartholomew, T. T., & Scheel, M. J. (2020). Culture and care: An illustration of multicultural processes in a counseling dyad. *Practice Innovations, 5*(1), 19–31. https://doi.org/10.1037/pri0000104

Gushue, G. V., & Constantine, M. G. (2007). Color-blind racial attitudes and White racial identity attitudes in psychology trainees. *Professional Psychology: Research & Practice, 38*(3), 321–328. https://doi.org/10.1037/0735-7028.38.3.321

Guthrie, C. (2006). Disclosing the therapist's sexual orientation: The meaning of disclosure in working with gay, lesbian, and bisexual patients. *Journal of Gay & Lesbian Psychotherapy, 10*(1), 63–77. https://doi.org/10.1300/J236v10n01_07

Haggerty, G., & Hilsenroth, M. J. (2011). The use of video in psychotherapy supervision. *British Journal of Psychotherapy, 27*(2), 193–210. https://doi.org/10.1111/j.1752-0118.2011.01232.x

Harris, J., Jin, J., Hoffman, S., Phan, S., Prout, T. A., Rousmaniere, T., & Vaz, A. (2024). *Deliberate practice in multicultural therapy.* American Psychological Association. https://doi.org/10.1037/0000357-000

Hatcher, R. L. (2015). Interpersonal competencies: Responsiveness, technique, and training in psychotherapy. *American Psychologist, 70*(8), 747–757. https://doi.org/10.1037/a0039803

Hays, P. A. (2016). *Culturally responsive cognitive behavioral therapy for promoting strengths and wellness (Session 1 of 6)* [Video]. APA PsycTherapy. https://doi.org/10.1037/v00525-001

Hays, P. A. (2022). *Addressing cultural complexities in counseling and clinical practice: An intersectional approach* (4th ed.). American Psychological Association. https://doi.org/10.1037/0000277-000

Hays, P. A., & Iwamasa, G. Y. (Eds.). (2006). *Culturally responsive cognitive-behavioral therapy: Assessment, practice, and supervision.* American Psychological Association. https://doi.org/10.1037/11433-000

Helms, J. E., Nicolas, G., & Green, C. E. (2012). Racism and ethnoviolence as trauma: Enhancing professional and research training. *Traumatology, 18*(1), 65–74. https://doi.org/10.1177/1534765610396728

Henry, W. P., Strupp, H. H., Butler, S. F., Schacht, T. E., & Binder, J. L. (1993). Effects of training in time-limited dynamic psychotherapy: Changes in therapist behavior. *Journal of Consulting and Clinical Psychology, 61*(3), 434–440. https://doi.org/10.1037/0022-006X.61.3.434

Heredia, D., Jr., & Rider, G. N. (2020). Intersectionality in sex therapy: Opportunities for promoting sexual wellness among queer people of color. *Current Sexual Health Reports, 12*(3), 195–201.

Hicks, E. T., de la Caridad Alvarez, M., & Domenech Rodríguez, M. M. (2022). Impact of difficult dialogues on social justice attitudes during a multicultural psychology course. *Teaching of Psychology.* Advance online publication. https://journals.sagepub.com/doi/full/10.1177/00986283221104057

Hill, C. E., Kivlighan, D. M., III, Rousmaniere, T., Kivlighan, D. M., Jr., Gerstenblith, J. A., & Hillman, J. W. (2020). Deliberate practice for the skill of immediacy: A multiple case study of doctoral student therapists and clients. *Psychotherapy, 57*(4), 587–597. https://doi.org/10.1037/pst0000247

Hill, C. E., Knox, S., & Pinto-Coelho, K. G. (2018). Therapist self-disclosure and immediacy: A qualitative meta-analysis. *Psychotherapy, 55*(4), 445–460. https://doi.org/10.1037/pst0000182

Hollingsworth, D. W., Cole, A. B., O'Keefe, V. M., Tucker, R. P., Story, C. R., & Wingate, L. R. (2017). Experiencing racial microaggressions influences suicide ideation through perceived burdensomeness in African Americans. *Journal of Counseling Psychology, 64*(1), 104–111. https://doi.org/10.1037/cou0000177

Hook, J. N., Davis, D., Owen, J., & DeBlaere, C. (2017). *Cultural humility: Engaging diverse identities in therapy.* American Psychological Association. https://doi.org/10.1037/0000037-000

Hook, J. N., Davis, D. E., Owen, J., Worthington, E. L., Jr., & Utsey, S. O. (2013). Cultural humility: Measuring openness to culturally diverse clients. *Journal of Counseling Psychology, 60*(3), 353–366. https://doi.org/10.1037/a0032595

Horvath, A. O., Del Re, A. C., Flückiger, C., & Symonds, D. (2011). Alliance in individual psychotherapy. *Psychotherapy, 48*(1), 9–16. https://doi.org/10.1037/a0022186

Jones, J. M., Sander, J. B., & Booker, K. W. (2013). Multicultural competency building: Practical solutions for training and evaluating student progress. *Training and Education in Professional Psychology, 7*(1), 12–22. https://doi.org/10.1037/a0030880

Kattari, S. K., Olzman, M., & Hanna, M. D. (2018). "You look fine!" Ableist experiences by people with invisible disabilities. *Affilia, 33*(4), 477–492. https://doi.org/10.1177/0886109918778073

Kelley, F. A. (2015). The therapy relationship with lesbian and gay clients. *Psychotherapy, 52*(1), 113–118. https://doi.org/10.1037/a0037958

Kendall, P. C., & Beidas, R. S. (2007). Smoothing the trail for dissemination of evidence-based practices for youth: Flexibility within fidelity. *Professional Psychology, Research and Practice, 38*(1), 13–20. https://doi.org/10.1037/0735-7028.38.1.13

Kendall, P. C., & Frank, H. E. (2018). Implementing evidence-based treatment protocols: Flexibility within fidelity. *Clinical Psychology: Science and Practice, 25*(4), e12271. https://doi.org/10.1111/cpsp.12271

King, K. M., Borders, L. D., & Jones, C. T. (2020). Multicultural orientation in clinical supervision: Examining impact through dyadic data. *The Clinical Supervisor, 39*(2), 248–271. https://doi.org/10.1080/07325223.2020.1763223

Kivlighan, D. M., III, & Chapman, N. A. (2018). Extending the multicultural orientation (MCO) framework to group psychotherapy: A clinical illustration. *Psychotherapy, 55*(1), 39–44. https://doi.org/10.1037/pst0000142

Koziol, L. F., & Budding, D. E. (2012). Procedural learning. In N. M. Seel (Ed.), *Encyclopedia of the sciences of learning* (pp. 2694–2696). Springer. https://doi.org/10.1007/978-1-4419-1428-6_670

Kronner, H. W., & Northcut, T. (2015). Listening to both sides of the therapeutic dyad: Self-disclosure of gay male therapists and reflections from their gay male clients. *Psychoanalytic Social Work, 22*(2), 162–181. https://doi.org/10.1080/15228878.2015.1050746

Kuo, P. B., Imel, Z. E., & Tao, K. W. (2021). An experimental analogue evaluation of Asian and Asian Americans' immediate reactions to therapist microaggressions. *The Counseling Psychologist, 49*(5), 754–780. https://doi.org/10.1177/00110000211001368

Kwon, H., Yoon, K. L., Joormann, J., & Kwon, J. H. (2013). Cultural and gender differences in emotion regulation: Relation to depression. *Cognition and Emotion, 27*(5), 769–782. https://doi.org/10.1080/02699931.2013.792244

La Roche, M. (2020). *Towards a global and cultural psychology: Theoretical foundations and clinical implications.* Cognella.

Lambert, M. J. (2010). Yes, it is time for clinicians to monitor treatment outcome. In B. L. Duncan, S. C. Miller, B. E. Wampold, & M. A. Hubble (Eds.), *Heart and soul of change: Delivering what works in therapy* (2nd ed., pp. 239–266). American Psychological Association. https://doi.org/10.1037/12075-008

Learning for Justice. (n.d.). *Social justice standards: Unpacking identity.* https://www.learningforjustice.org/professional-development/social-justice-standards-unpacking-identity

Lee, D. L., Rosen, A. D., & McWhirter, J. J. (2014). Assessing changes in counselor trainees' multicultural competence related to service learning. *Journal of Multicultural Counseling and Development, 42*(1), 31–41. https://doi.org/10.1002/j.2161-1912.2014.00042.x

Liu, N. H., & Herndon, J. L. (2022). A framework for culturally humble therapeutic responses using the deliberate practice multicultural orientation video prompts. *Practice Innovations, 7*(3), 178–187. https://doi.org/10.1037/pri0000177

López, D. J., Yuan, Y., Booth, J., Wei, K., & Friedman, M. R. (2022). Discrimination and rejection: The effects of ethnic and sexuality-based discrimination against Latino gay and bisexual men. *Journal of Homosexuality.* Advance online publication. https://doi.org/10.1080/00918369.2022.2081105

Lorde, A. (1982). *Learning from the 60s.* https://www.blackpast.org/african-american-history/1982-audre-lorde-learning-60s/

Love, M., & Farber, B. A. (2019). Honesty in psychotherapy: Results of an online survey comparing high vs. low self-concealers. *Psychotherapy Research, 29*(5), 607–620. https://doi.org/10.1080/10503307.2017.1417652

Lukianoff, G., & Haidt, J. (2015, September). The coddling of the American mind. *The Atlantic.* https://www.theatlantic.com/magazine/archive/2015/09/the-coddling-of-the-american-mind/399356/

Mankus, A. M., Boden, M. T., & Thompson, R. J. (2016). Sources of variation in emotional awareness: Age, gender, and socioeconomic status. *Personality and Individual Differences, 89*, 28–33. https://doi.org/10.1016/j.paid.2015.09.043

Markman, K. D., & Tetlock, P. E. (2000). Accountability and close-call counterfactuals: The loser who nearly won and the winner who nearly lost. *Personality and Social Psychology Bulletin, 26*(10), 1213–1224. https://doi.org/10.1177/0146167200262004

McGaghie, W. C., Issenberg, S. B., Barsuk, J. H., & Wayne, D. B. (2014). A critical review of simulation-based mastery learning with translational outcomes. *Medical Education, 48*(4), 375–385. https://doi.org/10.1111/medu.12391

McGeorge, C. R., Coburn, K. O., & Walsdorf, A. A. (2021). Deconstructing cissexism: The journey of becoming an affirmative family therapist for transgender and nonbinary clients. *Journal of Marital and Family Therapy*, *47*(3), 785–802. https://doi.org/10.1111/jmft.12481

McLeod, J. (2017). Qualitative methods for routine outcome measurement. In T. G. Rousmaniere, R. Goodyear, D. D. Miller, & B. E. Wampold (Eds.), *The cycle of excellence: Using deliberate practice to improve supervision and training* (pp. 99–122). John Wiley & Sons. https://doi.org/10.1002/9781119165590.ch5

Mesquita, B., Boiger, M., & De Leersnyder, J. (2017). Doing emotions: The role of culture in everyday emotions. *European Review of Social Psychology*, *28*(1), 95–133. https://doi.org/10.1080/10463283.2017.1329107

Mosher, D. K., Hook, J. N., Captari, L. E., Davis, D. E., DeBlaere, C., & Owen, J. (2017). Cultural humility: A therapeutic framework for engaging diverse clients. *Practice Innovations*, *2*(4), 221–233. https://doi.org/10.1037/pri0000055

Nadal, K. L., Davidoff, K. C., Davis, L. S., Wong, Y., Marshall, D., & McKenzie, V. (2015). A qualitative approach to intersectional microaggressions: Understanding, influences of race, ethnicity, gender, sexuality, and religion. *Qualitative Psychology*, *2*(2), 147–163. https://doi.org/10.1037/qup0000026

National Institute for the Clinical Application of Behavioral Medicine. (2020a). *Helping a patient with racial stress* [Video]. YouTube. https://www.youtube.com/watch?v=lBxYs2a2Ibo

National Institute for the Clinical Application of Behavioral Medicine. (2020b). *Working with the trauma of racism* [Video]. YouTube. https://www.youtube.com/watch?v=egr2279UiAI

Norcross, J. C., & Guy, J. D. (2005). The prevalence and parameters of personal therapy in the United States. In J. D. Geller, J. C. Norcross, & D. E. Orlinsky (Eds.), *The psychotherapist's own psychotherapy: Patient and clinician perspectives* (pp. 165–176). Oxford University Press.

Norcross, J. C., Lambert, M. J., & Wampold, B. E. (2019). *Psychotherapy relationships that work* (3rd ed.). Oxford University Press.

Ohio University. (n.d.). *The ADDRESSING model.* https://www.ohio.edu/cas/psychology/diversity/addressing-model

O'Keefe, V. M., Wingate, L. R., Cole, A. B., Hollingsworth, D. W., & Tucker, R. P. (2015). Seemingly harmless racial communications are not so harmless: Racial microaggressions lead to suicidal ideation by way of depression symptoms. *Suicide & Life-Threatening Behavior*, *45*(5), 567–576. https://doi.org/10.1111/sltb.12150

Orlinsky, D. E., Rønnestad, M. H., & Collaborative Research Network of the Society for Psychotherapy Research. (2005). *How psychotherapists develop: A study of therapeutic work and professional growth.* American Psychological Association. https://doi.org/10.1037/11157-000

Owen, J., Drinane, J., Tao, K. W., Adelson, J. L., Hook, J. N., Davis, D., & Fookune, N. (2017). Racial/ethnic disparities in client unilateral termination: The role of therapists' cultural comfort. *Psychotherapy Research*, *27*(1), 102–111. https://doi.org/10.1080/10503307.2015.1078517

Owen, J., & Hilsenroth, M. J. (2014). Treatment adherence: The importance of therapist flexibility in relation to therapy outcomes. *Journal of Counseling Psychology*, *61*(2), 280–288. https://doi.org/10.1037/a0035753

Owen, J., Imel, Z., Adelson, J., & Rodolfa, E. (2012). "No-show": Therapist racial/ethnic disparities in client unilateral termination. *Journal of Counseling Psychology*, *59*(2), 314–320. https://doi.org/10.1037/a0027091

Owen, J., Tao, K., & Rodolfa, E. (2010). Microaggressions and women in short-term psychotherapy: Initial evidence. *The Counseling Psychologist*, *38*(7), 923–946. https://doi.org/10.1177/0011000010376093

Owen, J., Tao, K. W., Drinane, J. M., Hook, J., Davis, D. E., & Kune, N. F. (2016). Client perceptions of therapists' multicultural orientation: Cultural (missed) opportunities and cultural humility. *Professional Psychology, Research and Practice*, *47*(1), 30–37. https://doi.org/10.1037/pro0000046

Owen, J., Tao, K. W., Imel, Z. E., Wampold, B. E., & Rodolfa, E. (2014). Addressing racial and ethnic microaggressions in therapy. *Professional Psychology: Research and Practice*, *45*(4), 283–290. https://doi.org/10.1037/a0037420

Owen, J. J., Tao, K., Leach, M. M., & Rodolfa, E. (2011). Clients' perceptions of their psychotherapists' multicultural orientation. *Psychotherapy*, *48*(3), 274–282. https://doi.org/10.1037/a0022065

Parr, N. J., & Howe, B. G. (2019). Heterogeneity of transgender identity nonaffirmation microaggressions and their association with depression symptoms and suicidality among transgender persons. *Psychology of Sexual Orientation and Gender Diversity*, *6*(4), 461–474. https://doi.org/10.1037/sgd0000347

Patterson, C. L., Anderson, T., & Wei, C. (2014). Clients' pretreatment role expectations, the therapeutic alliance, and clinical outcomes in outpatient therapy. *Journal of Clinical Psychology*, *70*(7), 673–680. https://doi.org/10.1002/jclp.22054

Patterson, C. L., Uhlin, B., & Anderson, T. (2008). Clients' pretreatment counseling expectations as predictors of the working alliance. *Journal of Counseling Psychology*, *55*(4), 528–534. https://doi.org/10.1037/a0013289

Pedersen, P. (1990). The multicultural perspective as a fourth force in counseling. *Journal of Mental Health Counseling*, *12*(1), 93–95.

Prescott, D. S., Maeschalck, C. L., & Miller, S. D. (Eds.). (2017). *Feedback-informed treatment in clinical practice: Reaching for excellence*. American Psychological Association. https://doi.org/10.1037/0000039-000

Psychotherapy Networker. (2019). *Handling microaggressions in therapy* [Video]. YouTube. https://www.youtube.com/watch?v=-4kODpuhngo

Roberts-Crews, J. (2020, June 8). *White academia: Do better*. https://medium.com/the-faculty/white-academia-do-better-fa96cede1fc5

Rosenthal, L. (2016). Incorporating intersectionality into psychology: An opportunity to promote social justice and equity. *American Psychologist*, *71*(6), 474–485. https://doi.org/10.1037/a0040323

Rousmaniere, T. (2016). *Deliberate practice for psychotherapists: A guide to improving clinical effectiveness*. Routledge. https://doi.org/10.4324/9781315472256

Rousmaniere, T. (2019). *Mastering the inner skills of psychotherapy: A deliberate practice manual*. Gold Lantern Books.

Rousmaniere, T., Goodyear, R., Miller, S. D., & Wampold, B. E. (Eds.). (2017). *The cycle of excellence: Using deliberate practice to improve supervision and training*. John Wiley & Sons. https://doi.org/10.1002/9781119165590

Sentio Therapist Training. (2020). *Multicultural orientation (MCO) deliberate practice webinar* [Video]. YouTube. https://www.youtube.com/watch?v=IJ1cWH88RI0&t=1622s

Shadick, R., Backus Dagirmanjian, F., & Barbot, B. (2015). Suicide risk among college students: The intersection of sexual orientation and race. *Crisis: The Journal of Crisis Intervention and Suicide Prevention*, *36*(6), 416–423. https://doi.org/10.1027/0227-5910/a000340

Shelton, K., & Delgado-Romero, E. A. (2011). Sexual orientation microaggressions: The experience of lesbian, gay, bisexual, and queer clients in psychotherapy. *Journal of Counseling Psychology*, *58*(2), 210–221. https://doi.org/10.1037/a0022251

Soto, A., Smith, T. B., Griner, D., Rodríguez, M. D., & Bernal, G. (2019). Cultural adaptations and multicultural competence. In J. C. Norcross & B. E. Wampold (Eds.), *Psychotherapy relationships that work: Evidence-based therapist responsiveness* (pp. 86–132). Oxford University Press. https://doi.org/10.1093/med-psych/9780190843960.003.0004

Squire, L. R. (2004). Memory systems of the brain: A brief history and current perspective. *Neurobiology of Learning and Memory*, *82*(3), 171–177. https://doi.org/10.1016/j.nlm.2004.06.005

Stiles, W. B., Honos-Webb, L., & Surko, M. (1998). Responsiveness in psychotherapy. *Clinical Psychology: Science and Practice*, *5*(4), 439–458. https://doi.org/10.1111/j.1468-2850.1998.tb00166.x

Stiles, W. B., & Horvath, A. O. (2017). Appropriate responsiveness as a contribution to therapist effects. In L. G. Castonguay & C. E. Hill (Eds.), *How and why are some therapists better than others? Understanding therapist effects* (pp. 71–84). American Psychological Association. https://doi.org/10.1037/0000034-005

Sue, D. W. (2017). Microaggressions and "evidence." *Perspectives on Psychological Science*, *12*(1), 170–172. https://doi.org/10.1177/1745691616664437

Sue, D. W., Rivera, D. P., Capodilupo, C. M., Lin, A. I., & Torino, G. C. (2010). Racial dialogues and White trainee fears: Implications for education and training. *Cultural Diversity and Ethnic Minority Psychology, 16*(2), 206–214. https://doi.org/10.1037/a0016112

Sue, D. W., & Sue, D. (2016). *Counseling the culturally diverse: Theory and practice* (7th ed.). John Wiley & Sons.

Sue, D. W., Sue, D., Neville, H. A., & Smith, L. (2019). *Counseling the culturally diverse: Theory and practice* (8th ed.). John Wiley & Sons. Videos to accompany chapter 2 available at https://higheredbcs.wiley.com/legacy/college/sue/1119448247/vss/ch02.html?new-window=true

Sunderani, S., & Moodley, R. (2020). Therapists' perceptions of their use of self-disclosure (and nondisclosure) during cross-cultural exchanges. *British Journal of Guidance & Counselling, 48*(6), 741–756. https://doi.org/10.1080/03069885.2020.1754333

Szlyk, H. S., Gulbas, L., & Zayas, L. (2019). "I just kept it to myself": The shaping of Latina suicidality through gendered oppression, silence, and violence. *Family Process, 58*(3), 778–790. https://doi.org/10.1111/famp.12384

Tatum, B. D. (2017). *Why are all the Black kids sitting together in the cafeteria? And other conversations about race.* Basic Books.

Taylor, F. (2019). As much space as we can imagine. *Therapy Today, 30*(8). https://www.bacp.co.uk/bacp-journals/therapy-today/2019/october-2019/as-much-space-as-we-can-imagine/

Taylor, J. M., & Neimeyer, G. J. (2017). The ongoing evolution of continuing education: Past, present, and future. In T. Rousmaniere, R. K. Goodyear, S. D. Miller, & B. E. Wampold (Eds.), *The cycle of excellence: Using deliberate practice to improve supervision and training* (pp. 219–248). John Wiley & Sons.

TED. (2015, April 20). *Jessica Dere: Challenges and rewards of a culturally-informed approach to mental health* [Video]. YouTube. https://www.youtube.com/watch?v=VrYmQDiunSc

TED. (2017, December 1). *Juliana Mosley, PhD: Cultural humility* [Video]. YouTube. https://www.youtube.com/watch?v=Ww_ml21L7Ns

Tervalon, M., & Murray-Garcia, J. (1998). Cultural humility versus cultural competence: A critical distinction in defining physician training outcomes in multicultural education. *Journal of Health Care for the Poor and Underserved, 9*(2), 117–125. https://doi.org/10.1353/hpu.2010.0233

Tracey, T. J. G., Wampold, B. E., Goodyear, R. K., & Lichtenberg, J. W. (2015). Improving expertise in psychotherapy. *Psychotherapy Bulletin, 50*(1), 7–13.

Tummala-Narra, P. (2015). Cultural competence as a core emphasis of psychoanalytic psychotherapy. *Psychoanalytic Psychology, 32*(2), 275–292. https://doi.org/10.1037/a0034041

UConn Racial/Ethnic Stress & Trauma Survey (UnRESTS). (n.d.). https://www.mentalhealthdisparities.org/docs/UnRESTS_0716_English.pdf

Vasquez, M. J. T., & Johnson, J. D. (2022). *Multicultural therapy: A practice imperative.* American Psychological Association. https://doi.org/10.1037/0000279-000

Velasquez, M. (2020, June 12). *Cultural humility in mental health: A move away from competence* [Video]. YouTube. https://www.youtube.com/watch?v=WXRGPSjMjWE

Wass, R., & Golding, C. (2014). Sharpening a tool for teaching: The zone of proximal development. *Teaching in Higher Education, 19*(6), 671–684. https://doi.org/10.1080/13562517.2014.901958

Watkins, C. E., Jr., Hook, J. N., Owen, J., DeBlaere, C., Davis, D. E., & Van Tongeren, D. R. (2019). Multicultural orientation in psychotherapy supervision: Cultural humility, cultural comfort, and cultural opportunities. *American Journal of Psychotherapy, 72*(2), 38–46. https://doi.org/10.1176/appi.psychotherapy.20180040

Weber, A., Collins, S. A., Robinson-Wood, T., Zeko-Underwood, E., & Poindexter, B. (2018). Subtle and severe: Microaggressions among racially diverse sexual minorities. *Journal of Homosexuality, 65*(4), 540–559. https://doi.org/10.1080/00918369.2017.1324679

Wiglesworth, A., Clement, D. N., Wingate, L. R., & Klimes-Dougan, B. (2022). Understanding suicide risk for youth who are both Black and Native American: The role of intersectionality and multiple marginalization. *Suicide & Life-Threatening Behavior, 52*(4), 668–682. https://doi.org/10.1111/sltb.12851

Wilcox, M. M., Drinane, J. M., Black, S. W., Cabrera, L., DeBlaere, C., Tao, K. W., Hook, J. N., Davis, D. E., Watkins, C. E., & Owen, J. (2022). Layered cultural processes: The relationship between multicultural orientation and satisfaction with supervision. *Training and Education in Professional Psychology, 16*(3), 235–243. https://doi.org/10.1037/tep0000366

Wilcox, M. M., Winkeljohn Black, S., Drinane, J. M., Morales-Ramirez, I., Akef, Z., Tao, K. W., DeBlaere, C., Hook, J. N., Davis, D. E., Watkins, C. E., Jr., & Owen, J. (2022). A brief qualitative examination of multicultural orientation in clinical supervision. *Professional Psychology, Research and Practice*. Advance online publication. https://doi.org/10.1037/pro0000477

Williams, D. R. (2016). *How racism makes us sick* [Video]. TED Conferences. https://www.ted.com/talks/david_r_williams_how_racism_makes_us_sick?language=en

Williams, M. T. (2020). Psychology cannot afford to ignore the many harms caused by micro-aggressions. *Perspectives on Psychological Science, 15*(1), 38–43. https://doi.org/10.1177/1745691619893362

Williams, M. T., Skinta, M. D., & Martin-Willett, R. (2021). After Pierce and Sue: A revised racial microaggressions taxonomy. *Perspectives on Psychological Science, 16*(5), 991–1007. https://doi.org/10.1177/1745691621994247

Winkeljohn Black, S., Drinane, J. M., Owen, J., DeBlaere, C., & Davis, D. (2021). Integrating spirituality as a multicultural component into time-limited psychotherapy: Two case studies. *Professional Psychology: Research and Practice, 52*(2), 121–129. https://doi.org/10.1037/pro0000369

Yeo, E., & Torres-Harding, S. R. (2021). Rupture resolution strategies and the impact of rupture on the working alliance after racial microaggressions in therapy. *Psychotherapy, 58*(4), 460–471. https://doi.org/10.1037/pst0000372

Zaretskii, V. (2009). The zone of proximal development: What Vygotsky did not have time to write. *Journal of Russian & East European Psychology, 47*(6), 70–93. https://doi.org/10.2753/RPO1061-0405470604

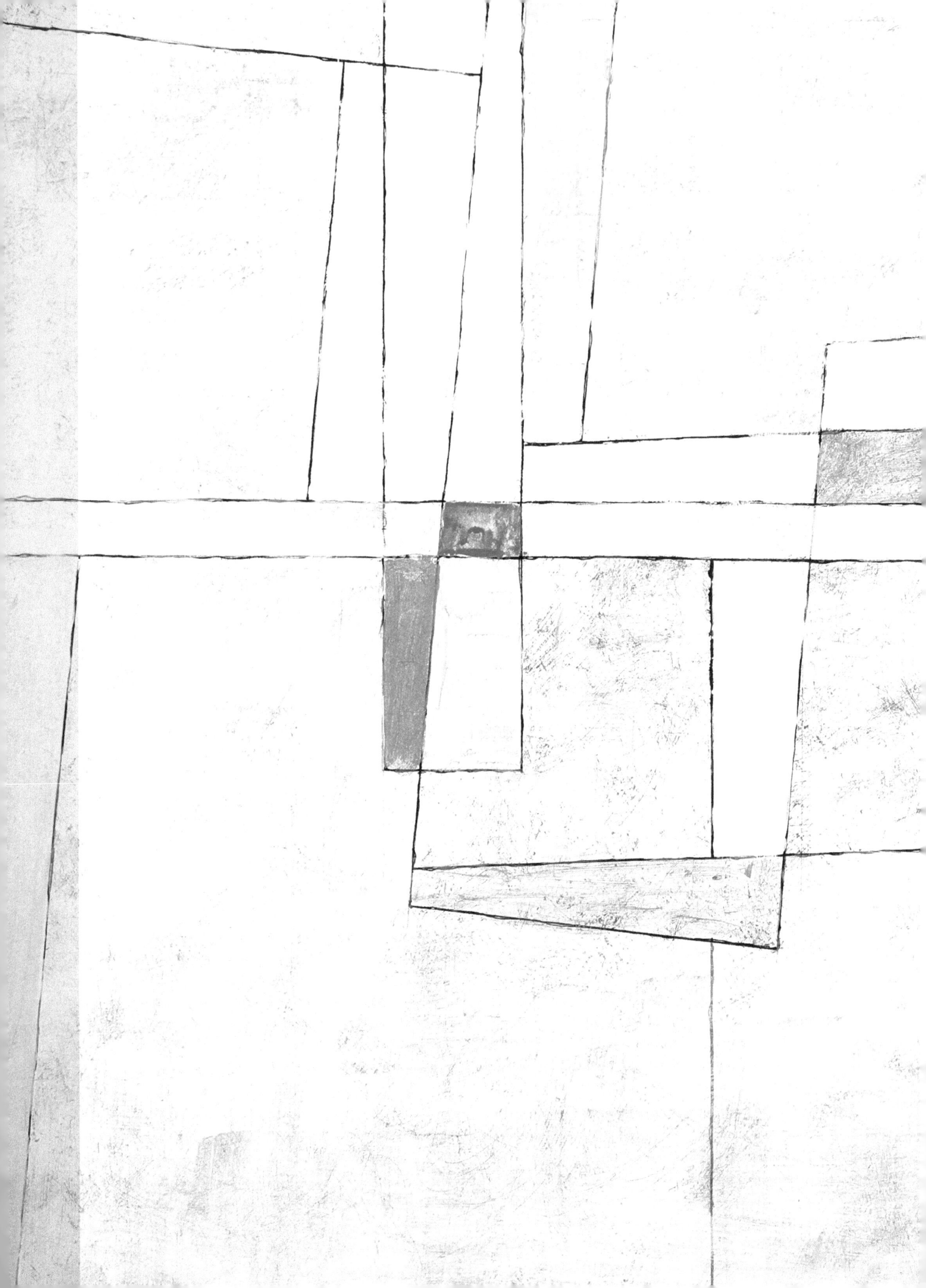

Index

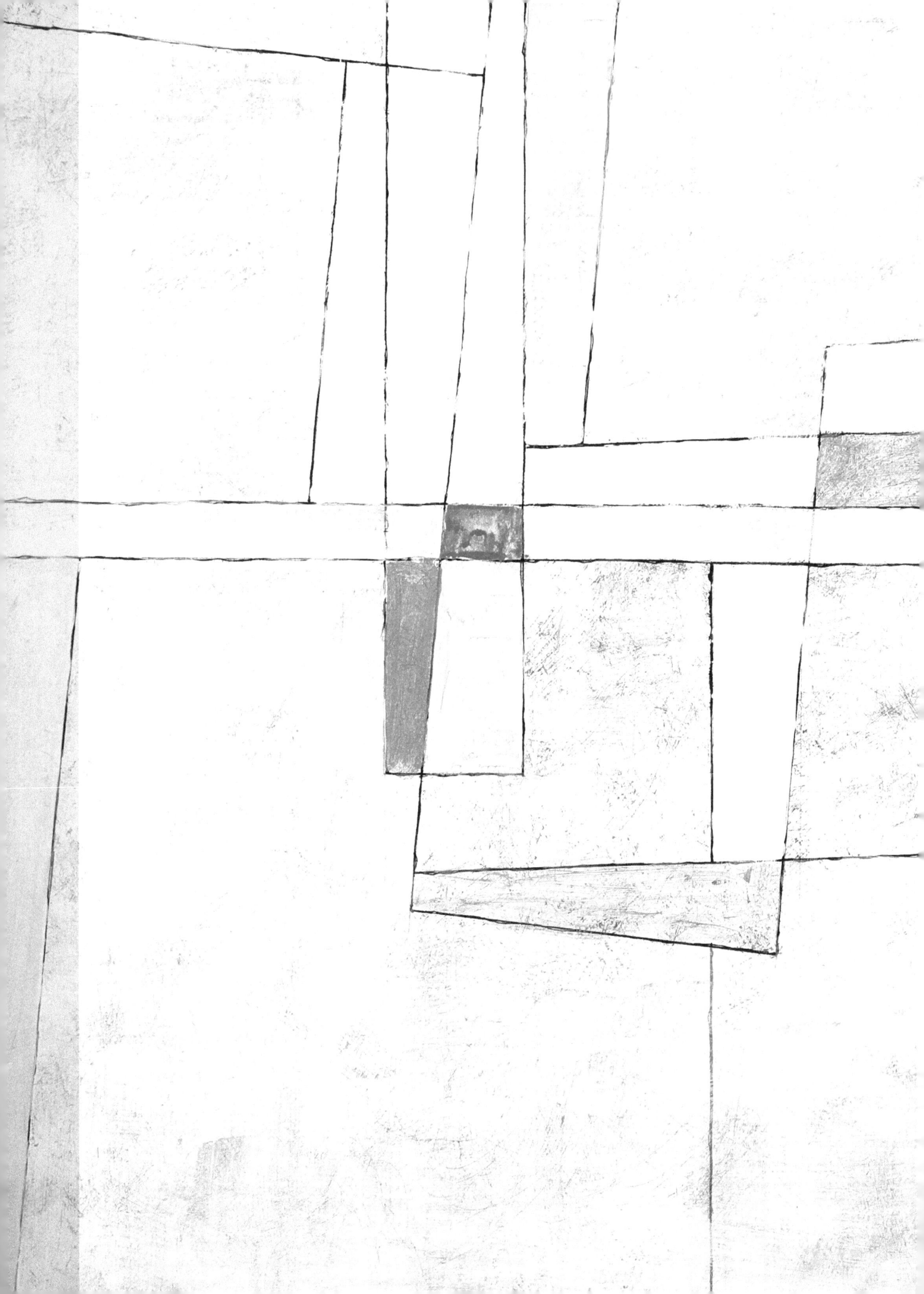

About the Authors

Jordan Harris, PhD, is the owner of Harris Counseling and Consulting, a private practice in northwest Arkansas specializing in couple therapy and hypnosis. Dr. Harris received his PhD in marriage and family therapy from the University of Louisiana Monroe. He also was an American Association of Marriage and Family Therapy (AAMFT) minority fellow and an AAMFT minority fellow mentor. He holds a master's of marriage and family therapy from Harding University and is dually licensed as a supervisor for licensed professional counselors and licensed marriage and family therapists. He blogs regularly at Jordanthecounselor.com, where he makes complicated research on therapy outcomes, common factors, and deliberate practice accessible to everyday clinicians. When not seeing clients, Dr. Harris offers deliberate practice trainings and coaches new therapists. His most recent training was "A Masterclass for Allies: Attuning to African Americans."

Joel Jin, PhD, is an assistant professor and the director of clinical practica of Seattle Pacific University's Clinical Psychology PhD program in Seattle, Washington. He has published several peer-reviewed journal articles on different aspects of culture and diversity, including race and ethnicity, religion and spirituality, and moral foundations. His research program focuses on addressing mental health disparities of racially minoritized populations by studying the role of stigma and perfectionism. With his graduate students, he is pilot testing a culturally sensitive, mindfulness-based intervention for high-achieving students who are racially minoritized. Dr. Jin teaches graduate-level courses on clinical foundations for psychotherapy using a deliberate practice framework, along with other courses about psychopathology, diversity and cultural competence, psychodynamic psychotherapy, and systems therapies. Clinically he has worked with children, adolescents, families, and adults across inpatient, community-based, and private practice settings. He received his PhD in clinical psychology from Fuller's School of Psychology. He also obtained an MA in theology and ministry. Dr. Jin is a second-generation Korean Canadian and a first-generation professional.

Sophia Hoffman, PhD, is assistant program director and the director of clinical training at the combined School-Clinical Child PsyD Program at Ferkauf Graduate School of Psychology at Yeshiva University, New York, New York. Dr. Hoffman works with children, adolescents, and their families in private practice at Lifespan Therapists of Brooklyn. She specializes in working with challenging behaviors in early childhood and consulting with parents about how those behaviors affect school experiences. Dr. Hoffman has extensive experience helping families manage childhood trauma and the subsequent challenging behaviors expressed at home and at school. Her doctoral research focused on implicit racial bias and disciplinary decision making in early childhood education. She currently teaches graduate-level courses in cultural humility, where she uses the deliberate practice framework to help students advance their clinical skills.

Selina Phan, MA, is a doctoral candidate in the School-Clinical Child PsyD Program at Ferkauf Graduate School of Psychology at Yeshiva University, New York, New York. Ms. Phan has experience working with children, adolescents, and their families across various settings, including schools, communities, and hospitals. Her doctoral research project aimed to evaluate the efficacy of deliberate practice training to facilitate greater multicultural orientation in clinicians. To support her research, Ms. Phan was awarded the 2021 Society for the Advancement of Psychotherapy Diversity Research Grant for Predoctoral Candidates. As a first-generation Vietnamese American woman and first-generation college graduate, she is committed to learning about and providing culturally responsive care to individuals across the lifespan and contributing to research that enhances psychotherapy training that fosters greater cultural humility.

Tracy A. Prout, PhD, is codirector of IMPACT Psychological Services (https://www.impact-psych.com/), a group practice that serves children, adolescents, and adults in Westchester and Beacon, New York. Dr. Prout received her PhD in clinical psychology from Fordham University, Bronx, NY. She earned a certificate in psychodynamic psychotherapy from the Institute for Psychoanalytic Education at NYU Medical Center. She has completed advanced research training through the International Psychoanalytical Association, the Anna Freud Centre, and Duke University's Center for Spirituality, Theology and Health. She also has a master's in counseling from Gordon Conwell Theological Seminary and graduated from Wellesley College with a double major in psychology and political science. Dr. Prout is the author of numerous books and articles on Regulation Focused Psychotherapy for Children, including the training of mental health professionals and psychotherapy integration. She is also coauthor of *Deliberate Practice in Child and Adolescent Psychotherapy*, part of the Essentials of Deliberate Practice Series (American Psychological Association), *Manual of Regulation-Focused Psychotherapy for Children (RFP-C) With Externalizing Behaviors: A Psychodynamic Approach* (Routledge), and *Essential Interviewing and Counseling Skills: An Integrated Approach to Practice* (Springer).

Tony Rousmaniere, PsyD, is executive director of the Sentio Counseling Center and clinical faculty at University of Washington. He provides workshops, webinars, and advanced clinical training to clinicians around the world. Dr. Rousmaniere is the author/coeditor of many books on deliberate practice and psychotherapy training and two series of clinical training books: The Essentials of Deliberate Practice (American Psychological Association [APA]) and Advanced Therapeutics, Clinical and Interpersonal Skills (Elsevier). In 2017, he published the widely cited article "What Your Therapist Doesn't Know" in *The Atlantic Monthly*. Dr. Rousmaniere supports the open-data movement and publishes his aggregated clinical outcome data, in deidentified form, on his website (https://drtonyr.com/). Dr. Rousmaniere is incoming president of APA Division 29 (Society for the Advancement of Psychotherapy).

Alexandre Vaz, PhD, is cofounder and chief academic officer of the Sentio Counseling Center. He provides deliberate practice workshops and advanced clinical training and supervision to clinicians around the world. Dr. Vaz is the author/coeditor of multiple books on deliberate practice and psychotherapy training and two series of clinical training books: The Essentials of Deliberate Practice (American Psychological Association) and Advanced Therapeutics, Clinical and Interpersonal Skills (Elsevier). He has held multiple committee roles for the Society for the Exploration of Psychotherapy Integration and the Society for Psychotherapy Research. Dr. Vaz is founder and host of "Psychotherapy Expert Talks," an acclaimed interview series with distinguished psychotherapists and therapy researchers.